T0173343

Unlocked

Also by Pete Etchells

Lost in a Good Game: Why we play video games
and what they can do for us

Unlocked

The Real Science of Screen Time
(and how to spend it better)

Pete Etchells

PIATKUS

PIATKUS

First published in Great Britain in 2024 by Piatkus

1 3 5 7 9 10 8 6 4 2

A CIP catalogue record for this book
is available from the British Library.

ISBN: 978-0-34943-293-9

Typeset in Sabon by M Rules
Printed and bound in Great Britain by Clays Ltd, Elcograf S.p.A.

Papers used by Piatkus are from well-managed forests
and other responsible sources.

Piatkus
An imprint of
Little, Brown Book Group
Carmelite House
50 Victoria Embankment
London EC4Y 0DZ

An Hachette UK Company
www.hachette.co.uk

www.littlebrown.co.uk

For Frances, Matilda and Patrick

Contents

Introduction

Over the last ten years or so, a conventional wisdom has taken hold about smartphones, video games, social media and the internet at large. Our screen-based lives, we have been persistently told, are unwholesome – unnatural and harmful, even. Kids shouldn't play video games because they might make them more aggressive, destroy their memory and attention span, or turn them into digital junkies. Social media makes us less resilient and more isolated and hateful towards one another. And we are addicted to our smartphones, unable to resist the relentless appeal of a tiny screen through which we can do anything, say anything, read anything or be anyone.

This very public debate is precisely mirrored in the research literature. While some scientists are actively looking into the best ways to harness digital technology to improve our lives, other, more vocal researchers are convinced that screen time – a simple measure of how long we spend in front of some sort of digital technology every day or every week – is linked to increases in teenage depression and suicidal thoughts, and problems in childhood social and neurological development, and displaces other offline activities that are much better for our mental and physical wellbeing. The one consistent casualty in all of this is togetherness: our ability to make meaningful connections with each other is only really possible when we meet offline, face to face.

All of that changed when coronavirus disrupted our lives. Overnight (literally), the screens won out: worries about the quality-of-life differences between talking to someone in person and interacting with them online were temporarily put aside, as digital technology became the only conduit through which we were able to keep in touch with our friends, family and workmates. More than that, though, the public narrative about screens seemed to shift. No longer were they something to be vilified or feared; instead, screen-based technologies were touted as the key to getting through the crisis. Video calls and recordings replaced in-person meetings, lessons and lectures. Online video games allowed us (well, some of us) to remain in contact with friends, de-stress and rest our minds through play. Social media kept us up to date with everyone's baking activities, as well as giving us minute-by-minute analyses of how the pandemic was being handled and who was being affected.

But, lurking in the background, the worries were still there, and as we emerged from the pandemic they started to regain prominence in our minds. Was it really OK that we were all spending so much time digitally connected? Lots of parents quietly felt terrible for letting their kids play video games so much – surely there was something experientially richer or more useful they could be doing with their time? And although our daily routines had changed, the internet hadn't: cyberbullying, body-shaming, porn, violence and extremism were all still there, just a few unsuspecting misclicks away. How should we balance what had become a necessity with the potential risks?

Thankfully, science is starting to help us in getting answers to those questions. Although the debate around screen time has largely been framed as good versus evil, all versus none, the best research we currently have paints a decidedly different picture about the effects that digital technology can have on us. Screen time, it turns out, isn't a key driving factor behind the apparent decline in our mental health and wellbeing; in fact, some screen time is better for us than none at all. And yet deeper investigation reveals that, far from being simple to quantify, screen time is a remarkably complex phenomenon. Measuring how much of our days we spend in front of screens has the potential to reveal our own biases and beliefs about this relatively new technology. But those numbers alone don't tell us much about the effects they can have on how we think, feel and act. Instead, an emerging – and contentious – field of study is only now just starting to get to grips with the important details: gross screen time isn't as important as what we *do* with that time, what apps we use, how and where we use them and with *who*. Far from making us slaves to our phones, ultimately digital technology is a tool – and, like any tool, it needs to be understood so that we can utilise it appropriately and avoid hurting ourselves and others.

Nevertheless, video games, social media and smartphones often – and seemingly inexorably – provoke confusion, concern, suspicion and contempt both among those who use them and those who religiously avoid them. There is a general sense that, by sheer design, they are fundamentally damaging for us. In part this is stoked by confusing messages from medical and psychological experts, alongside stories of Silicon Valley executives – the very people creating these technologies – having low-tech homes or sending their kids to screen-free schools in an apparent attempt to mitigate the damage of their creations. Such ideas have been promulgated by a handful of science communicators and wellbeing experts, as well as a famous and much-shared *Atlantic* article, to the point that they have become a kind of default for conversations about technology. Even as far back as 2010, Apple supremo Steve Jobs was apparently reluctant to let his kids use iPads at home. It is easy to understand, then, how the conversation around screens has become so derailed.

In this book I'm going to argue that collectively, as a society, we have become too apprehensive – and even fearful – about screens. The beliefs that people hold concerning the effects that screens have on us can often be deeply idiosyncratic, grounded firmly in anecdote and lived experience. But while we shouldn't disregard our own feelings, we need to be mindful of their impact on our understanding of, and relationship with, digital technology. We all come to this debate with deep-seated worries, concerns, opinions and questions about the effects that screens can have. Through the course of this book, together we'll address some of those worries head-on; we'll look at why we've got the narrative around screens so wrong, and we'll uncover what the best science can tell us about their true impact. In a way, this is a guidebook for our digital lives. I want us to move away from generalised worries about screens becoming a controlling influence in our lives that we're unable to do anything about. In order to push past this feeling, though, we need to understand what the scientific evidence base actually has to say, clarifying what specifically we should be concerned about and, crucially, giving us tools with which to think more deeply and practically about how to make screens best work for us.

In my previous book, *Lost in a Good Game*, I laid out an argument that video games have been unfairly treated and vilified by the media – and society at large – for too long. Rather than being the digital equivalent of junk food, they are a powerful medium through which we can connect with each other, live, love and remember those we've lost. *Unlocked* builds on this argument by looking at the wider issue of digital technology through a similar lens. But because we're now talking about something much more complex and endemic within society, the story is going to be more complicated. So we're going to break down screen time into its constituent pieces and then rebuild it to see if the whole is more than the sum of its parts. In Chapter 1 we'll take a look at how we've got to our present state, and try to understand why a polarising narrative about screens has evolved over the past few years. Chapters 2 and 3 will tackle one of the big questions about our relationship with screens, and take a deep dive into the problems faced by research attempting to uncover how they impact our mental health. Chapters 4 and 5 will examine two prominent concerns that we often have about digital technology – how it affects our sleep and our ability to focus – and take a critical look at the extent to which the current scientific evidence base can speak to those worries, as well as how the wider public debate aggravates them. Chapter 6 will focus on the world of online algorithms and video game monetisation, two areas where I believe there are real issues that technology companies should rectify for the sake of our health and wellbeing. In Chapter 7 I'll explain why I think we've got stuck in thinking about screens in addictive terms, why that's unhelpful, and whether there's a better approach to using them. In the closing chapters I'll build on those arguments, and introduce more practical ways of thinking about digital technologies so that we can start to develop healthier relationships with them.

It's impossible to discuss the science on the effects of screen time without examining the reasons why we, on an individual level, find them so compelling. While other books have suggested that the science is clear and confirmed, I will take a different approach. Through telling personal stories about how we use digital technology – or rather, how we can *best* use it to focus on improving our lives – this book will dissect our complex and sometimes contradictory relationship with screens. On a cultural timescale, let alone an evolutionary one, they are startlingly new, and it's unsurprising that our default status is to view them with caution. I'm not going to pretend that I have all the answers here – no one does. Nor am I saying that there is nothing to worry about when it comes to our screen-based lives; this is not an apologia for big tech. But a lack of understanding of digital technologies, while taking perhaps too conservative and precautionary an approach towards them, means that we risk missing the myriad benefits that they can afford. My hope is that this book will prompt you to consider your association with digital technology more rationally, reflectively, and yes, more critically, because although screens are now very much a part of the fabric of society, we still remain uncertain about what category of experience to place our use of them *in*. If we want to change the narrative about screens, if we want to build the foundations for better relationships with them – both for ourselves and for younger generations – then we need to find a remedy for that. So let's begin.

1

Of pandemics and panics

It's 6 a.m., and even after nine months I am not used to being awake at this time. I have always been a late starter, preferring the quiet comfort of dark nights over early-morning sunshine. But I am up, with an essential, steaming cup of coffee in hand, because my daughter is too, and I always take the morning playtime shifts. She is a light sleeper and an early starter, as many babies are. Strewn across the living-room floor are all the usual items in an infant's arsenal of amusement; stacking cups, wooden blocks, a single-octave xylophone that has a couple of irritatingly flat bars, soft toys and our pet dog Willow, snoring lightly in one corner, desperately trying to get a nap in before she once again becomes the focus of tiny grasping hands.

Matilda is not playing with any of these things. She is playing with one of *my* toys instead.

She is standing by the sofa, balancing somewhat unsteadily using her hip as an anchor, while she holds my phone. She managed to pickpocket it from me earlier (she's worryingly good at that), and now she clasps her trophy in both hands, staring at it triumphantly, a quiet 'eeee' escaping her lips, the sound she makes whenever she successfully acquires something she has been on the hunt for. She slowly turns it over and over, inspecting front and back with equal interest. Eventually, her thumb sits on the camera icon long enough to switch it on and she stares, mesmerised by the screen. A flash lets me know that another masterful blur of colour and light has been added to my photo album. As she takes the event in she begins to repetitively, relentlessly jab at the screen, changing options that I had long forgotten existed, before the lock screen flicks back on. She prods long enough for the emergency call option to flash up and I eventually step in, holding out my hand to gently ask for it back. I get a reproachful look, and as she enthusiastically throws the phone – away from me, not towards – I watch it skitter across the floor and come to rest underneath the armchair. I put my coffee on a shelf – to be forgotten, like many before it, for the rest of the day – before scrabbling underneath the chair to rescue my phone, and then chase after my daughter as she toddles off on her next adventure.

When I watch the way in which Matilda interacts with my phone, it's easy to understand why so many people are worried about the allure of screens. While, at nine months old, she has no understanding of how to use it or what it can be used for, she nevertheless finds it fascinating, almost hypnotic. She doesn't interrogate any other toy with nearly as much intense concentration and focus as she does a smartphone. It is hard, then, not to wonder whether this is deliberate design: that these machines have been built to steal our attention, to mould us from an early age into conspicuous consumers of throwaway tech that needs to be updated as fast as we can afford it. It's also difficult not to worry that maybe it's my *own* tech use that I see reflected in her captivation. Is she just mimicking what she sees me do? Am I witnessing the results of being a terrible father? These sorts of anxieties are being voiced today by many parents, old and new. They're also exacerbated by a culture that often shames us for the way we've apparently let screens dominate our lives – countless articles breathlessly claim that it's *our fault* that kids are glued to their screens, because we've been sucked into them ourselves.*

Over time, these anxieties have coalesced into a general feeling that many of society's ills can be explained by our increasing reliance on screens. One of the most prominent examples of this is in *The Coddling of the American Mind*, a 2018 book by social psychologist Jonathan Haidt and economist Greg Lukianoff. In it they cite work by psychologist Jean Twenge suggesting that depression and anxiety rates in US teenagers started to uptick noticeably from around 2011 onwards, which corresponds to the explosion in smartphone and social media use around that time. According to Twenge, the links are undeniable. In her data, teenagers who use screens for more than two hours per day are at a much higher risk of becoming depressed, whereas for those who don't use screens at all the risk is much lower. For Haidt and Lukianoff the implications are clear: 'we don't want to create a moral panic and frighten parents into banning all devices until their kids turn twenty-one. These are complicated issues and much more research is needed. In the meantime ... there is enough evidence to support placing time limits on device use (perhaps two hours a day for adolescents, less for younger kids).'

---

* A 2018 article in *The Atlantic* did just this, arguing that 'parents should worry less about kids' screen time and more about their own'. It's an anxiety-provoking read, citing, for example, observational studies which showed that adults in dinner-table situations were more likely to ignore their kids if they were checking their phones, and less likely to socially interact with them. We've all been there; silently judging families we see at a restaurant who are glued to their screens. But the thing to remember about observational studies is that they are just a snapshot of social interaction, bereft of much-needed context and detail. More on this later.

At face value, this is a sensible suggestion. Except for two things. The first is that Twenge's work is but one strand in a tapestry of mixed results – some studies have shown that a certain amount of screen time is better than none at all (and that the amount which corresponds with 'peak' wellbeing is different depending on the time of week and type of activity), while others have suggested that while there is a correlation between screen time and mental health issues, the negative effect of smartphone use is actually quite small in comparison with other factors. The second is that the evidence suggesting that imposing strict limits on screen time will have any meaningful impact on our wellbeing is even more shaky. Perhaps the most fascinating example of this comes from South Korea. Fuelled by concerns that teenagers were spending too much time playing games on the internet at night, in 2011 the country implemented what became known as the 'shutdown policy'. Between the hours of midnight and 6 a.m., children and teenagers under the age of sixteen were effectively barred from accessing the web. When later research was conducted on the effects of this policy, scientists found that it resulted in a whopping 1.5 extra minutes of sleep per night for boys, 2.7 minutes for girls, and had the net effect of actually *increasing* the amount of time they spent on the internet during the day.

So there's something about these broad-strokes narratives that just doesn't sit right with me. Aside from being a new parent, I'm also a scientist. I conduct research on the behavioural and mental-wellbeing effects that playing video games can have on us, as well as how screen time can impact issues such as depression and anxiety. And as I've suggested, concrete scientific evidence to back up stories about the terrible outcomes of screen time simply isn't there. Let's continue with sleep as an example. We're often told that blue light before bedtime is bad for us because it disrupts the release of a hormone called melatonin, which is important for making us feel drowsy. This has become totally accepted wisdom: *Dragon's Den* entrepreneurs have made investments on the basis of blue-light-blocking tech, and health gurus writing about sleep begin the relevant chapter of their books by expounding on the disruptive effect of exposure. Screens emit blue light, so if we use them late into the evening, common sense would dictate that we're not going to get a decent night's rest. The trouble is, though, that while the relationship between blue light and melatonin is incontrovertible, research linking that to an appreciable effect in terms of screen time usage is less conclusive. And in fact, a number of studies – albeit small ones – have shown that if you give people blue-light-blocking glasses to wear for a few hours before bed, *it doesn't result in more sleep*, or feeling more refreshed in the morning. For example, a 2021 study from researchers at Montana State University found the opposite: participants who used blue-light-blocking glasses ended up having about fifteen minutes' *less* sleep per night compared with those who used control glasses with clear lenses. A similar study from six years previously asked male teenage participants to wear either blue-light blockers or control glasses and spend about three hours before bed staring at an LED screen. While the blockers appeared to suppress the effects that blue light has on melatonin production (that is, participants reported feeling sleepier before bed if they wore them), there were no differences in subjective sleepiness levels the morning after, and the participants' sleep cycles remained unchanged compared with the control condition. Then there's a study from 2019 which drew on data from over 50,000 children in the US to look at the effects of screen use on sleep. One of the key take-home messages from that research was that each hour of screen time seemed to result in between three and eight fewer minutes of sleep, which hardly feels like it's, well, worth losing sleep over. Of course, our conclusion here shouldn't be that screens *don't* impact our sleep, or that we shouldn't worry about their effects, or that we shouldn't be reflective and interrogate our use of them. It's more that, very often, our common-sense intuition that digital technology is *definitely bad* for us comes into conflict with what scientific research might actually have to say on the matter. There are no definitive answers yet, because the science of screens is young, evolving, contentious and conflicting. But it's also worth considering that, maybe, some of our suspicions about screens are wrong.

Sleep is just one of the many important areas where psychologists are trying to investigate the potentially detrimental effects that certain types of screen use can have. But before we delve deeper into the many and varied ways in which they pervade our lives, it's worth pointing out that when it comes to the fledgling science of screens, things are a bit of a mess at the moment. Part of the reason for this is the fact that it's remarkably hard to study the effects of screens in the lab, with the vast majority of research on the topic focusing instead on longitudinal data – that is, surveying large numbers of people, over time, about what proportion of their day they spend using their digital devices, how they feel their mental health is, their ability to concentrate on their work or schooling, their academic performance, and so on. Such studies have revealed a complex array of findings; some, such as Jean Twenge's, appear to show that there are clear links between screen use and mental health issues – even suicidal ideation – among US teens. Others indicate that the magnitude of the effect that screens have on mental health is of a similar order to that of eating potatoes (this isn't a flippant remark, and we'll come back to that particular study later).

Some studies have argued for something known as the

displacement hypothesis – that a linear relationship between longer amounts of screen time and increases in depression or poor mental health exists because our time on screens supplants other, more beneficial activities, like going for a walk in the woods or socialising with friends in person. Conversely, there are also studies that argue for what's called the Goldilocks hypothesis: just as in the fairy tale, too much or too little time spent online can be worse for our wellbeing than 'just the right amount'. Or, to put it another way: despite our reservations, it's important to realise that some screen time is better than none at all. It's helpful to think about this in terms of childhood benefits; if you're not allowed *any* screen time at home, then inevitably you're going to be out of step with your classmates and friends when it comes to the latest cartoon craze, game phenomenon or video sensation. While it feels like something unnatural that disconnects us, participating in the online world actually does the opposite: it's an intrinsic part of our modern-day 'real-world' lives. It's a tricky research literature to navigate, so in one sense it's unsurprising that the stories we see in the news about the effects of video games, smartphones, social media and the like often fall back on anecdata: personal accounts from individuals who have had particularly negative experiences, or (much more rarely) extremely positive ones, used implicitly as paragon examples of the effects that screens have in the main. Human-interest stories are a powerful storytelling tool when it comes to digital technology, because by and large we've all got a personal lived experience with screens, and we can often see shades of our own interactions with them in the accounts of people who have had more consequential relationships with *their* devices. Countering that narrative can be a very difficult thing to do.

Nevertheless, there is emerging research that points to the

beneficial effect that screens can have in our lives. For example, work led by Leonard Reinecke at Johannes Gutenberg University Mainz looked at this in the context of authenticity, or the way that we (truthfully) present ourselves in our day-to-day activities. The impact of being 'true to yourself' has been one that has fascinated psychologists for decades (and philosophers for even longer), and the general consensus is that authenticity is linked to increased levels of positive wellbeing. Reinecke extended this idea to our online lives: Facebook users were tested over the course of six months, and authenticity on the social networking site was linked to significant improvements not only in subjective wellbeing but also positivity and life satisfaction. Other studies have shown that in some cases screen use, at a more general level, can similarly have a net positive impact on our wellbeing. For example, in 2019 researchers based at Cardiff, Oxford and Cambridge Universities looked at survey data from caregivers for more than 50,000 children in the US and found that, rather than there being a negative linear relationship between screen time and wellbeing – i.e., as screen time goes up, wellbeing goes down – instead it was U-shaped. For low levels of screen use there was a positive relationship – that is, wellbeing went up – peaking at between one and five hours per day, depending on the type of activity (watching TV shows, playing video games, using computers to check emails and so on). It was only after much higher levels of engagement that a subjectively noticeable decline in wellbeing started to occur – around four and a half hours for watching TV, and more than five hours for spending time on the phone, on computers or playing video games.

While this is by no means the final word on the matter, it does at least show that the way we use screens is complex and nuanced, with as much potential for good in our lives as bad.

In part, this is why the concept of 'digital detox' as a proposed solution to our online ailments doesn't sit particularly well with me. The idea itself is rooted in a sort of technological determinism – the notion that the technologies we use essentially act as the fundamental basis for the development of social and cultural structures in society. When a technology becomes more advanced, or a completely new one comes into play, it acts as the principal driver for societal change. Critically, because technology is so powerful in this regard, we end up feeling as though society is largely powerless to stop it. This, of course, is a huge oversimplification of the tangled web of social, psychological, economic and political factors that underpin societal change, but it's also unsurprising that some feel the need to push back against a tangible causal agent.

As screen-based technologies have become more prolific, so too have we seen an increase in the number of people who preach abstinence, eager for us to expunge this blight from our psychological systems. Digital detox articles abound on the internet, all with a similar message: screens are inherently damaging for us, so take a break for a week, a month, a year, and you'll feel less stressed and much more in control of your life. By and large, though, these stories fall back on anecdotal experiences: seemingly reasonable and sensible suggestions, but ones that aren't supported by research. Large-scale studies – those which track people's digital technology usage over a long period of time – simply don't exist yet. Instead, where studies do exist, most ask people to quit temporarily for a much shorter period of time: say twenty-four hours, or a week. The results are mixed, but there's a growing body of evidence to suggest that abstaining from things like social media doesn't result in an automatic improvement in people's mental health. Nor does it seem to be the case that they

replace their social media time with other forms of socialising. In fact, some studies have shown that if you ask people
to refrain from using Facebook for a few days, they have
reduced levels of the hormone cortisol (which is involved in
the body's stress response), but they also report decreased
life satisfaction. These findings, and others, lead to a general
sense that digital technology *isn't* inherently harmful in the
way we might have been led to believe. And in turn, digital
detoxes are meaningless, because the problem they're trying
to fix doesn't really exist.

The whole ethos of digital detoxing borrows heavily from
the diet and wellness industry, which is ironic because the
same criticisms can be levelled there: 'detox' diets, we are
told, help us to clear toxic sludge from our bodies – leftover
poisons from sinful overindulgences, like eating too much at
Christmas. If we fast, or cut out impure things like caffeine,
or restrict ourselves to eating nothing but bone broth, we will
magically and permanently lose weight, look more beautiful,
be more energetic and generally be more ideal versions of
ourselves. A wonderful idea, save for the fact that detox diets
are utter hogwash, devoid of any evidence that they actually
work. There are no quick fixes when it comes to weight loss,
just as there are no quick fixes when we want to change things
in our digital lives for the better.

Pseudoscientific nutritional advice aside, though, there's
nevertheless some mileage in considering issues around screen
time in dietary terms. In fact, in 2020 Cambridge University
psychologist Dr Amy Orben did just that, putting forward an
argument for a 'digital diet' approach to frame our reasoning
about the effects that digital technologies can have on us. 'The
funny thing is, the whole diet literature is kind of like the
screen time literature, in that anything prescriptive ends up
being out of touch with reality,' Amy tells me. 'But also, the

difficulty with our current approaches to researching screens and digital media mirrors the fact that there's been no real scientific progress in the diet literature, or how it's communicated to the public,' she adds. The digital diet approach that Amy espouses is somewhat tongue-in-cheek, but nevertheless provides a useful metaphor for shaping meaningful questions about digital technology. In order to understand how our diet influences our development, she explains, there are a number of specific questions that we should ask: for example, about the types of foods, and how much of each, we're eating. We need to know what the interaction is between different food groups. We need to take individual variations into account, because people can have very diverse reactions to certain foods – nuts are fine for most people, for instance, but not for those with a nut allergy. We also need to think about the context in which we eat things – an energy bar is great if you're running a marathon, but perhaps not so good just before bed, when you want to get to sleep. And lastly, we need to know about population-level factors: food and financial inequalities across the globe mean that in some countries dietary challenges focus on malnutrition, in others on obesity.

Those same questions can be asked of our digital diets. Just as some foods are healthier for us than others, so it is the case that different forms (and amounts) of screen time can have varying potential effects on our health and wellbeing. If used correctly, screens can offer us a wealth of situation-specific advantages and benefits, and we all have stories of connecting with loved ones via Zoom or FaceTime during lockdown as an obvious example. At the same time, absent-mindedly scrolling through social media in the middle of the night is perhaps not such a good idea when you would be better off getting some sleep. And, like global dietary challenges, digital inequalities are faced by diverse populations both within and across countries: screen time studies, and the ensuing advice, which fit well in one area might not translate appropriately in other places and populations.

So here's the thing: screens aren't in fact ruining our lives, or those of our children. The discussions we have about them shouldn't be all-or-nothing affairs; we shouldn't be starting from the position that either they are destroying our minds and society or that they are uniquely, wholly good for us. Neither stance allows us any insight into what's truly going on, thus denying us the potential to identify and develop beneficial digital technology habits. In order to get to grips with what the effects really are, we need to keep a calm mind and take a level-headed approach while maintaining a healthy dose of critical thinking. That criticality begins with interrogating what 'screen time' really means in the first place.

Take a moment to look at your immediate environment and the digital technology that's lying around. For me, it's everywhere. I'm writing this on my laptop, which is connected to two external monitors. An iPad sits off to one side, displaying my daily to-do list. My phone, precariously balanced on the edge of my desk, occasionally pings with an email notification, a WhatsApp message or an announcement that someone's just rung my doorbell. These are echoed by the occasional buzz of the smartwatch on my wrist. A digital photo frame cycles endlessly through pictures of friends and family on a nearby shelf, and next to it my Nintendo Switch lies idly waiting for someone to come along and charge it. All screens, but all very different from one another. What exactly do we mean then by 'screen time'? And, perhaps more to the point, how do we even begin to assess it in terms of the impact it can have on us?

This is not a trivial problem. The vast majority of research on the effects of digital technology essentially takes the form of self-report questionnaires, and here's where our troubles begin. The simplest way to define screen time is as the number of hours during which we use some sort of screen-based technology per day. That's an enticing definition for the scientists doing the research because it's so simple: ask people how much they use their digital devices, and you get a number between zero and twenty-four. But as my current working environment – and perhaps yours – shows, this would be meaningless. On this particular Tuesday, over the past hour, for the most part I've been looking at my laptop screen as I write. I've also glanced at my phone an indeterminate number of times to check messages, emails or social media. In between writing paragraphs, I've idly shuffled a music playlist on one of my secondary screens ... *Who am I kidding*, I've sometimes been doing that mid-sentence when the right words have eluded me. Does all that count as one hour of screen time? According to my basic definition above, yes. Does that measure tell us anything meaningful about what effect the last hour of screen time has had on me? Probably not.

So maybe we can be smarter about this. Let's try to break down my last hour in a more meaningful way. I'm going to liberally claim that I spent thirty minutes writing. For the sake of argument, let's say that I spent about ten minutes flicking through my song playlist, five minutes checking emails, three minutes on WhatsApp, and the remaining twelve minutes scrolling through Twitter. Of my Twitter time, four minutes consisted of idle 'doomscrolling' through my feed, absorbing an onslaught of bad news about the world in general. Five minutes were spent chatting to colleagues in private messages about some ongoing project ideas, one minute watching a video of someone performing a 1980s-style rendition of 'Wonderwall', and, after clicking a website link, the last two minutes quickly flicking through a news article.

That, I think, is a fairly comprehensive account of my last hour of screen time. If we were able to take the same level of detail across an entire day, we'd have a pretty reasonable starting point for working out which uses might have had a beneficial impact on me, which weren't so great, and whether, on balance, I had a fairly good day or my mental health took a bit of a hit.

That rather long-winded example highlights a crucial point about screen time research: getting this level of detail about an individual's daily screen diet is a near-impossible task, and *no* studies do this well. I was able to provide these tremendously exciting details because I've just spent the last few minutes thinking quite hard about what I'd done over the preceding hour, but scientific studies which rely on self-report question-naire methods don't do this – can't do this. They instead ask questions like 'Thinking over the past week, how many hours or minutes per day did you spend on social media?' If you came back next week and asked me how I'd spent my Tuesday afternoon, I'd likely just say that I spent an hour working on my book. All of that nuance would be lost, because we don't keep accurate, internalised, minute-by-minute records of our daily routines. It's just not how our memories work.

But, for the sake of argument, let's just say that we *could* remember. You come back next week, ask me what I did on Tuesday afternoon, and I accurately tell you that I spent twelve minutes on Twitter. But *even then*, this doesn't tell you much. The five minutes that I spent privately talking to colleagues left me feeling positive about some upcoming pro-jects. The four minutes of doomscrolling left me feeling a bit miserable. Critically, these things didn't happen in sequence; they *happened at the same time*. How do we even begin to disentangle their effects?

You can see where I'm going with this. Research that

attempts to catalogue the time we spend on digital devices and compare that against measures of things like mental health and wellbeing is flawed at a fairly fundamental level. It's an elephant in the room that we're only just starting to acknowledge, highlighted quite neatly in a 2020 paper by a team led by Dr Heather Shaw at Lancaster University. 'I used to be a psychology technician, before I started doing my PhD,' explains Shaw – we're talking about her work over a Zoom call, and in the back of my mind I can't help wondering whether we should be counting this towards our daily screen time estimates. 'I was really interested in behavioural analytics research – so what we can learn about people's psychology from digital traces of behaviour – and I got drawn to smartphones because they're ubiquitous, we use them so much during the day,' she explains. 'There are lots of potential applications for health here – so, things like if you can infer whether a certain type of person or a certain type of usage can lead towards issues like anxiety or depression.' When a researcher starts out on a new avenue of enquiry, the first thing to do is an in-depth, detailed search of the existing scientific literature in order to figure out what we already know, what we don't know and how studies are typically run. 'Because I used to be a technician, I believe that there's a technical solution to these sorts of questions,' Shaw points out. 'But I found it quite outstanding that hardly any studies were using these digital traces that you can now collect, and instead most were based on psychometric scales, or estimates of how people *thought* they were using their phones.' I understand this, because it's something that I've fallen foul of in my own research on video games. It's much easier to ask someone how much time they think they've been playing a game over the past week than it is to get a more objective measure drawn from the actual technology they use. And when a project is time-critical, we tend to fall back on what we know will be quick, even when it doesn't quite achieve what we want it to.

Focusing on smartphones, Shaw's study compared three different measures of screen time: a single question asking participants to estimate how many hours per day they used their smartphone over the preceding week; a self-rated questionnaire measure of smartphone addiction; and an objective measure, which either involved participants downloading an app that tracked how often they picked up their phone and used it, or using Apple's built-in Screen Time app. They also asked participants to fill out measures of anxiety and perceived stress. 'The thing in my mind was: "Why are there so many discrepancies?" Why is one research result saying one thing and another saying something else?' explains Shaw. 'One thought was that it could be down to the measurements everyone was using, so I wanted to put that to the test.'

Across two experiments, Shaw and her team found that the method by which smartphone use was determined had a profound effect on its observed relationship with mental health. The first study, of forty-six Android users, showed that the correlation between smartphone addiction and anxiety, depression and stress was only significant in the subjective measure – in other words, when participants were asked to assess their own use. Indeed, the extent of the correlation *quadrupled* when that method was used, compared with either the self-rated measure of screen time or the objective measure of phone use. The second study rolled this out to nearly 200 iPhone users and found a similar result: a threefold increase in the size of the correlation when using self-rated smartphone addiction as a measure, as opposed to the subjective screen time estimate or objective logs from Apple's Screen Time app. Further statistical modelling corroborated this:

while measures of people's self-rated worries about smart-phone addiction seemed to predict mental health scores, using objective measures of the actual time they used their phones didn't. In other words, conflating how someone *thinks* they are using their smartphone with how they are *actually* using it produces very different findings about the potential effect on their mental wellbeing. This isn't a trivial problem that the research field can ignore – a recent review of studies in the area by Sara Thomée at the University of Gothenburg showed that 70 per cent of them use some version of a self-report-style smartphone addiction scale.

As we will come to see, the emerging research on screen time and whether it has positive or negative effects on us is starting to shift: whereas earlier work raised concerns about clear, potentially causal negative impacts on various facets of mental wellbeing, recent studies temper those worries with more nuanced and reassuring findings that allude to milder effects and, in some cases, actual benefits. Where problems are being noted, these are starting to become more specific, more targeted, and therefore more actionable. And while mental wellbeing is obviously a hugely important topic, the story of our screen-based lives is one that touches on a wealth of other factors. So, like anything in psychology, the science of screens needs to be examined within the wider context of the rest of our lifestyle. Screen use doesn't occur in isolation – it happens alongside work, play, relaxation, major life events, minor life events and everything in between, all of which may be moderated, in some way, by our use of screens. And vice versa; our attitudes and approaches towards our own screen time are very likely impacted by the day-to-day situations we find ourselves in. This is not a particularly novel revelation, and one that I am sure most of us, consciously or otherwise, already know. But it came into stark focus in the early months

of 2020, when a new coronavirus, SARS-CoV-2, made a devastating entrance on to the world stage.

When the first lockdown came into effect in the UK, at the
beginning I didn't really appreciate the impact that it would
have on the little everyday things we took for granted, not
least in terms of what it meant for Matilda's growth and
development. Prior to that point, her diary was a busy one: if
she wasn't going to a coffee shop with her mum to meet other
recently mummified friends she was at swimming classes,
sensory classes or music sessions. All of that stopped in the
spring of 2020, though, and we were faced with the realisation that she wasn't going to be seeing anyone, her age or
otherwise, for quite some time. How would it affect her social
development? And, dear God, how would we stop her from
getting bored? It was a rising sense of anxiety that I'm sure
many parents across the country, across the world, began to
experience – much more so those of older children who, virtually overnight, had to figure out how to juggle their own work
life with the prospect of becoming a de facto schoolteacher.

We all quickly pivoted to a digital life. Schools and universities made a Herculean effort to shift classes online.
Where people could work from home, they rapidly became
well versed in the art of Zoom video calls, Google meets,
Microsoft Team sessions and the like. Some of us even managed to remember our Skype passwords.* Driving all of this
was a need to stay connected, to maintain some sense of
normality in the most extraordinary of situations. Screens
became the central hub of our lives, and with that came an
amplified urge to get the balance right, to temper our preconceived notions of what constitutes 'good-quality' playtime,

---

* Alas, too few of us were able to fully use this time to master the art of
not hitting 'reply-all' to large group emails.

or work time, or relaxation time, with the simple fact that we were limited to what was possible within the boundaries of our own homes. I was lucky, in a sense – having spent a lifetime in the company of computers, I was immediately comfortable with transferring most of my social interactions online. I was worried about Matilda, though. Suddenly her world had shrunk to all of two people: Mum and Dad. She was ten months old when lockdown hit. Did she understand that when we were video-calling with family, those moving pictures she saw on our phones were her grandparents, her aunties and uncles, cousins, friends? In those early days she didn't really seem to comprehend this, or recognise the real people on the other end of the call. How would it play out?

As a scientist, I often find solace in evidence and research. There is a certain comfort in learning something new, objectively getting to grips with an evidence base, separating the good science from the anecdotal pseudoresearch. It takes time, but the end result is – hopefully – a more informed opinion, a drop of enlightenment in what would otherwise be a sea of uncertainty. And while there is no science (yet) to tell us about the effects of moving our lives online specifically in the context of a pandemic, I did take heart in the broader evidence base for screen time effects. For example, a 2018 study published in the *Journal of Experimental Child Psychology* looked specifically at the effects of video calls, versus pre-recorded videos, in the context of toddlers' word-learning skills. Nearly ninety two-and-a-half-year-olds took part in an experiment in which they were either shown a video or had a video call with an experimenter, with the aim of teaching them some new words. For one half of the toddlers, their parents took part and played along with the instructions, whereas for the other half their parents simply sat in the room with them. The results showed that live video calls were better than the pre-recorded videos at keeping the toddlers' *attention*, but it was only when parents were taking part alongside them that they were actually able to learn new words. This is a study that has stuck with me for a while now: whenever Matilda watches TV, for example, when possible I try to watch along with her and share in that experience.*

Another potentially useful source of evidence came in the form of guidelines from paediatric associations – although this is a somewhat mixed bag of suggestions. For nearly twenty years the American Academy of Pediatrics took a 'digital abstinence' stance, suggesting no screen time at all for children aged two or younger, and no more than two hours a day for those older. More recently, in 2016, they shifted this position, suggesting no screen time at all until eighteen months old, a 'limited' amount of screen time for those aged eighteen to twenty-four months, and no more than an hour a day for two-to-five-year-olds. Neither of these policy positions were based in meaningful evidence, nor were they particularly useful in the context of the pandemic. Thankfully, the Royal College of Paediatrics and Child Health (RCPCH) introduced much more level-headed and evidence-based screen time guidance in 2019. Rather than try to suggest hard time limits, the focus here was to approach conversations about screen time based on a child's developmental age, their individual needs, and the amount of importance and value that the family placed on other activities like socialising or exercise. Basically, the RCPCH's approach was much more reasonable: there's no clear evidence base for a 'toxic' effect of screen time, there's no good evidence to suggest that screen time thresholds work, so the next-best thing to do is to look at how our own families use

---

*   Also, it means I get to watch cartoons for a bit, and you're never too old for a good cartoon.

screens, figure out where it's working and where it might be interfering with home life, and adjust accordingly.

In the absence of solid, robust research that could tell me what the potential effects of lockdown screen time were for me and my family, I took the RCPCH's advice: don't panic, be mindful of what we were doing on screens, when, and for how long, and prioritise face-to-face interaction. By necessity, sometimes this was FaceTime-to-FaceTime, but you get the idea. It was Matilda's first birthday right in the midst of the first lockdown. While some politicians in the UK were partying away in their offices, on that day our dining room felt a little quieter; filled with pom-poms, bunting and streamers for a party that couldn't happen the way we wanted it to. A helium-filled '1' balloon floated gently in a tight circle, anchored to her high chair, which was positioned at the head of the table. The table itself was adorned with multi-coloured paper cups, plates and napkins, and a picnic feast for the three of us. As she munched on a cucumber sandwich, Mum sneaked off into the kitchen to light a candle on the Paddington Bear cake she had made the day before. I had my phone in hand, ready to record the moment. 'On three! One, two, three – happy birthday to …' A wonderfully disjointed singing chorus blared out from the laptop, placed close enough to the birthday girl for her to see her family, but just far enough away for it not to get covered in crumbs. Although we couldn't have everyone we loved physically in the house to celebrate, Zoom meant that we could share that special, fleeting moment with those we wanted to.

Still, as much as those video calls with friends and family had been necessary, did we really need to have so many of them, or were we using them as an excuse to fill the time, on occasion, when we were exhausted? Was that also true of the TV time we had allowed her? Sure, either my wife or I would watch it with her whenever we could, but in all honesty there were times – there still are times – when we needed a brief distraction so that we could get a chore done or take a breath. It's easy to think about these things in the abstract, when we're detached from the situation, but some time later the country started to tentatively open up, and all those anxieties about Matilda's development came into sharp focus. She was about to go back to nursery and see a lot of people – real, flesh-and-blood people – for the first time in months. Had we got it wrong?

Among many information sheets and forms to fill in upon Matilda's return, the nursery had also told us that we could download an app which we could use to track her progress, and into which they would upload photos of her antics during the day. After I dropped her off that first morning back, I remember spending much of the next few hours constantly refreshing the program, worrying and wondering whether she was getting along with nursery friends or whether she was struggling being around so many people.

Eventually, an update popped up.

'This morning Matilda enjoyed playing with her friends. The first thing she did was to give every one of them a cuddle and say "Ahh"'.

The reality of the situation was that, although those anxieties about Matilda's screen time had been in the back of my mind throughout the pandemic, and particularly as we moved back into a more normal way of life, so too had that guidance from the RCPCH. Try not to panic, try not to take an all-or-nothing approach, but instead be reflective about her digital technology use (as well as my own around her) – and, critically, have conversations about the when and where of its use. Those are the things that ultimately allayed my fears.

Being mindful about our digital technology use – by which

I mean being persistently reflective about what we're doing, as well as how, why and when we're doing it – is one of a few better habits that we can all start developing if we want to have healthier relationships with screens. We'll come across more in due course, and I'll elaborate on why that particular habit is, I think, one of the more important ones in our toolkit. I also appreciate that, at this point, it may well come across as the sort of thing that's easier said than done. In the years I've spent researching the effects of digital technology, I've come to understand that the answers aren't so much about the technology itself as the people involved – both those who use it and those who study it. People are messy, unpredictable, biased and surprising, and scientists are no different. As much as this is a story about technology, it's a story about *us* – why we rely on screens to such an extent, why we have concerns about that, and why we find it hard to see the positives in our habits. I'm not going to tell you that there's nothing to worry about, because that's simply not true. But my hope is that in picking apart the science of screens, we might all be better equipped to understand how to best use them in our lives and gain confidence in our ability to get real benefits out of them. After all, screens aren't going away any time soon.

So let's make them work for us.

2

Are smartphones destroying a generation?

Someone likes your entry.

It was a subject line that had all the hallmarks of your run-of-the-mill scam email. Devoid of context, slightly enticing, but also a little bit creepy. Normally I wouldn't have given it a second thought before consigning it, with a swipe, to my junk folder. But then I saw the sender: LiveJournal.

Oh my God, does that website still exist? Wait – does my account still exist?!

For the uninitiated, LiveJournal was a proto social network that emerged at the turn of the millennium. Back then, it felt like a counter-culture mini-blogging site, in some ways a predecessor to Substack but with more grungy teenage angst, and less potential to make a viable living out of it. Blog entries could be as long or as short as you wanted them to be, and you could even tag on a little animated GIF to express your current mood, if you were in the habit of wearing your heart on your sleeve. It was generally available for any and all to see, but I vaguely remember that back when I started using the site it was an invitation-only system, and you could protect posts so that only 'friends' (followers, basically) could read them. For a few years in the early 2000s LiveJournal was the centre of my digital life, where I would talk about my hopes and dreams, my deepest fears, and post the occasional (by which I mean frequent) 'what Pokémon/Hogwarts house/condiment are you?'-style 'personality' quiz to a select group of friends, some of who I'd never met in person and who lived on the other side of the world. Back in those days, the idea that you could just casually talk to someone who lived literally anywhere still felt like something out of a sci-fi movie. It was intoxicating, at least for a while. As I grew up and grew older I moved on, and eventually forgot that I ever even had a blog on that site.

Until now. I'm not only looking at my old entries, I'm looking at them as *someone who isn't logged into the site.* With a rising sense of horror, I realise that these thoughts and intimate insights about my life have just been sitting there, ready for anyone to read, for the past twenty years. I frantically go through the process of deleting the account, as though if I don't do it right away someone, now, after two decades, is going to find it and broadcast it to the world. Although it takes a while to lock it down, finally it's done. But not before I make a copy of the entries to scour through.

It transpires that I wrote somewhere in the region of 35,000 words over the course of three years in my late teens, during my first stint at university, when arguably that time might have been more appropriately spent working on my studies. It's a time in my life which I can now barely recall. Sure, there are pockets of recollection – the big things, mostly – but for the most part, when I try to think back to that time there are only shards of memories, distortions that no longer seem to properly fit together to make complete impressions in my mind. As I pore over the blog entries, I start to understand why. I read through the musings of this past version of me and my heart starts to break a little. This kid was *miserable*. There's all the usual juvenile malaise in there: unrequited love, worries about schoolwork, arguments with family. But there's something else, just under the surface of it all. Something that feels a little more insidious.

3rd December 2002. 9:52p.m.

You stare at a screen. That's all you do every night. No one wants to talk to you, and they get annoyed whenever you call. That's understandable, because whenever you do call, all you ever end up talking about is yourself and how everything's wrong with your life.

You're selfish. What have you got to show for your life? Nothing. You're a failure, and your father would be quietly disappointed with the way you turned out. You're a mistake, and a stupid one at that.

People like you, sure. For a while. Then you become unwanted baggage. You'd like to think it's because you're drifting apart, that people change. But you know why. You're an idiot. You just do a good job of hiding it for the first few months. And here's the killer part. You've found that you can hide it perfectly on the internet. So you have all these people across the world who think you're great. Why? It's easy to lie to them. To show them something you're not, and make them think you're a better person than you really are. But, through it all, you know the truth, and it eats at you. You're a liar.

You stare at a flickering screen. Every night, the same routine. You think about everything that's wrong with your life, and get depressed. Then you stick on some depressing music to make yourself feel worse. Then you load up livejournal, and moan about all the shit that happens to you and how it's not fair and how you don't deserve it.

The truth is, you do.

It's hard to read that back. While I don't remember much from that time, I do remember feeling that way. Not long after I wrote that post, I plucked up the courage to talk to a doctor. I was diagnosed with depression, and spent the next ten years or so on various types of therapy and medication. It's something that I still deal with on occasion now – depression is something that's always there, at best just ebbing into the background of your life – but reading posts like the one above, I can't help but feel the urge to reach back in time to help that kid, to tell him that things would get better, that he would be OK. Such is the benefit of hindsight.

You stare at a screen. That's all you do every night. With the advent of smartphones and how much we worry about them, those words are eerily familiar to so many of us. Was I depressed because I spent too much time on screens? Or did I spend my evenings scouring the internet for some sort of greater meaning, or social connection, because I was so low? Trying to understand that relationship, and in particular which direction it flows, is at the cutting edge of psychological research into the effects that digital technology can have on us. It is also an issue that plays out in a very public manner in the wider discourse that we see around screens, and smartphones in particular. Because they are a relatively new technology, it is unsurprising that we view them with wariness and uncertainty. Add that to the fact that smartphones, as the most overt manifestation of our digital lives, are everywhere we look, and it's hard not to worry. We worry that because of that little device we store in our pockets, we are no longer willing or able to take interest in the world around us. That social media and video games bring out the worst in us, more antisocial than social activities – ones that are turning us into baser, angrier versions of ourselves, and in the process making the world that little bit less manageable to live in. That we could be doing something better with our time. And, ultimately, we worry that all of this is breaking our mental health.

These are entirely reasonable fears to have, in part because they fit so succinctly with our lived experience of screens. Next time you're out and about, take a look around at what everyone's doing. How many people do you see fixated on their phones? Or, more to the point, how many people do you see fixated on their phones when it looks and feels like they probably shouldn't be? And I'm sure many of us have had moments when, after absent-mindedly scrolling through a social media feed, or a retail website, or a news app, we've caught ourselves in the act (or maybe someone close to us has) and felt like maybe we've overdone it a bit. It's little moments like these that feed into our perception of screens as something unwholesome, designed simply to steal our attention and our time. So when a scientist comes along and validates those fears, telling us that screens *are* actually eroding our mental health, it's hard not to do anything but listen to them, precisely because it fits in with our perceptions of the world. And then we worry even more.

For as long as I've been a psychologist, I've seen this play out in the media. Every so often, someone comes along and proclaims that screens are bad for us in some way, or ruining society, or ruining our kids. They are usually, although not exclusively, dystopian affairs that leave readers with a hopeless feeling of the inexorable influence that digital technology has on making everything worse. They are also usually, although again not exclusively, based in anecdote, cherry-picked data, or appeals to authority. One of my favourite examples was a news article from 2011 with the headline 'Computer games leave children with dementia, warns top neurologist', which was neither based on research (there is no study showing that children will get dementia if they play video games), nor declared by a top neurologist (the person in question, Professor Susan Greenfield, is a neuroscientist with no background research expertise in the psychology of media effects). Stories like this gain significant traction, tend to be rebutted relatively quickly by science writers interested in screen time effects (although, due to Brandolini's Law,* these counterpoints are rarely publicised as widely as the original article), and then fade into relative obscurity until a few months later, when essentially the same drama plays out in the media all over again.

Something about this cycle changed in the latter half of the 2010s. While we continued to see the usual sorts of scare stories about screens in the news, it felt as though they were now coming at us with a much greater sense of urgency. It seemed that we were nearing a point of no return: today's kids have never known a world without internet-connected screens, it is fundamentally changing the way that they live their lives, and they are experiencing significant distress as a result. One of the most important articles in this genre was published by *The Atlantic* in the summer of 2017. 'Have smartphones destroyed a generation?', written by Professor Jean Twenge, made the case that the post-millennial generation, or iGen as she referred to them, are suffering from an apparent suspension of adolescence – they report spending more time at home and less time working, driving (or learning to drive), dating and having sex. Concurrent with this apparent rejection of independence and responsibility, there has been a ruinous increase in psychological vulnerability in teenagers: they are less likely

---

* Also known as the 'Bullshit Asymmetry Principle'. First coined by Italian computer programmer Alberto Brandolini in 2013, this states that the amount of energy needed to refute bullshit is orders of magnitude bigger than that necessary to produce it in the first place.

to get enough sleep, more likely to feel alone, depression rates are soaring and, perhaps of most concern, so too are levels of suicidal ideation.* What set this article apart from most other such scare stories was the fact that these weren't just idle musings: Twenge was drawing on data from at least two extensive datasets, one of which is called the Monitoring the Future survey, which is a long-running nationally represent-ative survey based in the US. On a yearly basis, Monitoring the Future asks thirteen-to-eighteen-year-olds about a range of topics – everything from drug use, to what they do in their spare time, to their opinions on religion. Crucially, the survey also asks how happy they are, and over the past few years how much time they spend on screens. By Twenge's reckoning, the trends across a range of mental wellbeing indicators were clear: teenagers who spent a greater than average amount of time engaging in activities like using social media, sending text messages or surfing the internet were more likely to report being unhappy. 'There's not a single exception,' she wrote. 'All screen activities are linked to less happiness, and all nonscreen activities are linked to more happiness.'

Twenge's article was, in many ways, the vanguard of a new anxiety about screens, and one that hasn't gone unnoticed by major stakeholders. In 2018, Apple shareholders published an open letter urging that the tech giant should do more to help parents and protect youngsters from the potentially harmful effects of too much screen time (Twenge's work was heavily cited in it). In response, that same year Apple introduced a new feature to its mobile operating system iOS 12, rather unimaginatively called 'Screen Time', which provided smart-phone users with information about what apps they are using,

---

*   Essentially, having thoughts about suicide, which might range from thinking that you 'might be better off dead' through to working out elaborate plans as to how you might go about it.

how often and for how long, alongside the ability to set time limits on the most frequently used apps.* At around the same time, the UK's House of Commons Science and Technology Committee launched an inquiry into the impact of social media and screen use on children and adolescent health. The inquiry saw over 150 written submissions from across the spectrum of interested parties: researchers, parents, teens, teachers, schools, technology companies and more wrote in to extol the virtues of screens or decry their wickedness, and in general give voice to the rising sense of concern around them. The ensuing report, published in 2019, was understandably wide-ranging in scope, covering everything from the importance of screens for creativity and learning, to harms around online hate speech and violence, to risks for mental health and wellbeing, to the onus on both government and industry to shoulder the responsibility to improve childhood outcomes. There was even a brief, and appropriately dismissive, section responding to worries about the effects of 'electrosmog'.† Prefacing all this was one important point. So important, in fact, that it formed the first substantive chapter of the report.

In an attempt to synthesise the evidence base for understanding the potential benefits or disbenefits of using screen-based technology, the Science and Technology Committee had come to the same conclusion that many researchers in this area, myself included, have been calmly, rationally trying to explain

---

* To date, it's still unclear as to whether this new feature was anything other than a response to that letter. According to reports at the time, rather than being grounded in anything resembling evidence-based research, the decision to implement the feature came largely off the back of consultations with advocacy groups and the likes of Ariana Huffington.

† Electrosmog, briefly, relates to the belief held by some that electromagnetic fields created by phones, wi-fi routers, telephone masts and the like can cause an array of physical illness symptoms in some particularly 'electrosensitive' people. There's no convincing evidence to date that this is accurate. Nevertheless, it hasn't stopped a parade of grifters hawking tin-foil hats to vulnerable people who have legitimate worries about their health.

for years now. That point is this: research which attempts to understand the links between screen time and mental health is so fraught with methodological problems and statistical limitations that we simply don't have anything near the sort of convincing evidence base necessary to come to firm conclusions about cause and effect. We certainly have nothing to reasonably support the outlandish claim that smartphones have destroyed a generation.

Twenge's research, along with some of the studies that were published in response, does a good job of highlighting many of the issues facing the scientific study of screen time effects, so let's take a look at what's going on in a bit more detail. The original 2017 *Atlantic* article was adapted from Twenge's book, published that same year and rather prolixly titled *iGen: Why Today's Super-Connected Kids Are Growing Up Less Rebellious, More Tolerant, Less Happy – and Completely Unprepared for Adulthood – and What That Means for the Rest of Us*. Within a few months of both being published, Twenge, with colleagues from San Diego State and Florida State Universities, also published a study in the journal *Clinical Psychological Science*. This, to me, seems the wrong way round: if you're going to publish a pop science book and a major magazine article decrying the effects of screens, then prudence would suggest that the research on which those claims are being made should be published first. Anyway, the study was based on data from Monitoring the Future and a second nationally representative survey called the Youth Risk Behavior Surveillance System, and therefore essentially forms the core scientific basis for both the book and article. As reported in both, the study purported to show that between 2010 and 2015 there were clear increases in teenage depressive symptoms, suicide-related outcomes and actual suicide. During that same period, teenagers were spending more time on screen-based activities. In a series of correlational analyses, Twenge and her team found that teenagers who reported spending more time on screen-based activities were significantly more likely to feel more depressed, and the team found at least one suicide-related outcome – that is, a positive correlation between increasing screen time and increasing mental health issues. Conversely, teenagers who reported spending more time on non-screen activities – things like exercise, attending church, having a paid job or meeting up with friends – were statistically significantly *less* likely to report mental health issues. When it came to suicide-related outcomes specifically, the analysis suggested an exposure-response relationship with what the authors termed electronic device use: 28 per cent of teenagers who reported spending an hour using screens per day also reported at least one suicide risk factor, which increased to 33 per cent of those reporting two hours of use per day, and up to 48 per cent of teenagers who used screens for five or more hours. 'It seems likely,' Twenge and her team concluded, 'that the concomitant rise of screen time and adolescent depression and suicide is not coincidental.'

There's an obvious point to make here, which we'll come to in a moment. The first thing to say is that, as scary as this all sounds, one detail which was overlooked in the Twenge study was that although the correlations were statistically significant – that is, the findings were unlikely to have occurred randomly or by chance – they were incredibly weak. The correlations reported between depressive symptoms and screen activities (either social media use, watching TV or browsing the internet for news) were between 0.01 and 0.06. Correlations can range from values between -1 and 1, where -1 implies a perfect negative correlation, 0 implies no correlation and 1 implies a perfect positive correlation. In other words, if you were to plot two variables against each other on a graph, and then draw a straight line through them that best captures the relationship between them, then a correlation of 1 would mean that your data points essentially all fall exactly on that line. A correlation of 0 would be a flat line through a messy cloud of dots. Generally, correlations above 0.5 are said to be strong, those between around 0.3 and 0.5 are medium, and below 0.3 they are weak. In this case, we have *very* weak correlations. Another way of thinking about this is to consider the amount of covariance that the correlations explain. Covariance refers, in our case, to the extent to which variation in social media use can account for the variation in depressive symptoms. A high positive covariance would mean that there was a strong relationship between the two – when social media use increases, depressive symptoms would also tend to increase in a more predictable way. On the other hand, low positive covariance would mean that there was essentially no consistent relationship between the two – in this scenario, changes in social media use couldn't reliably be used to predict any consistent changes in depressive symptoms. In a reanalysis of Twenge's data, Amy Orben showed that social media use explains 0.36 per cent of the covariance in depressive symptoms for teenage girls. That is, less than half a per cent of the variation in depressive symptoms that teenage girls report can be accounted for based on the amount of social media they're exposed to. For the data from teenage boys, that amount is even smaller – by Orben's analysis, social media use explained about 0.01 per cent of the variability in depressive symptoms – and in fact, by Twenge's own reporting, while depressive symptoms broadly seem to be increasing in girls over time, for boys the trend seems to be *downwards*. Once we start to take a more careful look at the data, then, it seems harder to justify a firm conclusion that screen time is clearly driving a meaningful aggravation of mental health issues.

The obvious point to make is one which we all know about and are probably fed up with hearing. And it's this: correlations don't tell us anything meaningful about causal relationships. A classic example of this, taught to many undergraduates, is that ice-cream sales correlate pretty well with crime rates – both go up during the summer months and down during the winter. Ice-cream sales clearly do not drive people to commit wanton illegal acts, though, nor is it the case that crime sprees fuel an anxiety in the population which people try to alleviate with a cold treat. As the lesson goes, there is a third variable that can account for both – the time of year. People like eating ice cream when it's warmer and sunnier, and longer summer days drive a shift in our activities, which means that there are more opportunities to commit crime. While Twenge's study attempted to account for some potential third variables – things like socioeconomic status, race and unemployment rate – it didn't account for all of them. This might be an unfair point to make – it would be incredibly difficult to take into account everything that you think could have an impact – but it's an important one. While there are many potentially significant factors that might reasonably impact both screen use and mental health, we don't yet have a clear idea of what the key ones might be. In order to gain that understanding, and come up with an appropriate or meaningful list of potential third variables, it's necessary to have some sort of theoretical framework in which to think about the research question. Twenge's study doesn't provide that, but this is true of most studies in the field, and is an issue that has dogged the study of technology effects for decades. We'll come back to this in more detail later on. Suffice to say that, given the issues in determining causality which the study faces, it takes a massive leap of faith to go from a set of weak correlations to claiming that smartphones are the likely culprit in ruining teenage mental health.

Since that 2017 study, we've seen a number of scientific papers published that all take a broadly similar approach to tackling the question of how screen time impacts various aspects of mental health and wellbeing. They all largely struggle for reasons that we've already come across; most are based on cross-sectional datasets, and so suffer from the problems facing self-report measures that we learned about in Chapter 1. It also means that, however fancy the statistical analyses reported seem to be, they are all essentially correlational in nature and don't tell us anything new about about what is driving changes in mental health. One of the best synopses of the state of the research area was published in 2019 by developmental psychologists Candice Odgers and Michaeline Jensen. In their far-reaching review, Odgers and Jensen note three overarching features of the extant research literature: first, that despite the commonplace assumption that there's a clear link between screen use and mental health, the research findings are mixed – some studies show a negative relationship, some show a positive relationship, and some show no relationship at all; second, that in studies which find a negative relationship, even when a statistically significant effect is found it is so small that it is unlikely to be practically or clinically meaningful; and finally, as we saw earlier, that it's extremely difficult, if not impossible, to establish cause and effect.

If we do want to establish cause and effect, then we need to look to experimental, laboratory-based studies. The value of this kind of research lies in the level of control that we have over the specific things we're interested in. Longitudinal and cross-sectional studies are great for gathering large amounts of data to look at population level trends, but as scientists we have very little control over who takes part in those studies, what unique characteristics they possess, and what they might be thinking about, or what their environment is like, when they're filling out the survey. Experimental studies give us back some of that control: by deciding precisely what things we are going to test, how we are going to test them and under what conditions, we are able to systematically change one thing in our study (say, the amount of screen time a participant has access to) and see whether or not this has an effect on another thing (for example, whether participants feel more or less depressed).

When it comes to screen time, such studies are relatively few and far between, and often don't quite fit our needs when it comes to looking at direct mental health outcomes, but Odgers and Jensen's review notes some. For example, in a 2013 study by Elisheva Gross at UCLA, participants were randomly allocated to play one of two versions of a digital social exclusion game called Cyberball. Cyberball is, essentially, a very simple game of pass-the-ball, but it's been used in countless psychological studies looking at the impact of ostracism. The basic set-up is that participants are told that they are playing a ball-tossing game with two other people on the internet (in reality, these people don't exist; everything is controlled by the computer). When they have the ball, the participant has the simple task of deciding who to throw it to. More interesting, though, is what happens when they *don't* have the ball. The game can be programmed to allow the participants to be included by their virtual co-players, or they can be excluded from the game by having the two other players just pass the ball between each other. By manipulating the number of times the participant receives the ball (if ever), researchers can control to what extent people feel socially excluded, and in turn see what impact this has on other behaviours or feelings. In Gross's study, participants were included in or excluded from the game, and then asked to spend twelve minutes either playing Tetris or talking to someone they didn't know over an instant messaging service. The idea here was to see whether talking to someone online, even if they were a stranger, would help people get over the effects of social exclusion. As it turns out, it did: teenagers who had been excluded and then assigned to the instant messaging condition reported higher levels of self-esteem replenishment and lower levels of negative mood than excluded teens who got to play Tetris for a bit. Elsewhere, work by researchers at the University of Haifa recruited teenagers who reported either being in a distressed emotional state or in a more positive state and looked at the emotional effects of taking part in instant messaging conversations with their friends. For those teens who didn't report being distressed, chatting online didn't have much of an effect on their mood. For the ones that were distressed, though, instant messaging provided a significant amount of emotional relief. In other words, some experimental studies suggest a net *positive* effect of screens on wellbeing.

What we have, then, is a literature that feels like a mess. One of the consistent lines through Odgers and Jensen's review is that if you look at the broad spread of experimental, cross-sectional and longitudinal studies on screen time, combined with meta-analyses and systematic reviews, the conclusion time and again is that, well, we don't really know what the link between screen time and mental health is. Findings are inconsistent across studies, and sometimes even across studies *based on the same dataset*. For example, a 2020 paper by a team led by Noah Kreski at Columbia University analysed data from an updated version of the Monitoring the

Future dataset and, contrary to Twenge's findings three years earlier, found that daily social media use wasn't a consistent risk factor for depressive symptoms. The only consistent association was between daily social media use and an increase in depressive symptoms in one particular subsample: girls who had been categorised as having the lowest risk of depression. And in a 2021 meta-analysis led by Christopher Ferguson at Stetson University, the authors go a step further than Odgers and Jensen, concluding on the basis of thirty-seven studies that the current body of data we have simply doesn't support the claim that social media or smartphones are associated with poorer mental health. Instead, Ferguson's team argue that the research field is stymied by a lack of methodological rigour that desperately needs to be addressed, noting that where studies used appropriate control variables* in their analyses, the effects of screen time tended to be much smaller than in studies which didn't.

All of this leaves us floundering somewhat. I don't want

---

* Briefly, control variables are other factors which you think might have an impact on your variable of interest, and which therefore you need to account for in your study. So if you're interested in the effect of screen time on mental health, then you need to consider what other sorts of things might come into play, and make sure that either they don't change over the course of your study or, if they do change, then that's factored into your analysis. Relevant controls here might be things like age, gender, family environment or even baseline mental health. Let's imagine you're doing a really basic experiment: you ask one group of people to spend at least five hours a day on their screens, and a second group to spend no more than thirty minutes a day doing the same. After a week you measure their levels of depression and find that the heavy screen time group have significantly higher levels of depression than the light screen time group. But because you are a smart scientist, you also asked participants in both groups to report their depression levels at the *start* of the study. You find that, out of sheer happenstance, all the participants in your heavy screen time group also reported significantly higher levels of depression *before the study began*, and when you take into account those baseline depression scores – your control for them – you find no overall effect. So does screen time cause depression? If we ignore our control variable, then yes. If we include it, then no. Put simply, control variables are really, really important if you want to figure out the right answer.

to tell you that there's nothing to worry about when it comes to screen time, that we should all happily, uncritically carry on spending our lives online without reflecting on its effects. There definitely are areas of concern, as we will come to see. And moreover, if we take the trend at face value, then we do seem to be seeing drops in mental wellbeing over the past few years – although a bit of caution is needed here. In 2023, work by the National Bureau of Economic Research showed that there was a rise in teenage suicide-related hospital visits in the US around 2012, but this corresponded to a change in medical screening practices that were implemented at the time. Similarly, a sharp uptick around 2017 corresponded to changes in the way that suicidal ideation was recorded, in line with international guidelines. The authors of the study suggest that it may well have been the case that adolescent mental health issues were always much higher than we were able to detect, and that rather than something external driving timepoint-specific increases, it's more the simple fact that screening changes made us better at spotting what was already there. Nevertheless, if there's a sense that our screen-based lives might even vaguely impact our wellbeing, then that's important to figure out, and it's right that we study it. But how do we make sense of a literature that at the same time tells us both that there is a clear link between digital technology and mental health *and* that there isn't? If we want to even begin to answer that question, then we need to acknowledge the fact that a rather big problem has been staring at us this whole time.

My suspicion is that you've already spotted it, and you're possibly getting annoyed by it. I know I am, because not only is it a problem with the research we've talked about so far (and will continue to be for most research that we come across from now on), but it's also a problem with this book itself. So far we've been talking about screens, screen time, digital technology, smartphones, social media, instant messaging, the internet and generally 'being online' as if these are all equivalent terms. They're not, though. The same goes for mental health and wellbeing: broadly, the research we've looked at so far covers things like depression, anxiety, suicide, happiness, emotional distress, self-esteem and social exclusion, and, just as broadly, we've been considering them all effectively as equivalent issues. These terms are not interchangeable, though, and assuming that they are means that we end up glossing over what are likely to be very meaningful distinctions between them. Asking what the effect of smartphones on depression is, for instance, is not the same as asking what the effect of using social media is on happiness. It's a problem that is regularly found in the sciences, and particularly in new areas of enquiry, where researchers don't yet have a strong theoretical or methodological base for investigating whatever it is they're interested in. Psychologists refer to it as the jingle-jangle problem and have been discussing it for well over a century.

Writing about the potential pitfalls of measurement in 1904, the famed US psychologist Edward Thorndike used the following illustration to explain what he called the jingle problem. The term 'college student' is often used in general discussions about university life. But 'college student' can refer to a number of very different groups: male versus female students; first-year versus final-year students; part-time versus full-time students; home versus international students, and so on. Each of these groups could reasonably be referred to as 'college student', because there is a verbal resemblance there. But in doing so we begin to assume that there is just one category of 'college student', and therefore ignore the potential differences between the actual groups we're interested in. The jangle problem is essentially the reverse. Truman L. Kelley (one of Thorndike's students) coined the term in his 1927 book *Interpretation of Educational Measurements*, and in simple terms it is when two words or phrases which sound different from each other, but which essentially refer to the same thing, lead to a situation where we think they are two different things. Or, to use some examples for our present purposes, using 'social media' when we're actually interested in Instagram, Mastodon or Facebook is a jingle problem, whereas using phrases like 'social media', 'social networking sites' and 'screen time' interchangeably when we're talking about one thing is a jangle problem.*

Jingle-jangle problems, as you've probably guessed, are a pretty big barrier to moving fledgling fields of research forward. If they aren't properly addressed they can make it difficult, if not impossible, to develop coherent theoretical frameworks within which to research and test a given phenomenon. We can already see this in the screen time literature we've covered so far. Some studies find negative associations between screens and mental health, some find positive associations, and some find no links at all, *because they're all measuring different things*. It may seem dire, but there have been some admirable attempts to overcome this issue. In a 2020 meta-review – a review of other review papers – by Adrian Meier and Leonard Reinecke at Johannes Gutenberg University Mainz, the authors attempted to produce a taxonomy of research approaches both to mental health and

---

*   With my deepest apologies, I'm still going to use these terms somewhat commutably throughout the rest of the book. I'll try to be as precise as possible where I'm able to, and where it's necessary. But if we're honest with each other, I'm sure you don't want to read the words screen time over and over until they become indecipherable blobs on the page, just as much as I don't want to write them.

what they termed 'computer-mediated communication', or CMC. They did this by first looking at the spectrum of CMC measures that have been included in a wide range of literature reviews, and then mapping out their similarities and differences. The aim here was to define a hierarchy of research approaches that can be applied to existing forms of digital technology, while also being flexible enough to be applied to new ones as they come along – a sort of road map, then, for thinking about screens both retrospectively and proactively.

Meier and Reinecke's approach started by outlining two main conceptual approaches to CMC. What they termed the *channel-centred approach* essentially refers to how most research in this area already treats screen use. Channels can be very broad, such as a particular device (smartphone, tablet, computer), or general software type (social media, email, and so on), or they can be more specific, such as certain apps or even features of apps (for example, Facebook's news feed, or Instagram's direct message function). However the channel is defined, in essence it is treated as a 'black box': it is studied as a whole and singular thing, with less regard for how the constituent parts might have an influence. Conversely, the *communication-centred approach* cracks open that black box and looks at two key subcomponents: how we use screens to interact and communicate with each other, and whether or what specific features of individual messages might be important.

Alongside these conceptual approaches, Meier and Reinecke also outlined what they termed 'operational approaches' to CMC. They distinguish between two key pipelines: technology-centred and user-centred approaches. *Technology-centred approaches* are essentially descriptive measures that capture data such as the amount of time spent on screens, and in doing so implicitly assume that mere exposure to digital technology will be directly related to mental health. On the other hand, *user-centred approaches* focus on how and why people use screens, and therefore attempt to explain the relationship between digital technology use and mental health by looking at the interaction between technology and an individual's psychological make-up. Already this is getting somewhat complex, but in a way that's the point. Most research in the area, because of the jingle-jangle problem, doesn't really acknowledge that there are myriad ways in which we can consider how digital technology is used, and therefore how it might have some sort of specific effect. Unless we start to move beyond screen time as a broad concept, it will be impossible to develop any sort of deeper understanding as to where those specific positive and negative effects lie.

The same is true when we consider mental health. Most studies of screen time effects use fairly disconnected measures – we've already seen this in the relaxed attitude towards using terms like wellbeing, life satisfaction, depression and so on. Broadly speaking, we can categorise research in this area along one of two streams. Some work focuses on psychopathology, which concerns behaviours, motivations or feelings that cause distress and impair an individual's abilities in everyday life. In contrast, work on psychological wellbeing focuses on the positives, by looking at the effect of optimal psychological functioning – literally, how well people are doing in life. The important thing to remember, though, is that psychopathology and psychological wellbeing are not two ends of the same spectrum. One is not the absence of the other, and some people can exhibit high levels of both at the same time. This is a crucial point that often gets lost in broader discussions. You can be vulnerable to developing depression, for instance, but because you have a strong support network around you that doesn't necessarily mean that clinical levels of depression manifest.

Digital technology use can impact both psychopathology and wellbeing in different ways – for example, certain types of online interactions might make us feel more stressed whereas others help us to relax. Some can reinforce our social support networks and some can undermine them. In other words, digital technology use isn't easy to simplify, but even if it was it would still sit within a complex ecosystem of other factors, all of which have the potential to boost or dampen our mental resilience.

Meier and Reinecke's paper was important for providing that much-needed depth of detail about digital technology use, but what they were really doing was a review of other review papers, all looking at the interplay between screens and mental health. It's nigh on impossible to do something like that without some sort of theoretical framework to guide our thought processes, because we have so many different ways of defining the variables we're interested in – the jingle-jangle problem, basically. So the framework they developed does two things: first, it forces us to start thinking hard about what, precisely, we mean when we're talking about screen effects. This can be different things in different situations, which is fine – it just helps to be more exact. Second, it provides a way to impose structure on the research on screens that we have to date, rather than assuming that all studies can be directly compared.

Using this approach, Meier and Reinecke's findings, although by no means conclusive, provide us with a slightly richer understanding of how screens impact our mental health. In general, there were three core take-home messages. First, that the vast majority of research in the area is concerned only with the effects of using social networking sites, treating them very much as a black box in the process. Given that there are so many more aspects of computer-mediated communication that we are exposed to, it really would be a good idea to broaden out our research to take this into account – we can't really come to a general conclusion about the effects of screens when we're not actually measuring most of the stuff that we do on them. Second, although it is often repeated in the literature that any screen effects probably depend on other moderating variables, the meta-analyses that Meier and Reinecke looked at didn't seem to find much evidence for those of either age or gender – two key variables that researchers like Twenge and Haidt seem to be fixated on. And finally, because there's such a tendency to conflate levels of analysis or conceptualisation within the field, it's likely that where effects on mental health are uncovered, they might be attributed to the wrong causes. In other words, how you measure screen time, and what you consider as your mental health outcome, have a considerable impact on the association you find. And an elegant demonstration of this idea can be found published in the research literature in 2019.

'There's no curiosity about a very boring fact, here. There's just no curiosity about the data generation procedure.' I'm talking to Professor Andy Przybylski, Director of Research at the Oxford Internet Institute and one of the world's foremost experts in digital technology effects. 'Look, when somebody in 2007, or 2011, or 2017 is sitting in a high school somewhere, and they're answering a questionnaire about screen time, do you believe that their answers contain meaningful information about their technology use that is at all logically possible to connect to how they say they feel?' We're talking about datasets like Monitoring the Future – vastly rich sources of information, but ones which are open to potential misuse or misinterpretation if they aren't treated with the appropriate care and respect that they deserve. 'You can either approach this in a deterministic sort of way – say, you'll take any tiny positive or negative correlation, look at it at face value and say, "tech is good" or "tech is bad" – or you can approach it with something vaguely looking like curiosity.' What Andy is talking about here is that if you barrel your way into a large, multi-year dataset, you will always find something, there will always be a correlation to uncover. But whether that correlation really means anything, whether it relates to some sort of real-world relationship or effect, requires reflection and interrogation. Do the questions that participants are asked change over time, and if so in what way, and what might this mean for their interpretation? What might these relationships mean in the context of what we know from other datasets? What are the limits of the knowledge we can garner in these contexts? Are our biases and preconceived notions about the relationships having an impact on what we find? And just how much does it matter how you define screen time or mental health?

In 2019, teaming up with Amy Orben, Andy published a hugely influential study in the journal *Nature Human Behaviour* which addressed some of these questions head-on. They pooled the information from three large-scale datasets – Monitoring the Future, the Youth Risk and Behavior Survey (YRBS) from the US, and the Millennium Cohort Study (MCS) from the UK – and applied a technique called Specification Curve Analysis to the data. Remember that these sorts of nationally representative datasets cover a great deal of ground, gathering data on everything from numeracy and literacy skills to education, housing situations, cognitive assessments and even in some cases biological samples. That means that there are a lot of potential outcomes when it comes to talking about both mental health and digital technology use. For example, in the YRBS there are two questions about 'electronic device use' and 'TV use', so you could take responses to either of these and make that your technology use variable, or you could maybe use the average of the two responses. The MCS has five questions, covering TV, electronic gaming and social media, as well as whether the respondent owns a computer and whether they have access to the internet at home. Monitoring the Future has *eleven* relevant technology use measures. If anything, the problem gets worse for measures of mental health: across those three datasets there are a considerable number of questions or items you could use, depending on how you define mental health or mental wellbeing. In a nutshell, Specification Curve Analysis involves mapping out all the possible ways in which an analysis can be reasonably conducted in datasets of this type and then goes ahead and actually runs all of them, using a form of correlational analysis called a multiple regression.

Brace yourself. Orben and Przybylski determined that there were 372 justifiable ways to specify the regression analysis using the data from the YRBS. For Monitoring the Future there were 40,966 theoretically defensible specifications. And for the MCS there were 603,979,752 plausible specifications. If you decide to include other variables which you suspect might also impact mental health in the analysis, then for the MCS the number of legitimate combinations of digital technology indicator and mental health outcome that you could analyse rises to 2,500,000,000,000. That's 2.5 *trillion* ways in which you could potentially, and reasonably, analyse the data.

Once the number of analytical paths has been identified, typically a Specification Curve Analysis will then go and run all those analyses. We're dealing with ludicrously large numbers here, though, so in order to finish the study in a reasonable time frame, Orben and Przybylski used all specifications for the YRBS and MTF data and then took a subsample of just over 20,000 combinations for the MCS data.* The approach here was to take all combinations of measures that had previously

---

*   It's sometimes difficult to get your head around just how big a trillion is. Assuming you're trying to do this analysis on a computer that allows you to run 1,000 regressions per second, then 2.5 trillion regressions would take around eighty years. You would also need an astonishingly large hard drive to store all the data – somewhere in the region of at least 280 terabytes.

been reported in other studies, combinations that included *all* measures, and then finally some other, randomly selected combinations. Each time the analysis is run an estimate of the relationship between digital technology use and wellbeing is obtained, and those estimates can then be pooled to see what the average relationship is across all specifications. By Orben and Przybylski's estimates, technology use accounted for less than 0.1 per cent of the variability in wellbeing scores in the MTF data, and at most 0.4 per cent in the MCS dataset. For analyses which included control variables, in general the relationships were weaker than for those which didn't include any controls. And for the MCS dataset, which included much more fine-grained measures than the other two data sources, the relationship between wellbeing and technology use was stronger for adolescent self-report measures of wellbeing than if parent or caregiver reports were used.

To put these numbers into context, Orben and Przybylski compared the size of the effect that technology use has with other factors that are known to be related to wellbeing in some way. Behaviours that we know definitely do have a negative impact on adolescent mental health include binge-drinking, getting into fights and smoking cigarettes or weed, whereas we also know that some things have a positive effect – eating fruit and vegetables, say, or getting enough good sleep. The researchers also included some factors which we don't have any particular reason to think will impact on mental health either way – your height, whether you wear glasses or not or whether you're right- or left-handed, for example. Taking the association between technology use and wellbeing as the baseline, the results of this analysis suggested, perhaps unsur-prisingly, that the effects of these better-documented factors are generally much greater than those of screens. For example, the negative effect of bullying was around four to five times that of screen use. Depending on the dataset, the positive effect of good sleep on wellbeing was between two and forty-four times greater. In terms of neutral factors, the YRBS, amazingly, has a question which asks whether respondents have eaten any potatoes in the preceding seven days. How did this compare with digital tech use? Well, the results were about the same – eating potatoes had an effect on wellbeing that was 0.86 times that of screen use.

This was an important study for many reasons. First and foremost it showed, in a systematic and near-exhaustive way, that although there is a negative association between digital technology use and psychological wellbeing it is small and, when considered alongside other human behaviours, not something we should worry about as much as we do. Second, and I would argue much more importantly, the study does a pretty comprehensive job of showing why we have to be careful when delving into large-scale datasets. They are powerful entities which can be incredibly enticing for researchers: treasure troves of information where the hard part – actually collecting the data – has already been done. All you need to do is get your hands on them and run the statistics. But with great power comes great responsibility. If you blunder your way into the numbers without thinking about how or why you're doing it, you run the very real risk of finding seemingly strong correlations which may well be spurious. And because of this, Orben and Przybylski highlight the critical next step. They note, rightly, that their study doesn't provide definitive closure to the question of whether screens impact our mental health. As well constructed as it is, at its core it's still a study based on correlational, cross-sectional data. If we want to move our understanding of screens forward, they argue, we need to rethink our approach. We need to be clear about what aspects of mental health we're focusing on, and for who. We need multi-laboratory projects and new, more detailed cohort studies. We need to stop relying on self-report measures of everything and find ways to get more objective data. In short, we need to be smarter.

Since that paper was published in 2019, by and large we have not been smarter. In the following two years, Orben and Przybylski ended up in a back-and-forth argument with Twenge and colleagues, including social psychologist Jonathan Haidt, that largely centred on whether the original paper included analytical justifications that effectively watered down the effects of screen time. Twenge and Haidt argued, for example, that because Orben and Przybylski had aggregated data across digital technology types and gender, important associations were getting lost in the overall results. Previous work by Przybylski has suggested a 'Goldilocks effect' for technology use – that is, both too much *and* too little are worse for wellbeing than 'just the right amount', so to speak. Why, then, did Orben and Przybylski only look at linear relationships? But it was the effect of social media use on the wellbeing of teenage girls that became the specific battleground which Twenge, Haidt and colleagues homed in on. They argued that the strongest negative links were seen here, and therefore it was inappropriate to lump these results together with other types of screen time (like TV use) and data from teenage boys, which showed much weaker associations. In a patient reply, Orben and Przybylski pointed out that some of their concerns had already been addressed in the original paper. They also directly tested many of the specific associations which Twenge and her team proposed, but found that the results didn't practically change anything. In additional analyses on technology-use intensity, for example, Orben and Przybylski found that there was a slight overall positive effect on wellbeing for low-intensity users, and a slight overall negative effect on wellbeing for high-intensity users. Addressing the gender question, they noticed that there was a slightly larger negative association for girls than for boys, but in all cases these were still tiny effects, explaining less than 1 per cent of variability in wellbeing scores. To their credit, Orben and Przybylski made all their data and analysis code free to access, open to anyone who wanted to rerun the analyses themselves.

And yet the debate continued. Not content with this reply, Twenge and various colleagues continued to publish papers that all essentially did and said the same thing – that various measures of mental wellbeing were generally getting worse in teenagers, with a concomitant general rise in different types of screen use. Rather than attempting to engage with the concerns and difficulties we came across earlier, it would seem instead that researchers on the 'everything is horrible' side of the debate were simply content with digging their heels in, churning out paper after paper in the hope that it would change everyone's mind. This academic equivalent of a Gish gallop* took a somewhat bizarre turn in 2022 in a paper by Twenge, Haidt and others which was published in the journal *Acta Psychologica*. It purported to rerun a Specification Curve Analysis on the same datasets used by Orben and Przybylski, but with a very different outcome: that the associations

---

* Basically, quantity over quality. Named after creationist Duane Gish, the Gish gallop is a rhetorical technique in which opponents are overwhelmed with a seemingly endless stream of arguments, many of which are specious or poorly evidenced. It causes a real problem, because anyone wanting to rebut the claims being made is faced with the task of countering each claim in turn, which we already know takes significantly more time and effort than it does to make the claim in the first place (remember the Bullshit Asymmetry Principle). In doing so, it can often make them end up looking like they don't know how to debate very well, or that they have some sort of vendetta against the person in question. In the context of academic research papers, grinding out article after article also causes other issues for evaluating the evidence base, which we'll look at in more detail when we talk about addiction later on.

between screen time and mental health were meaningful enough to be of considerable concern.

I say that the study purported to rerun that analysis, and well, it did and it didn't. It did, in the sense that the authors reran Orben and Przybylski's analytical code on the same datasets and, unsurprisingly, found the same numbers. It didn't, in that following this 'replication' Twenge's team proposed an 'alternative set of specifications', which they claimed were theoretically justifiable choices to set limits on the sample space. One could argue they picked specific data combinations which they thought would produce the strongest effects – for example, separating analyses by gender or specific screen activities. In their version of this analysis the team determined that for girls electronic device use had a stronger link with poorer mental health than, among other things, obesity, having sex before the age of thirteen or using injectable drugs. The association, they argued, was similar to that between mental health and heroin use.

If you are looking at the results from a statistical analysis, and those results tell you that screens are worse for you than heroin, then either we've got the debate around screen time *very* wrong or I would gently suggest that you've borked your analysis. The reality is that this paper didn't really conduct a Specification Curve Analysis, or at least didn't implement it in the typically accepted way. Remember, the whole point of this technique is to address the fact that when researchers are translating a scientific hypothesis into a practical and testable prediction, a number of decisions need to be made about how to characterise the data they're interested in. For example, they need to decide how to define their variables of interest, or whether other variables should be accounted for (and if so, which ones). In an ideal world, these decisions should be justified based on existing theory and defensible as such; but in reality, and certainly in psychological research, data can be very messy, with no clear or obvious basis on which to make those decisions. Inevitably, bias can creep into the process, and researchers are prone to making decisions that result in data analyses which support their preconceptions. They are much less likely to report findings that run counter to those prior beliefs. In their *Acta Psychologica* paper, Twenge's team essentially ran a restricted Specification Curve Analysis that focused on a subset of specifications that they claimed were theoretically defensible, but for which no extant theoretical grounding actually exists. The result was a study that was simply a rehash of previous correlational analyses but under a different name, with the associated claim that it was therefore more rigorous. In reality it just added noise to an already chaotic literature.

At face value, it might seem unfair that I'm picking on Twenge's research here, and in particular her work with Haidt, but I think it's important to do so because it is these studies that invariably make it into the mainstream news and therefore have the disproportionate potential to influence public understanding. Moreover, when this does happen, the story that is told has, over time, shifted the goalposts in unhelpful ways. It started with Twenge's *Atlantic* article in 2017, which was about screens, but a series of graphs showing declines in mental health were clearly linked to the launch of the iPhone in 2007. Haidt has published similar articles; but with titles like 'The dangerous experiment on teen girls' that squarely point the finger at social media having a causal effect on mental health, there's a subtle shift in where the blame is being laid – it's not just screens any more. Likewise, in 2023 the *Financial Times* ran an article titled 'Smartphones and social media are destroying children's mental health', drawing on Twenge's work, and including graphs based on those in the 2017 *Atlantic* article; although instead of pegging the start of the decline in mental health to the iPhone, this time the line was drawn at 2010, labelled somewhat vaguely as 'the smartphone era'.

What we're left with is a confusing picture – we're told that something is going badly wrong when it comes to mental health (which is scary!), and that it's to do with smartphones. Or maybe social media. Or maybe iPhones specifically. Or maybe screen time generally. That level of inadvertent obfuscation and uncertainty does a real disservice to those of us who have very real anxieties about digital technology. There are important questions to answer about whether different types of screen time, used in different situational contexts, have differing effects on our mental health – and by 'our', I don't just mean teenagers here, I mean everyone. And people care about these questions. But we are never going to be able to answer them if researchers who do robust and open work are sucked into recursively having to address the same misconceptions. Nor are we going to make progress if those who have privileged access to major news platforms keep trying to change the goalposts without ever offering up anything even vaguely resembling a decent theoretical framework within which to generate testable and meaningful predictions about screen effects. What we need, then, is to clear the air a little bit, and think about this in a more objective and grown-up way.

One of the many things that remains unanswered here is a simple 'why'. Why have we got into this situation? Not just in terms of the mess in the scientific literature, but why, generally, are we so worried about screens when it comes to mental health? It could be just another generational panic, in the same vein as comic books, telephones, video nasties, Dungeons & Dragons, violent video games and the like. Or it could be that in this case parental instincts are right – there is something rum about screens, but the science hasn't quite got to the point where it can tell us what the problem is. Or maybe it's not that screens themselves are worrying us, but that because they're such a salient part of our everyday lives they end up forming a focal point for what causes us distress. In other words, it is better not to think about this in simple cause-and-effect terms, but instead consider how the things that are happening to us in our offline worlds are mirrored in our online lives. If that's the case, then as much as screens have the potential to bring us distress, they also have the power to help us. That help might come in the form of a targeted therapy app, or it might be as simple as releasing your feelings on a small blog in a long-forgotten corner of the internet. So, as we'll come to see, maybe we've been looking at this from the wrong perspective all along.

You stare at a flickering screen. Every night, the same routine. You think about everything that's wrong with your life, and get depressed. Then you stick on some depressing music to make yourself feel worse. Then you load up livejournal, and moan about all the shit that happens to you and how it's not fair and how you don't deserve it.

The truth is, you don't.

3

The mirror in your pocket

I didn't have the most successful of starts when it came to my university career. For a significant chunk of my teenage years, I had imagined that I would go on to study for a degree in Physics and Philosophy, two subjects that I adored at school. My family were less enamoured by those choices. When I first told my grandfather about what I wanted to do, although he was supportive of my decision to go to university (and proud – I was the first in my family to consider it), he was less enthusiastic about the subject. 'Oh, you don't want to do Physics,' I remember him telling me. 'There's no money in it.' The evidence for this largely came from a story regaled by his barber, whose daughter, after having completed a Master's degree in the discipline, was now working in a local grocery store. 'Computers, that's where you want to be!' he rhapsodised.

My grandfather was an amazing man – gentle, kind, full of worldly advice. He was eighteen when he went off to war, serving in communications on a *Bittern*-class sloop, and after returning home had a long and fruitful career working in a building society. He was always a solid, dependable person to go to when you needed counsel, and after my dad died when I was in my early teens, he took on the father figure role in my life without question or complaint. I depended on him a lot. So when he said that I should do something in computing, it never even occurred to me to doubt his advice. Without thinking much more about the matter, I dropped my earlier ambitions and started researching degrees in Computer Science. I had no experience in coding, but I had spent many a year playing video games, so that had to count for something, right?

It did not.

My first year of university was one of the most miserable times of my life. It wasn't my grandfather's fault in the slightest; my choices, and my mistakes, were my own to make and take responsibility for. I struggled to adjust to life away from home. I struggled to make friends. I struggled with the course. I was a smart kid at school, but at university things just didn't click. Computer programming was an alien process to me, and a good chunk of that first year was learning how to code in various programming languages.* One of the most vivid memories I have of that degree, which features often in the cringe-moment highlight reel that plays in my head whenever I'm feeling particularly anxious, is submitting a piece of code that we had to self-mark. I scored myself 15 per cent on that one. When I spoke to the lecturer in charge of the module, he looked at my score sheet with something resembling a mixture of incredulity and pity. 'You only gave yourself 15 per cent ... ?' he enquired as I passed him a USB stick

---

* One such language was Haskell, which is a functional programming language that, to this day, I am convinced will only work for people who the computer senses are fundamentally able to grasp coding. If you got coding – by which I mean, if you appeared as someone capable of understanding the concept – Haskell could see that and would make life easy for you. Show it even the slightest bit of ineptitude, though, and it would punish you for your sins. You know how horses can smell fear? Haskell can smell incompetence.

containing the offending item. I could feel my face burn as he asked, although there was a small spark of hope that maybe I'd undersold myself and he'd find something, somewhere in those lines of code that would scrape me a few extra marks. That feeling quickly evaporated as soon as he tried to compile my program, and everything crashed.

Things weren't great at home, either. As much as I was finding it difficult being so far away from the only place I'd ever really known, there was a certain reprieve in not being around while my mum's second marriage crumbled to dust. Not long after that disastrous coursework experience, she called one evening to say that she and her partner were getting a divorce. What little I had in terms of a family support network seemed to ebb away, and with it the last remaining reserves of mental resilience. I sank into a deep depression, one that would take years to get out of. With no one to reach out to – no real friends at university, and none to lean on back home – I turned instead to the internet, in the vague hope I might find solace there. This led me to setting up my LiveJournal account, where I'd pour my heart out night after night. Not to anyone in particular, but always with a quiet hope that if I kept at it some kind soul would magically stumble upon my blog and reach out.

They did, of course. What I hadn't fully realised at the time was that I wasn't a lone voice on some unknown corner of the web. I had joined a community, and in doing so it was inevitable that I would gravitate towards like-minded people, and they me. Scrolling through my old posts, it's easy to see that now; over time, the reflections that I published slowly gathered more and more comments. I'm not talking huge numbers here, but a consistent amount, and increasingly from the same few people. People who, like me, were struggling. People who understood why it was important to provide words of comfort and encouragement. It's clear that the blog had become a sort of therapy, a place to express emotions and thoughts in a safe and welcoming environment, in the absence of any similar support in the offline world.

I want to tell you a nice straightforward story here about how, in reliving and revisiting those LiveJournal articles, at a meta level I could see how things, over time, got better. How, through my writing, eventually I got out of the affective mire I was in, improved my outlook on life, and started talking about happier things. That's a somewhat rose-tinted view of how therapy works, though, and the reality is that while my mental health did start improving, this wasn't something that was overtly captured in the words I wrote. Instead it was reflected more subtly, in the simple fact that over time I ended up posting less and less frequently, and the group of friends I had come to know started to drift off into other ventures. And so one day, without fanfare or warning, I just stopped posting. The need for that particular outlet, that specific support net-work, had gradually dropped away, its purpose served. And it was absolutely fine.

We have a common-sense view that our online lives are detached from our offline world, that those two versions of ourselves are different; the former difficult to change, the latter completely malleable. In some ways, there's a certain truth to that – for example, it often feels as though we're inundated with nothing but positive things happening in other people's lives on Facebook or Instagram, which can be particularly grating if we're going through a tough spot. The idea that we can be who we want to be online stems from the early days of the internet and the lack of experience that came with it, perhaps best summed up by the quip from a famous 1993 *New Yorker* cartoon that 'On the internet, nobody knows you're a dog.' But the online world has evolved into a more socially connected one in which we reveal our true personalities constantly but almost imperceptibly. The types of photos we share, the status updates we post, the messages that we repost – all of these things reflect who we really are, often without us noticing what information we're giving away.* The more complex reality, then, is that while we like to think that we can present ourselves in an ideal form online (whatever our own personal definition of ideal is), our digital personas are all reflections, in whole or in part, of our core identity. For example, research by Lucia Lushi Chen and colleagues at the University of Edinburgh has shown that extroverted people tend to post more positive content on Facebook, whereas more neurotic people tend to alternate between positive and negative content. Some studies have taken this further, suggesting that personality traits can actually be predicted by looking at patterns of social media use (for instance, what types of Facebook posts we tend to hit the Like button on, or the specific types of content posted in tweets). Others have suggested that people who reported that they enjoyed trolling others online were more likely to score highly on measures of what's known as the Dark Tetrad of personality – narcissism, Machiavellianism, psychopathy and sadism. In other words, internet trolls are pretty horrible people in the offline world too.

Our online world is a reflection of our offline life in ways that go beyond personality factors, though. This has important implications for thinking about how we approach the question of how digital technology use is linked to mental

---

* This, of course, is the basis of many online scams. Whenever you see one of those innocuous-looking memes that get you to post your combination of superhero powers, or *Harry Potter* persona, or whatever, by looking up the phrases that match the day and month you were born, remember that if you post the results you've just told a lot of random strangers on the internet when your birthday is.

health, and again particularly when it comes to teenagers and young adults. For example, while parents often worry about who their kids are interacting with online, studies have consistently shown that adolescent social networks are very similar both online and offline. That is, they are using social media and messaging services largely to maintain and manage existing social relationships, as opposed to talking to random strangers. Today's adolescents are in a unique place in that they were 'born digital', unaware of what life was like before the age of the internet. That means that they are more comfortable than previous generations with using digital technology to find information about mental health (or, well, anything really), and to seek out online sources of support. To a certain extent, I've been there myself: my own online experiences at an earlier age mirrored events going on in my physical life. I was depressed offline, and in turning to the internet for some hope of support I wrote about depression online. One didn't cause the other – that's the wrong way of thinking about it. Instead, both were intrinsically, almost symbiotically connected. I was lucky, in a way. I didn't have any master plan in mind when I started writing on my blog; there was just a hazy desire to find something or someone that would help. That I found this support was largely a product of chance; thinking back, had I used a different website or come across a different group of people, then it's quite easy to see how opening up about my emotional life in that very public way could have backfired disastrously. So the question is not whether screen time affects mental health or vice versa, but why do some people thrive online and others struggle?

'The biggest thing we see is that offline risk mirrors online risk,' says Candice Odgers, a Professor of Psychological Science at the University of California, Irvine, whose work has been hugely influential in shaping our understanding of digital technology effects. 'So kids who have early trauma, or are from families with high levels of substance use or criminality, or have early trouble with their peers – those are the types of things that predict riskier experiences online. It's a selection into environment.' We've already come across some of Candice's work, but the main focus of her research is in understanding how things like social inequality and early-life adversity have an influence on future health and wellbeing, particularly when it comes to online behaviours. In a 2015 review co-authored with Dr Madeleine George, Odgers argued that despite our common conceptions about our online and offline worlds being separate, the vast major-ity of online threats to wellbeing (and particularly adolescent wellbeing) find their basis in similar offline factors.

Let's take cyberbullying as an example. As teens have started to spend growing amounts of time online, particularly in terms of their social media use, so parental fears about the risks of children facing abusive behaviours have increased. Cyberbullying feels – and is – more insidious than face-to-face abuse, for a wealth of reasons: it's much more difficult to keep tabs on, bullies can hide behind a cloak of digital anonymity, and it can conceivably happen anywhere, at any time, and so invade the potential safe space of home. Unlike other areas of research into digital wellbeing, there's actually a large evidence base of studies looking at the prevalence and impact of cyberbullying; and while estimates of its reach vary quite widely (depending on the country where the data were collected, or the definition of cyberbullying that was used, for example), most peg it at somewhere between around 11 per cent and 58 per cent of the teens surveyed. This is a real cause for concern – but it's important to note that there also seems to be a considerable amount of overlap between the risk of being victimised online and experiencing bullying offline; for example, a 2012 study of nearly half a million US and Norwegian teens suggested that around 90 per cent of kids who reported that they had been bullied online also said that they had experienced it offline, and about the same overlap was reported for perpetrators of bullying. A 2017 study published in the journal *Lancet Child and Adolescent Health* found similar results: data from just over 120,000 UK teenagers showed that 406 participants reported experiencing only cyberbullying, whereas 3,655 disclosed experiences of both online and traditional bullying – in other words, 90 per cent of the total number of teens who experienced cyberbullying were also being victimised offline. For context, the *Lancet* study also revealed that traditional bullying was much more prevalent: 27 per cent of the total sample reported experiences of it. And while both types of abuse were related to declines in mental wellbeing, traditional bullying was by far the stronger factor: 5 per cent of the variability in wellbeing was accounted for by offline bullying, whereas 0.1 per cent of the variability could be put down to cyberbullying.

More broadly, studies have shown that teenagers who have various offline vulnerabilities – for example, those who have communication difficulties, physical or mental health difficulties, special educational needs or are young carers or in care themselves – are more likely to engage in a range of higher-risk online behaviours. Work by Adrienne Katz, an online safety consultant, in collaboration with Aiman El Asam at Kingston University London has shown that not only does offline vulnerability predict online vulnerability, but that specific types of offline difficulties can be predictive of specific high-risk online scenarios. In a study of nearly 3,000 ten-to-sixteen-year-olds, El Asam and Katz showed that, for example, children with a physical disability or communication difficulty were more likely to engage in what they termed 'conduct risks' – using chatrooms or online gambling sites, or illegally downloading music and movies, or visiting websites not intended for children. Children with special educational needs were at higher risk of getting involved in unhealthy or inappropriate online relationships ('contact risk'), whereas children who had family-related vulnerabilities were at higher risk of cyberscams – issues like having social media accounts hacked, or being tricked into giving people money. Finally, children with mental health difficulties didn't seem to be more susceptible to one type of online risk over any others, but were more likely in general to face some form of danger online.

What we're starting to see here, then, is a much more complex and reciprocal relationship between screens, our mental health and our behaviour. Taking the results for children with family and social vulnerabilities as an example, El Asam and Katz provide some insight into why we see the relationships that we do. We know from other research that children who are young carers, for example, tend to be more withdrawn and anxious, and often feel like they're missing out on social lives with friends their own age. It also means that they're spending a lot of their day at home, and therefore, potentially, on the internet. Along with other challenges, such as living with their own disability needs or having a low socioeconomic status, kids in these sorts of situations are much less likely to have access to meaningful education about how to stay safe online, and are given relatively little parental support when using the internet. In turn, this increases the likelihood of falling victim to a cyberscam. In a similar vein, El Asam and Katz suggest that children who have been victims of neglect and are subsequently taken into care can go on to display a range of developmental and behavioural problems; and, lacking appropriate education in online safety, these children are more likely to seek out new relationships online. If they aren't doing that in the right places, there's clearly an increased risk of them being the victims of online scams and predation.

This idea – that there are inequalities in the ability to navigate online worlds, and that these arise in part because of offline, 'real-world' inequalities – is one that is starting to gain increasing traction in the research field. It also highlights the need to approach the question of the relationship between screens and mental health in a much more considered way. Research has consistently shown that young people are more likely to seek out information about mental health issues online, and that in the right conditions this can be a powerful form of support. But it can also go very wrong. El Asam and Katz's work offers a clear example: in their study, adolescents who reported having mental health difficulties weren't at a higher risk of online harm of a specific sort, but were generally at greater risk of *any* category of harm. To try to unpack why this might be the case, they cite a 2013 review which showed that teens who went online in a constructive attempt to get more information and support about self-harm and suicide were, in so doing, also more likely to come across harmful content – for example, forums where people share posts about the techniques, or concealing the effects, of self-harm. Without support systems which help adolescents understand how to navigate online interactions in a safe and positive way, the balance between the benefit and harm of screen use can tilt drastically in the wrong direction. That support system starts at home – or, to be more precise, the type of home in which you find yourself.

'I think that's one of the biggest concerns,' says Candice. 'Middle- and upper-class families curate their children's online experience around that risk/opportunity divide, and then there are a whole group of children living in lower-resource homes who don't have that kind of scaffolding. They don't get to benefit in the way that they could or should, and that opens up risk.' Consistent research has shown that household income levels are an important predictor of adolescent mental health, both now and in the future. But socioeconomic status also has a huge impact on the ability to access and understand digital technology. For example, recent survey work by Victoria Rideout and Michael Robb for the non-profit organisation Common Sense Media has shown that, in the US at least, 73 per cent of adolescents from lower-income households (defined as earning less than $35,000 per year) have access to a computer, and about the same percentage access to a smartphone. In contrast, 94 per cent of teens from higher-income households (that is, those earning more than $100,000 per year) have access to a computer, and 89 per cent access to a smartphone. Despite this gap, on average teens from lower-income households are spending around one and a half to two hours per day longer on screen-based media than their higher-income counterparts, and about 50 per cent less time using digital devices for homework. Elsewhere, survey work from the Net Children Go Mobile project suggests that children and adolescents from lower-income back-grounds tend to be less supported in terms of their parents actively mediating their internet use: across 3,500 nine-to-sixteen-year-olds sampled in Europe, 73 per cent of those in higher-income homes reported parental input, versus 64 per cent of those from lower-income backgrounds. 'Active medi-ation of internet use' in this case refers to situations in which parents talk to their kids about online content while they're engaging with it, and stay nearby while they're online. The same survey also reported data on active mediation of internet safety, which involves parents doing things like explaining why some websites might be good or bad, suggesting tips for behaving nicely to other people online, and generally being around to talk to their kids if something has bothered them. The results were broadly the same – this sort of mediation was less likely to be reported by young people from poorer homes by about 17 percentage points.

Hopefully, we're starting to make some headway when it comes to understanding the relationship between screens and mental health. There is a wealth of risks that can potentially be encountered online, particularly for children and adolescents, as we've been focusing on, but there's no reason to think that the same isn't true for adults too – and in some cases, these risks can have an impact on our mental well-being. It's not necessarily the case that encountering those risky situations will inevitably lead to harm, and in fact the Net Children Go Mobile survey suggests just that: young people who report such encounters online don't necessarily experience harmful consequences as a result. But pre-existing vulnerabilities can lend themselves to greater levels of problems online, which can in turn amplify or maintain those offline. All this is moderated, among other things, by levels of household wealth, and the quality and types of support systems that are available. In other words, some people thrive online because they've got the necessary support structures around them to, in essence, shake off negative experiences when they come their way. But others struggle, because the building blocks of developing that online resilience were never as readily available to them. Which category you fall into depends on a range of interacting factors, many of which you can't control.

If we start to think of digital technology in this way – not as the sole or root cause of mental health issues, but as a lens through which the impact of pre-existing vulnerabilities and inequalities can be lessened or intensified – then not only can we start to see why many of the correlational arguments we encountered in the last chapter are essentially futile endeavours, but we can begin to think about ways in which screens could be leveraged to provide better opportunities to support and improve mental health. Screens aren't going to disappear any time soon. Much the opposite, in that they have become an integral part of the fabric of our daily lives. Numerous studies have shown that although the ways in which we connect with each other are fundamentally different now than they were thirty, twenty or even ten years ago, the reasons why we use digital technology to do so are largely the same: to maintain existing relationships, to do and discuss work, to arrange meet-ups, to tell people that we care about them and to look for support when we need it. More and more, we find ourselves turning to the internet when we're struggling, and those who have grown up not knowing a world without digital technology feel much more at home in seeking information and support through internet forums and social media.* As we've already seen, there are clear risks in those situations – but there is also tremendous opportunity to create meaningful and effective interventions.

While I'm excited about this possibility, the current evidence base is, unfortunately (and perhaps unsurprisingly) a little shaky when it comes to assessing the utility of mental

---

* It's worth adding here that, just as today's teens have grown up in an increasingly digital world, they've also experienced a gradual erosion of offline 'third spaces' – places that aren't home or school (or work), where they can meet up with friends and create or reinforce those support networks. Playgrounds and parks are disappearing, as are youth centres and the like. In my own home town, half of the swings in the local play areas were removed during the pandemic, presumably in some misplaced effort to enforce social distancing. It took a long time post-lockdown to get them back, only for one of the few soft-play centres we had to then be closed down in favour of a gym. We often talk about getting kids off their screens and 'going outside' as though this is a good thing, but the reality is that, increasingly, there isn't anywhere 'outside' for them to go. It's no wonder, then, that we end up looking for those spaces online instead.

health-based apps and online interventions. As with many issues in digital psychology, some studies find some evidence of effectiveness in certain cases whereas others do not, and it largely depends on what type of mental health issue you're talking about, what population you're targeting, and what the intervention actually looks like. For example, a 2017 meta-review by a team led by Chris Hollis at the University of Nottingham suggested that there was some evidence that digital interventions focusing on cognitive behavioural therapy provided benefits for adolescents with anxiety and depression, but found less convincing evidence that digital interventions worked for other sorts of mental health issues like ADHD, psychosis or eating disorders. More recently, a mammoth meta-review led by Simon Goldberg at the University of Wisconsin-Madison incorporated results from 145 randomised controlled trials covering a range of treatment modalities (smartphone apps, meditation apps, text messaging-based interventions and the like) and health outcomes (including, among other things, stress, depression, anxiety and suicidal ideation). The top-line finding from this work (and the one most repeated on social media) was that, overall, the researchers found little in the way of any convincing evidence that such interventions were effective. 'Overall' is doing a lot of leg work here, though, because that summary finding averages out effects across quite a broad range of issues and treatment vectors. Drilling down into the results with a little more specificity, we do find promising signs and useful detail: in line with Hollis's review, there was good evidence that both smartphone interventions and meditation apps had a small-scale effect on depression and anxiety. Depending on the types of controls used, smartphone interventions either showed some evidence of effectiveness for stress (if inactive controls were used), or no evidence (in the case of studies using active controls).* The evidence was weaker for text-messaging-based interventions generally, and in the case of suicidal ideation there was no evidence that apps were particularly effective.

While these results might not sound particularly earth-shattering, Goldberg's team were cautiously optimistic in their conclusions. There was, they argued, some evidence that digital health interventions held promise for common mental health issues like depression and anxiety. While their findings showed that the effects were modest at best, this has to be considered in the context that things like smartphone apps are relatively cheap to implement and can be easily scaled to reach large numbers of people. This is important when it comes to mental health interventions like cognitive behavioural therapy, because traditionally these are done face to face, which means they're often time-intensive and require significant resourcing in terms of physical space and human involvement. If you can effectively target a lot of people who need a specific type of help quickly and easily, then even modest benefits have the potential to transform into appreciable improvements in public health.

Nevertheless, we're only starting to scratch the surface when it comes to this kind of work, and there are a lot of unknowns that we still need to answer. We don't know the true extent to which digital health interventions have any meaningful 'real-world' impact. We *do* know that drop-out rates for such interventions tend to be pretty high (if you're not in a good place, then it's a lot easier to stop using an app than it is to stop other types of treatment), but at this point

---

* In studies using active controls, one group (the treatment group) gets the intervention you're interested in, while the other (control) group gets a comparable treatment that's already generally used as standard. This differs in studies using inactive controls, wherein the control group gets no comparable treatment (or at least, they don't get it until after the study has finished).

little work has been done on figuring out how to keep people engaged. We also don't know much about the potential negative impacts of these sorts of therapies – adverse events or unanticipated problems that might arise during a course of therapy are important things to track and understand in any form of medical treatment, and screen-based interventions are no exception. Overarching all these unknowns is the issue of privacy; the use of such interventions necessarily entails sharing sensitive personal data, and there are very serious consequences if that data is used improperly, insecurely, or in a way that runs counter to the benefit of the patient.

Digital technology is never going to be a panacea for mental health issues, just as it isn't the root cause of them in the first place. But if we're going to make any sort of headway in figuring out where and how it can help us, we must fill these gaps in our knowledge. What we need is a multi-pronged approach that acknowledges the messy and incomplete picture that we currently have, brings together key players in a positive and constructive way, and ultimately allows us to make real advances in leveraging digital technology as a way to improve mental health.

In a review paper published in 2020, Candice Odgers along with other colleagues at the University of California, Irvine, put forward some useful solutions. One of the key issues here is that although the data researchers need in order to answer basic questions about how, when and why people use digital technology (and therefore how it might affect them) are already out there, they're nigh on impossible to access. The keys to that data are held very firmly by big tech companies, who are either unwilling to share it or are reticent to do so because of their proprietary nature. At the same time, scientists working in this area tend to be extremely cagey about working directly with these companies because of the spectre of collusion and compromise. There's currently no clear framework, anywhere in the world, within which researchers can access the data they need without it resulting in a conflict of interest, perceived or actual. This isn't an idle worry: researchers are frequently criticised on social media about perceived biases. It's something I've had experience of myself. After I published work on the associations between violent video games and aggression a few years ago, one particularly prominent scientist argued that a conflict of interest would have necessarily biased my study – that 'conflict' being that I play video games myself. So it's easy to understand how there's a reluctance to engage with big tech companies at the level needed in order to get anything nearing useful data.

One solution to this put forward by Odgers and her team, which is often echoed throughout the research community, is for independent third parties to step in and act as mediators. These could be national funding bodies, charities, think tanks or even governmental organisations, who can bring together any and all relevant stakeholders – researchers, tech companies, policymakers and users – in order to figure out how to share data in such a way that individual privacy is upheld, proprietary software isn't exposed, and robust research can be conducted without undue influence. A potential stumbling block here, though, is that there isn't much of an incentive for technology companies to sign up to a programme like this. That can only change if we create a shift in public thinking about screens. We need to move away from the unhelpful cycle of fear-based moral panics that focus almost exclusively on digital technologies as a negative force. If nothing else, rather than driving action, such panics end up promoting inertia, because they can be easily dismissed as sensationalist nonsense by the tech industry. Instead, we have to start thinking and talking about screens more rationally; if we can more reasonably consider the balance between potential benefits and realistic risks, we are in a much better position to put constructive political pressure on the industry. Tech companies make a lot of noise about being socially responsible, but we've yet to see that translate into meaningful action on their part. Whether by carrot or stick, we need to show them that this isn't just something that we care about, but something that they need to *do* something about. Some countries are making inroads into creating research frameworks or regulatory systems that will help achieve this, but they are largely embryonic in nature right now.

Once this starts to happen, we can start to develop more robust research programmes – ones that combine meaningful industry data with insights from objective data gleaned in a more targeted way from individual users. We've already started to see proof-of-concept studies showing that, far from being a pipe dream, this is an achievable goal. For example, recently a team led by Niklas Johannes at the Oxford Internet Institute were able to obtain objective data from video games companies Nintendo and EA about the amount of time people played two games, Animal Crossing: New Horizons and Plants vs Zombies, and combine this with subjective reports of mental wellbeing from those same players. Their results showed that, contrary to popular belief, there's actually a small *positive* correlation between game play and mental health. Moreover, despite the common-sense view that people underestimate the amount of time they play video games, players in fact tend to quite significantly overestimate their game time. Aside from the specific research findings, though, this study is one of the first to provide concrete evidence that collaborations with the tech industry can be achieved in an open and transparent way, and in which research integrity isn't compromised. It was followed up by a study from members of the same team in 2023 which looked at the timecourse of Facebook adoption across seventy-two countries, and how this tracked general mental wellbeing. The results showed again that, counter to our common assumptions, there wasn't a negative relationship between the two: in a very broad sense, there were positive associations between country-level Facebook uptake and mental wellbeing. Studies like this provide us with some much-needed optimism that, when it comes to understanding the broader links between digital technology and mental health, we're tantalisingly close to getting the sort of solid research we need and deserve.

None of this is to say that, while we wait for the research field to get to the point where it can provide us with more definitive answers, we, individually, should just give screens a pass and sit idly by. If you're worried right now about the impact that digital technology might be having on your own mental health, or on that of the people around you, then there are some more concrete things you can do to help in the short term.

Hopefully, one thing that has become clear over the course of these last couple of chapters is that it's good, every now and then, to take stock of your digital life. Don't worry so much about the gross amount of time you spend in front of screens; instead, focus more on what you're doing with that time. Think about what you're getting out of the experience, and whether you feel it has a net positive or net negative effect for you. If you have kids, talk to them about what they're doing online, and what they're getting out of it too. If there are struggles there, remember that, as we've come to see, much of the time it may be likely that the things that are going wrong for us online are echoes of problems that we might not have noticed in our offline lives. So be reflective. Cut out those negative online interactions, just like you would (or should, or could) with any sort of negative relationship. It might take some time, but if you need support, then it's worth investing effort into figuring out what that might look like for you, and where the best places are to find it online. Keep that knowledge for the times when you might need it most. That device in your pocket isn't destroying a generation; whether you like it or not, it's an integral part of it. So the next time you see a doom-laden headline about the supposedly deleterious effects of digital technology, don't just blindly agree (or even disagree) with it; instead, consider what the evidence might be for such a claim, and whether this presents an opportunity to think about how best to make screens work for you in your own life.

4

The light in the darkness

Two across. Get off second to add the French record. Five letters.

I have a ... well, let's charitably say that I have a complex relationship with sleep. Don't get me wrong, I love it (when I can get it), and generally speaking, being able to drop off at a moment's notice is my totally banal superpower. It's just that when I do sleep, it's not very rejuvenating. There are at least two good reasons for this. One is that I have a sleep disorder, and the other is that I now have two kids under the age of three. In the seven months since our little boy arrived into the world, sleep has been seriously downgraded for both my wife and me (and to be honest, mostly for my wife). Any decent chunk of slumber feels like a precious commodity, or an elite luxury to aspire to. As any new parent can relate to, you don't truly appreciate the wonder of sleep until you're up at 1 a.m., desperately trying to get a newborn to settle, all the while secretly knowing that you're going to have to dig deep and figure out a way to stay awake while they inevitably decide that the only way they're going to nod off is if they are lying on top of you as you recline in a muscularly inadvisable position on the sofa. The main thing that keeps me going in these moments is the knowledge that I'm so sleep-deprived, I probably won't remember any of this in a few months. That, and I've downloaded a cryptic crossword app on to my phone to help me stay awake during the witching hours.

Four down. Tired out, Drake twisted neck like this. Nine letters.

One saving grace for both these issues is that they are fixable: medical treatment can help with a sleep disorder, and time will eventually favour us when the kids start sleeping through the night. But if I fall into the trap of having a little moan to unfortunate nearby people about our sleep woes, more often than not something else comes up: *Are you on your phone before bed? It's probably the light from your screen that's keeping you up. Have you tried leaving your phone somewhere else, or doing something else for a bit before you go to sleep?*

Look. My wife and I definitely *are* on our phones. It's because we're desperately trying to find some sort of panacea for overtired little ones, or one of us is staring obsessively at the baby monitor app* in nervous anticipation of the inevitable wake-up and meltdown. These are the things keeping us up. There's a common trope that screens are terrible for our sleep because they emit blue light, blue light interrupts the production of a hormone called melatonin, and melatonin is important for governing our sleep/wake cycles. For a long time I've largely been dismissive of this claim – in part because I'm generally cautious when it comes to *any* claims made about screens. We've just spent two chapters looking at the messy nature of research on screens and mental health, and it's reasonable to think that things will be similar in other

---

* We also have a dedicated monitor unit that came with the baby camera. It is one of many trivial banes of my life. It barely ever connects properly, which would be a problem save for the fact that the battery only lasts about ten seconds anyway.

domains of our digital lives. And while the broader research literature on blue light and melatonin is pretty solid, it's a lot shakier when it comes to talking about direct associations with screen time. Some studies argue that there is a clear link: for example, in 2014 a major study published in the *Proceedings of the National Academy of Sciences (PNAS)*, led by Professor Anne-Marie Chang at Harvard Medical School, compared the effects of reading on an iPad versus reading a book for four hours before bed across five nights. The results showed that in the iPad condition, participants' melatonin levels were suppressed by about 50 per cent, they took around ten minutes longer to get to sleep, felt less sleepy before bed and more sleepy at wake-up.

Elsewhere, though, studies are not so conclusive. We've already come across a couple of examples of these in Chapter 1; remember, there was a study in which teenagers spent about three hours prior to bedtime looking at a computer screen while wearing either blue-light-blocking glasses or controls, which found that although there were reported differences in pre-bedtime sleepiness levels, this didn't translate into a meaningful effect on sleep or post-wake-up sleepiness levels. There are problems with both these studies (and others) which we'll come back to in a bit, but if there's even a slight possibility that there's a meaningful link between screen time and sleep, then it's important to get to the bottom of it for two reasons. First, understanding the effects means that we can then figure out helpful guidelines on what to do (and what not to do) with screens before bed – much more so than saying 'screens are bad'. Second, and I'll be honest here, if there's even a slight chance that I can do something to get even an iota of extra sleep right now, I will take it without any hesitation whatsoever. So with that in mind, let's take a look at the science of what we know about screens and sleep.

As a starting point, it's probably useful to look at some of the biological mechanisms involved in sleep, and in particular what are known as 'circadian* rhythms'. Humans, and other living organisms, essentially have a built-in biological clock that regulates the twenty-four-hour cycle of sleep and wakefulness that we go through. There's a whole field of research dedicated to the study of these rhythms, pleasingly called chronobiology, that largely finds its origins in work by the French scientist Jean-Jacques d'Ortous de Mairan in the 1700s. De Mairan was interested (among other things – he was also a geophysicist and an astronomer) in the behaviour of a heliotropic plant called *mimosa pudica*, otherwise known as the shameplant or touch-me-not, because its leaves close up and slump when they're touched. In the absence of any tactile stimulation, shameplants nevertheless show quite curious rhythmic movements – their leaves drop when it goes dark at night and perk back up again during the daytime. To try to understand what might be causing this, de Mairan did what any good scientist would do and shut his plant inside a dark cupboard for a few days, periodically checking in to see what it was doing. And here was the weird thing: that regular cycle of leaves periodically dropping and rising carried on happening, even though it was dark all the time. The cautious conclusion that de Mairan came to was that, given the absence of an external cue such as light, there might be some sort of internal mechanism driving the plant's activity. I say 'cautious' here, because even though light had been factored out of the equation, he couldn't be certain that other external variables, things like temperature or humidity, might instead be driving the effect. Nevertheless, on the basis of early work like this, over the next 300 years of systematic and careful

---

*   From the Latin words *circa* and *diem*, meaning 'about a day'.

study chronobiologists built up a rich understanding of the
biological mechanisms that link behaviour to the sheer fact
that the Earth rotates on its axis once every twenty-four
hours or so.

In humans, although biological clocks can be found
in nearly every cell type in the body, in general circadian
rhythms are governed by two key areas of the brain: the
suprachiasmatic nucleus,* or SCN for short, and the pineal
gland. The SCN essentially acts as a 'master' biological clock,
using information about whether it's light or dark outside to
synchronise and coordinate a whole raft of bodily rhythms:
aside from our sleep/wake cycles, it also helps to organise
things like alertness levels, temperature levels, even periodic
variations in immune system function and digestive system
activity levels. This all makes sense from an evolutionary
point of view – we're awake when it's light and asleep when
it's dark, so other body systems need to be coordinated with
that so we don't end up having, say, our most necessary and
productive bowel movements when we should be in the arms
of Morpheus.† In part, we know about the crucial role that
the SCN plays in circadian rhythms through pioneering work
by the biological psychologist Curt Richter in the 1960s,
who suggested that an area of the brain called the hypothalamus, of which the SCN is a part, was a likely source of the
biorhythms involved in sleep/wake cycles. Richter conducted
work on rats which showed that surgically destroying the
hypothalamus resulted in disruptions to that rhythmicity;
later work in the 1970s narrowed this down to the SCN in
particular, which is located towards the front of the hypothalamus, sitting just on and above the optic chiasm, where the

---

*   Not, as my brain and fingers keep insisting on typing, the super-
charismatic nucleus.
†   The Greek god of sleep and dreams, not the one from *The Matrix*.

optic nerves from each eye cross over each other – hence the name ('supra' means 'above', so literally 'the nucleus sitting above the chiasm'). In a way, the SCN has a direct line to the outside world, in that it receives light information from specialised cells in the retina, at the back of the eye. This information is then passed on to other areas of the brain, and importantly for our present purposes, up to the pineal gland.

The pineal gland is perhaps one of the more famous areas of the brain, due to the dubious distinction conferred on it by Cartesian dualist philosophies as the 'seat of the soul'. This, scientifically speaking, is not correct. René Descartes, as influential a philosopher as he was, unfortunately got many things wrong when it came to the pineal gland. Writing in the mid-1600s, he surmised that blood vessels surrounding the gland deliver to it tiny particles that, upon entry, turn into animal spirits. This, scientifically speaking, is also not correct: as far as we can ascertain with the most up-to-date brain-scanning methodologies, you do not have the ghost of Mufasa riding around the centre of your brain. Instead, the much more scientifically accurate view of the pineal gland is that it is an important part of the endocrine system: a network of glands and organs that essentially forms an information superhighway in the body. Glands produce hormones, which are chemicals important for controlling major functions like metabolism, growth, mood, energy levels and sleep (among other things). At night, the pineal gland produces the hormone melatonin, which in turn acts throughout the brain and body (including having a feedback effect on the SCN), increasing sleepiness and lowering our core body temperature – getting us ready for sleep, basically. Melatonin starts to enter the bloodstream fairly soon after darkness falls, and in adults, reaches peak concentration levels between 2 and 4 a.m., before gradually falling off in the early hours of the morning. During daylight hours, incoming light information from the SCN suppresses melatonin production, thereby making us less sleepy and more alert. A wealth of research over the past forty years suggests that if we're exposed to light at night, the SCN kicks in to inhibit melatonin synthesis in the pineal gland, and in the early 2000s studies started to show that while all wavelengths of light can affect sleep cycles, it's short-wavelength 'blue' light that seems to have the most impact. In part, this is because there are a special class of light-sensitive cells at the back of the eye which are especially responsive to light at the blue end of the spectrum, called intrinsically photosensitive retinal ganglion cells (or ipRGCs for short).

In other words, artificial light at night is not so good for us, because its spectral profile differs from natural light, specifically in that it tends to contain higher proportions of shorter-wavelength, 'bluer' light. And because melatonin production is particularly sensitive to blue light, it seems reasonable to make a short logical leap here: if artificial light interrupts melatonin, and screens produce artificial light, then screen time at night is going to be bad for sleep. We need to be careful here, though, because that logical leap masks some important information. In that simple formulation, we might reasonably assume that any light at night time is going to be bad for us; but this assumption implies that all light is equal, which is not the case. If we want to really understand the effects of night-time light on sleep we need to drill a little deeper and consider the effect of three interacting factors: the type of light, its intensity, and duration of exposure. If we don't, we run the risk of using the wrong sort of evidence to come to a conclusion that might not be warranted.

As an example, a study was published in 1989 titled

'Quantal melatonin suppression by exposure to low intensity light in man'. At face value, this seems like it's going to be a useful source of evidence for thinking about screens: if you're concerned about the effects of a dimly lit screen in a darkened bedroom, then looking at 'low-intensity' light levels seems a reasonable thing to do. In that study, researchers at the University of Melbourne exposed participants to three intensities of light, ranging from 200 to 600 lux,* from midnight until 3 a.m. While significant melatonin suppression occurred for light intensities of 400 and 600 lux, no statistically significant differences were found for 200 lux light when compared with control conditions. For reference, according to British Standards, 200 lux is the recommended light level for a self-service restaurant or airport waiting area, and 400–600 lux is what you would normally expect to find in an office environment. Perhaps not that useful for our present purposes, then. Now, to be fair to the researchers at the time, 200 lux was indeed considered 'low-intensity' – until around the mid-1980s, scientists believed that human circadian rhythms were largely insensitive to ordinary indoor light environments. But hopefully you get my point here: a study which suggests that low-intensity light levels impact melatonin production might, at a surface-level reading, seem to support the viewpoint that screens are bad for sleep. On the other hand, a deeper reading of the study reveals that it's probably not that relevant, because we're probably talking about a different type, or at least a different intensity, of light. So if we want to plug that logical gap, we need to know three things. First, we need to figure out how intense screen light is. Next, we need to

---

*   Lux is a measure of illuminance, equal to one lumen per square metre, or, just under a tenth of a foot-candle, which is an actual real scientific term from the field of photometry. Essentially, lux gives you a measure of how intensely a given amount of light illuminates a surface.

know what sort of light intensities have a meaningful impact on melatonin suppression over what sort of time durations. Finally, we need to know what practical effect that level of melatonin suppression has on sleep.

At this point, you might reasonably expect that I'm going to tell you about a bunch of studies that give us the answers to those questions. As you might have realised by now, though, this isn't that sort of science book, and the answers are not straightforward. Part of the problem is that lux is not the simple(!) concept I've just made it out to be – there's photopic lux (which is probably what most people mean when they just say 'lux'), melanopic lux (a much-debated way of measuring the biological effects of light), scotopic lux (referring to light intensity in very dim conditions), and rhodopic, chloropic and erythropic lux (referring to light intensities weighted towards different parts of the visible light spectrum). So, for example, I could talk about research published in 2017 by a team led by Michitaka Yoshimura at the Keio University School of Medicine, which looked at how viewing distance and angle impacted illuminance for a single smartphone, the iPhone 5. Yoshimura's team found that you could get light intensities of anything between 2 lux (if you're viewing the phone at 30cm and an angle of 150 degrees) all the way up to 150 lux (if the phone's 10cm away from your face and at a 90-degree angle – that is, directly facing you). On average, the researchers estimated that the participants in their study – twenty-three university students – were exposed to somewhere between 50 to 80 lux from their smartphones. But what sort of lux are we talking about here? Is it relevant to melatonin suppression? And bloody hell, now we need to start thinking about viewing distances and phone angles. And that's just for one type of phone! What about other models, what about other screen devices? It's a problem for the research literature writ large, and is explained quite neatly in a recent review by researchers from the Centre for Chronobiology at the Psychiatric Hospital of the University of Basel. 'It is important to keep in mind that there are multiple ways how light is quantified and reported in the literature in particular when focussing on its repercussions on human physiology,' they write, adding, somewhat dishearteningly: 'Unfortunately, until recently, there have been no standard quantities that experimenters were asked to report, and therefore, summarising the chronobiological and somnological literature on the effects of light remains a challenge.'

It sure does. To try to get a sense check of what we can actually get from the research, I enlist the help of Professor Brant Hasler, Associate Professor of Psychiatry, Psychology and Clinical and Translational Science at the University of Pittsburgh. For the past twenty years he has been conducting work into the science of sleep and circadian rhythms, with a particular focus on adolescent sleep.

'We know there are obviously very clear effects of light levels, and blue light, on circadian rhythms – I mean, I wear glasses that have a blue-light filter,' I tell him. 'Do you get a sense from your work that this translates well into studies that have looked at the effects of light from things like iPads or iPhones?'

'Those glasses that you're wearing right now?' he asks.

I nod.

'Yeah, my guess is that they're not going to have a measurable effect in suppressing circadian influences,' Brant says. 'There's a huge market out there for really cool-looking glasses that just don't really do anything. Not to try to criticise you!'

I laugh, trying to hide my disappointment that I've inadvertently forked out a not-insubstantial amount of money for something which probably doesn't do what it's supposed to.* Anyway, back to screens. 'I don't know of any great studies that I'm aware of that really have hard data in terms of the difference,' he explains. As it turns out, it's not as simple as looking at the blue-light output, or even the overall brightness of a screen. Visual pathways are important, obviously, but so too are other routes through the brain. 'There are non-visual pathways that involve these intrinsically photosensitive retinal ganglion areas, so even if you were to block blue light, you can't completely get away from the effects on melatonin suppression and the circadian system,' he adds. One important aspect of this system is that while the eye does a fairly decent job of filtering out short-wavelength light, that ability changes over time; as we get older, our natural lenticular filters gradually become denser, meaning that it's increasingly harder for blue light to reach the retina at the back of the eye. This might have important consequences for thinking about screen effects across our lifespan, and particularly the impact of blue light in adolescence.

The effect on teens is something that Brant focuses on. 'The main point here is that the amount of light exposure, the light intensity, that comes out of smartphones is enough to have an impact on the circadian system. But it's not always clear what effect that translates into,' he tells me. While a number of studies suggest that, especially in teenage populations, screens can affect factors like actual bedtime, or the time it takes to get to sleep once you're in bed, the key sleep-related thing that we're interested in is not always well defined. Obviously,

---

* I'm also laughing, because while I appreciate the compliment about my glasses, they are very much not cool. I thought they were when I bought them. They were a brand I'd never heard of before, and in the heady excitement of the possibility of some nifty new specs, I looked up the company after I'd returned home from the opticians. To my thirty-something-year-old dismay, they were branded as 'designed and targeted specifically for the mature male'.

things like bedtime are important, but perhaps what we really care about here is the *quality* of sleep, or the amount that we actually get. The findings there are less clear-cut, but one consistent effect that does seem to appear across the litera-ture is the effect on daytime sleepiness: using screens at night seems to translate pretty dependably into feeling groggier the next day.

As an example, let's go back to the 2014 *PNAS* paper I mentioned earlier. In that study, twelve young adults were invited to spend two weeks living in a private room based in Brigham and Women's Hospital in Boston. Each night they were required to have a fixed eight hours of sleep, from 10 p.m. until 6 a.m., which they were also asked to maintain for a few weeks prior to the start of the experiment. In one condition, the participants were asked to read a book on an iPad in dim lighting conditions (around 3 lux) for about four hours prior to bedtime, five nights in a row. The other condition involved them, under the same lighting conditions, reading a printed book for the same amount of time. During the day, the ambient light level in the room was increased to around 90 lux. The study was a randomised crossover design, meaning that all participants took part in both conditions but were randomly assigned to which one they did first. On day one, as well as the seventh and thirteenth days (once a five-night condition block had been completed), the participants took part in what was called a 'constant posture' procedure, which involved them staying sedentary for about four hours both before and after sleep in the same dim-lighting con-ditions. Precise lighting measures were noted for the room, the iPad screen (set to maximum brightness levels) and the light reflected by the book, hourly blood samples were taken through the night to test for plasma melatonin, and the participants had various sensors attached to them to measure brain activity, eye movement, muscle tone and breathing, among other things. Needless to say, it was a highly rigorous and involved study, and one that would be particularly intensive for the participants* involved.

In general, the results showed that, compared with reading a print book, in the iPad condition participants took about ten minutes longer, on average, to get to sleep, and melatonin levels were suppressed by about 50 per cent. The iPad condition also resulted in about ten minutes' less REM† sleep per night, but there was no difference in non-REM sleep compared with the print book condition. There was also no difference in the total amount of sleep participants had. In terms of sleepiness levels, about an hour before bed participants reported feeling less sleepy in the iPad condition, and then reported feeling sleepier the morning after. They also took quite a few hours longer to get to full alertness levels. Finally, the researchers also looked at the spectral profile of light either being emitted by the iPad or being reflected by the book and found, perhaps unsurprisingly, that the light from the iPad was blue-light-rich, with an average illuminance level around 30 lux (compared with the less than 1 lux reflected by the book).

Phew. There's a lot to take in there, so let's break it down. Over the course of two weeks, participants were exposed to a tightly controlled light environment. For some segments of the experiment they used an iPad during the evening, and the effect that this had on their melatonin levels and sleep was compared with the segments when they instead read a traditional print book. Under the conditions of the experiment,

---

*   The upside was that they got the chance to do nothing but read, get eight uninterrupted hours of sleep each night, with the occasional four-hour lie-in. I would have signed up in a heartbeat.

†   Rapid eye movement sleep, which is basically the portion of the night where dreaming usually (although not exclusively) happens.

then, the only thing that differed between the two treatment conditions was exposure to tablet screen light, which seemed to have a direct impact on sleep: in the iPad condition, participants were less sleepy at night and sleepier in the morning, as a result of quantifiable changes in the amount and timing of melatonin production. It's fairly convincing evidence of a direct link between screen use and changes to sleep.

As with most digital technology research, though, if we dig a little deeper than the simple take-home message we're presented with on the surface, a more complicated reality emerges. The study was undoubtedly a highly rigorous and admirable attempt at looking at the relationship between screens and sleep in a systematic manner, but it does leave some key factors unaccounted for, while at the same time highlighting that there are other issues that we might not have considered before. For example, because participants were restricted to a fixed eight hours of sleep per night, it's still not clear whether total sleep time is an important factor or not – or even whether it's the case that people modify their sleep patterns in response to screen use at night. And as rigorous as the study was, perhaps it was too controlled in some respects; in a commentary reply to the study published in 2015, Jamie Zeitzer, Associate Professor of Psychiatry and Behavioural Sciences at Stanford University, pointed out that participants were spending their entire days in a controlled laboratory environment in which they were exposed to a constant 90 lux of light. This, he explained, is the equivalent of spending your day in quite a dimly lit room, and therefore not what most people would normally experience on a daily basis. Remember, 400–600 lux is about the standard for a typical office space, and an overcast day would be about 1,000 lux. Zeitzer went on to argue that the typical levels of light we're exposed to can desensitise us to the sort of light levels participants were exposed to in the study, meaning that under typical day-to-day lighting levels, the iPad condition might not have resulted in as much of a pronounced effect on the melatonin system. Or in other words, when it comes to understanding how screen light might impact sleep, it's not just illuminance in the moment that's important; an individual's 'light history' needs to be taken into account too.

We know that prior light history is important because two of the authors of the *PNAS* paper also published work on this a few years earlier, in 2011. In that study, participants were exposed to one of two 'light history' conditions – either very dim (1 lux) or very bright (90 lux) lighting during daytime hours over the course of three consecutive days. On 'light exposure' days, rather than lights out at bedtime, participants were exposed to either very dim or very bright light for around six and a half hours during the night, with blood melatonin levels sampled every hour or so. All seventeen participants were exposed to every combination of light history and light exposure, and the entire study required them to stay in the lab for thirty-two days. On average, melatonin production was suppressed by about 50 per cent (with a range of between 15 to 94 per cent across individuals) when participants had been exposed to brighter light for the preceding three days, whereas when they were exposed to very dim light, melatonin suppression was much greater – around 85 per cent (with a range of 60 to 96 per cent). That is, while the biological rhythms which govern sleep are sensitive to current light levels, the magnitude of that sensitivity is dependent on at least two things: the recent levels of light in the surrounding environment and, given the quite wide range of melatonin responses exhibited across participants, potential *individual differences* in light sensitivity.

None of this is to say that we should therefore completely

disregard the results of an otherwise robust study. It's just to emphasise that we need to be careful in getting too excited about the findings from a single source. For instance, we can be equally critical of studies I've mentioned here that suggest relatively little effect of short-wavelength screen light on sleep. Back in Chapter 1, I mentioned a study, led by Stephanie van Der Lely and colleagues at the University of Basel, which looked at the effects of wearing blue-light-blocking glasses. In that study, thirteen teenagers were asked to wear either blue-light blockers or clear-lens controls for a week at a time, and prior to bedtime each night they sat in front of a blank, bright-white computer screen for three hours while periodically completing cognitive tests, questionnaires, or providing saliva samples.* They then went to sleep for eight hours, and in the morning completed some follow-up tests. Participants reported feeling sleepier (and had higher levels of salivary melatonin) just prior to bedtime when they were wearing the blue-light blockers, but in the morning their subjective sleepiness levels (and melatonin levels) were comparable to those reported in the control condition. At the same time, the authors witnessed no differences across the conditions in terms of total sleep time, sleep quality or sleep cycles. Nevertheless, the authors concluded that 'the impact on the circadian system implicates that multimedia screen use may be harmful for adolescents' health'. Quite an assertion to make based on an objective reading of the results, but there we go.

In Chapter 1, I also reported the results of a similar study, led by Jeremy Bigalke at Montana State University, in which twenty participants were given either blue-light blockers or control glasses to wear for a week at a time, from 6 p.m. until bedtime, while otherwise going about their normal evening

---

* Don't ever let anyone tell you that science isn't exciting.

routines. Given that this study didn't happen in a tightly controlled lab environment, the authors relied instead on the use
of actigraphy watches* and self-reported sleep diaries. The
results showed that, subjectively, participants reported being
able to get to sleep more quickly, and waking up fewer times
during the night, when they wore the blue-light blockers. The
more objective measurements from the actigraph suggested
the opposite, though: in the blue-light-blocker condition,
participants didn't actually fall asleep more quickly *or* wake
up less often. Moreover, the actigraph data suggested that
although there were no statistically significant differences
in the total amount of sleep between the two conditions,
nevertheless the trends seemed to go in the wrong direction:
participants were getting around fifteen minutes' *less* sleep per
night after wearing blue-light blockers.

When I asked Brant Hasler about these studies, he empha-
sised one critical flaw present in both of them, and quite an
obvious one when you think about it. 'Both studies have a
number of strengths, but they lack a convincing measure of
adherence to wearing the glasses,' he explained. 'The Bigalke
article doesn't even try to measure adherence as far as I can
tell.' The van der Lely study does talk about adherence, noting
that the authors asked participants to keep a diary of when
and for how long they wore the glasses. This was checked
against the use of a device called a 'Luxblick' attached to the
glasses, which measures light exposure. As Brant told me,
though, it's not clear how that device distinguishes between
the glasses being worn (and therefore being exposed to light)
versus being plonked on a table in front of the participant

---

*   Essentially, watches which record the gross amount of movement that
happens during sleep. Nowhere near as accurate as the gold-standard method
of polysomnography (which was used in the *PNAS* study), but much cheaper
and less burdensome on participants.

(and still exposed to light). 'The adherence issue is a giant one, in my opinion,' he said. 'Having run two pilot studies using bright-light glasses, and presently running two large studies using both those and blue-light blockers, I've learned not to trust self-reports of adherence.' He also cautioned me about lending too much credence to objective measures of sleep over self-reported diaries. 'Actigraphs are notoriously unreliable at assessing sleep onset latency,' he explained, 'and even polysomnography has its limitations.' In that sense, self-report measures, despite their shortcomings, can still give us useful information about sleep where other gold-standard measures might not be able to.

At this point, let's try to take stock of where we are. What is hopefully becoming clear by now is that the research literature on screen light and sleep, like many other areas of work on digital technology effects, provides two conflicting viewpoints. Taken at face value, some studies seem to provide fairly convincing evidence that late-night screen time does have an effect on sleep. In a way, this is unsurprising, because it has to. Light levels definitely affect our circadian rhythms, circadian rhythms play an integral role in regular sleep, screens emit light – particularly blue light – and so on. Less clear is what that effect specifically looks like, and whether there is an appreciable effect on sleep. If we think deeply about what those studies can actually show us, then we get a much more complicated picture, because the relationship between light and sleep is itself so complicated. Simple light intensity and duration are important, but so are differences in sensitivity to light across our lifespan, as well as individual variability in sensitivity, and even the nature of the light environment we've been in over the past few days. Condensing all of this in an attempt to tell a relatively simple story about screens and sleep has the potential to unravel very quickly.

In a way, though, this is understandable, because light is just one, albeit important, facet of the story. Sleep is more than circadian rhythms, just as screen use is more than simply whether or not you're looking at one.

A series of findings that highlight this wider issue particularly well centre on evaluating the impact of Apple's 'Night Shift' feature in its iOS operating system. While there's considerable disagreement about whether or not screen-based technology emits enough blue light to have a meaningful impact on sleep, in a sense there's a potentially easy win here. If you can modify a screen display to emit less blue light, then by the logic we've been following up to now we might expect to see some sort of improvement in sleep. Night Shift does just that – allowing you to change the colour temperatures on your smartphone or tablet display to the 'warmer' end of the light spectrum. Basically, you can make your screen look more yellow, less blue. At least one study has shown that using Night Shift mode makes a difference to the amount of blue light emitted from Apple devices: work by a team led by Andrew Smith at University of California, Irvine showed across three devices (two iPhone models and one iPad) that using Night Shift mode at maximum setting decreased blue-light intensity by up to 90 per cent. But the key question is whether this has any sort of significant effect on sleep – and the answer here, somewhat surprisingly, is that it doesn't. A number of studies published between 2018 and 2022 have found, with fair consistency, that Night Shift doesn't impact melatonin suppression or sleep quality, among other things. In particular, a 2021 study by researchers based at Brigham Young University looked at sleep outcomes for seven consecutive nights after participants were asked to use an iPhone for an hour before bed, either with or without Night Shift on, or to abstain from using their phones at all. In general, there were no appreciable differences across those three groups in terms of sleep onset latency, sleep efficiency, or total sleep time. Where there was any sort of effect, in real terms it was pretty small – participants in the no-phone condition were, on average, getting two more minutes of sleep, and spending ten fewer minutes in bed, per night than those in the phone conditions.

It's tempting to conclude, on the basis of this study, that using screens before bedtime doesn't have an impact on sleep – after all, although the research was focused on the effects of Night Shift mode, the fact that there were no meaningful differences between either phone use condition and the no-phone condition seems to imply that there isn't a problem. We have to be careful with that conclusion, though. The research team note that, although the participants in the study were asked to try to get at least eight hours of sleep per night, on average they were getting about 6.8 hours per night across the experiment, with an average sleep efficiency of 82 per cent. Most guidelines* tend to state that anything lower than 85 per cent constitutes poor sleep, which suggests that the participants weren't getting enough good-quality sleep here. If it's the case that they were getting insufficient sleep over the long term, then changing things up for a week during the experiment won't have had much of an impact. Why might they not be getting enough sleep generally? The argument that the researchers put forward here is that the participants were in late adolescence, aged between eighteen and twenty-four, and adolescent sleep is generally pretty poor. They're also likely to be using their phones and other digital

---

* There's a caveat with this cut-off criterion, though, which is that it's not exactly clear where it comes from. Where I have found guidelines that provide a citation for that number, they all tend to point to a research paper in the *Journal of Clinical Sleep Medicine* which doesn't actually suggest 85 per cent as a cut-off for 'poor sleep', so it's debatable here whether a sleep efficiency of 82 per cent can reasonably be classed as suboptimal.

technology a lot, perhaps at night – although this was veering into conjecture, because none of this was actually measured in the study. Nevertheless, there are other studies to suggest that aside from light-specific arousal, smartphone use before bed might create psychological arousal and alertness depending on what you're doing on your phone.

As someone who is chronically sleep-deprived, I was really hoping for an easy win here: stick Night Shift on and coast my way to better sleep. The reality of the situation, though, is that very often I'm *not* on my phone before bed, so it probably wouldn't have mattered anyway. The last screen-based technology I tend to look at before I try to sleep is the baby monitor, because I'm on edge wondering whether we're going to get woken up by a crying baby in the next half an hour, hour, or whenever.* So while I think we should be cautious about how conclusive our interpretation of the results from the above study are, I do agree with one of the core arguments the authors put forward: namely that rather than considering sleep purely in the context of light emissions, it's also important – if not more important – to look at the effects of *what* we're doing on our phones just before bed.

As with research focusing on mental health, the vast majority of studies looking at the relationship between screen use and sleep concentrate on children and adolescents as the populations of interest. The reasons for this are largely

---

* Important side note: I am convinced that manufacturers of baby monitors have never, ever spoken to a new parent. There are no good baby monitors on the market. They all do stupid things, or have stupid features, or generally fail to show you a camera feed when you really, really need to see what's going on. When would you ever want to play a teeth-rattling synthesised rendition of 'Twinkle Twinkle Little Star' through the camera speaker? Why, in the age of Zoom and Teams, am I forced to make do with a feed that looks like some dimly lit 1980s CCTV footage recorded on to a VHS tape that's been used a few too many times? And, most importantly, why is the monitor so bright that it can be seen from the moon, even on the lowest setting?

unsurprising: the persistent worry is that if digital technology does have any sort of effect, it will be these populations that are exceptionally vulnerable. It is also a particular cause for concern in adolescents because the biological systems regulating their sleep undergo huge changes during this time. Across numerous studies, it has been consistently shown that as children move into adolescence, their bedtime tends to become increasingly later, due both to a phase delay in the circadian timing system (that is, they don't start to feel the sleepiness-inducing effects of melatonin until later in the evening) and a slowdown in the rate at which the biological pressure to sleep builds up during the day (in other words, they find it easier to stay awake for longer). Later bedtimes are coupled with school start times that stay the same, or in many countries get progressively earlier as children grow older. In the US, for example, 2016 data from the Department of Education showed that the average start time for primary or elementary schools was 8.17 a.m., which pushed back to 8.04 a.m. for middle schools and 7.59 a.m. for high schools. This combination of later bedtimes and earlier morning wake-up times has the potential to put significant pressure on the amount of sleep teens are able to get, and there is consistent evidence to suggest that this is precisely what's happening. For example, while the American Academy of Sleep Medicine recommends that children aged between six and twelve should regularly be getting at least nine hours of sleep per night, 2015 data from the Youth Risk Behavior Surveillance System, or YRBSS, reported that of some 52,000 children surveyed, 60 per cent of them weren't getting this minimum. For those aged thirteen to eighteen the Academy recommends at least eight hours sleep, and YRBSS data from 15,000 teenagers showed that things were worse, with just over 70 per cent not getting enough.

In an influential 2011 paper, noted sleep researcher Professor Mary Carskadon referred to this situation as the 'perfect storm'. As children enter adolescence, changes in their biological systems mean that it's easier for them to be more awake later into the evening. This, coupled with psychosocial pressures – parent-set bedtimes start to slacken off, homework demands require more time, social networks need maintaining – means that bedtime gradually creeps later and later. At the other end, school start times get earlier and earlier, meaning that the window for sleep shrinks. Given that sleep needs don't change that much across adolescence – on average, teens need just over nine hours for decent cognitive function and emotional regulation – this inevitably creates a tension between the amount of sleep adolescents require and how much they are likely to be able to get. The question of interest for us here is whether or not screen-based activities act as another psychosocial pressure, because if they do, then that's a relatively easily modifiable factor to improve sleep. Moreover, given the relatively tight window that adolescents have for sleep, if screen time *does* have any effects they will be much more pronounced for this population than for older adults.

There are two plausible effects that we can reasonably suppose screen time might have on that sleep window. The first is displacement: if teens are using digital technology instead of trying to go to sleep, that window dwindles even further. The second is that if what they're doing on their phones, tablets or computers is cognitively or emotionally stimulating, it might be harder for them to get to sleep once they start trying to do so. Moreover, displacement and stimulation aren't mutually exclusive, and there could well be an additive effect of the two together. A recent review by Lisbeth Lund and colleagues at the University of Southern Denmark suggested that across the literature there is some evidence for a general association between screen time and both these factors, although, as ever, it depends on the type of screen time we're talking about. Some studies, for example, report that using a computer doubles the odds of having less sleep per night and chatting on the phone triples the odds. In others, though, talking on the phone increases the amount of sleep, whereas texting reduces it. Where some studies show a link between having a TV in the bedroom and less sleep, others indicate that it's having a computer in the room, not a TV or a games console, which can have a negative impact. Age seems to be an important factor too: while Lund and her team found stronger evidence for an association between digital technology use and later bedtimes for children aged six to twelve, for thirteen-to-fifteen-year-olds there was instead stronger evidence for an association with difficulties in actually *getting* to sleep – active forms of screen use, like social media, were more often associated with poor sleep than passive forms such as watching TV.

Work led by Dr Holly Scott at the University of Glasgow has tried to decode what it is about bedtime screen use that might drive this difficulty in getting to sleep. Her research, involving focus groups with teenagers, has identified two core themes that the youngsters highlight when talking about, in particular, their use of social media at night time. One, which can broadly be thought of as 'fear of missing out', or FOMO, concerns the idea that teenagers worry that if they aren't active on social media around bedtime, which is when their friends and peers are active, they'll miss important things happening. This carries a significant 'real-world' cost, because the risk of missing something online – anything from an important social drama down to a simple shared joke – might bleed into face-to-face conversations the following day.

If you weren't there at the time, the risk is you'll end up feeling (inadvertently or deliberately) excluded or isolated from your group of friends. FOMO at night is a constant source of pressure and anxiety, and when it comes to sleep creates a no-win situation: either teens buckle under the pressure and hop back on to social media, thereby delaying bedtime, or they don't, but end up not sleeping anyway because they're worried about missing out on something.

The second core theme identified in Scott's research concerns social rules and expectations around what a 'normal' teenage life on social media looks like. Among other things, one unspoken norm is the requirement to be always available, and ready to respond to messages as soon as possible. Logging off at bedtime, and therefore not instantly replying to conversations as they come in, violates unspoken rules of online social etiquette. For some teenagers in Scott's focus groups, this wasn't a big deal – it was a manifestation of their burgeoning independence, coupled with a pinch of rebelliousness. For others, though, rule violations could result in quite negative emotions, with some teens saying that in such circumstances they would feel guilty or anxious. The upshot here is that in many cases, because of the perceived need to be 'always on', teens can feel deprived of a sense of agency or control; even if they want to switch off and go to sleep, there are strong social pressures preventing them from doing so. These pressures have a double-whammy effect in that they both push bedtime later and make teens feel more wired once they do get to bed. And because adolescents don't really see a difference between social relationships online versus offline – one is basically an extension of the other – then any negative feelings they experience when trying to use their smartphones less might be more acute than in older adults, who tend to care less about this sort of stuff.

Screen time seems to have an impact both in terms of displacement and stimulation, then. But there is an important question remaining: what is the magnitude of this effect? How much sleep are teenagers losing over social media? Well, here's where things get a little confusing. In 2020, Amy Orben and Andrew Przybylski attempted to answer just that question using data from the Millennium Cohort Study. We came across this dataset and these researchers earlier, when they used a special sort of statistical method called a Specification Curve Analysis to look at the relationship between screen time and mental health. They applied the same technique to sleep-related data by conducting 120 analyses that represent the spectrum of reasonable combinations of technology-use measures, sleep measures and control variables. Overall, the researchers found that both weekend and weekday digital technology use had a small negative association with sleep, weekday use being slightly more negative. Unsurprisingly, they also found that the patterns of those associations varied depending on what sleep outcome measure was used. For example, there was a small negative association between delayed bedtime and technology use for both weekdays and weekends, whereas the total time spent asleep was more strongly associated with technology use on weekdays. This makes sense: the things teenagers do online will largely stay the same across the week, but on weekdays, because wake-up is anchored to school start times, they can't make up for it by having a lie-in. In terms of the total time teens spent asleep, though, these effects were small: Orben and Przybylski estimated that every extra hour of screen time throughout the day corresponded to approximately nine minutes' less sleep on weekdays, and around 3.5 minutes' less on weekends. Moreover, teens who used screens in the half-hour before they went to bed went on to report around one minute less sleep per night, across the week. These estimates are in line with previous research using data from some 50,000 US adolescents, which found that every hour of screen time during the day was associated with between three and eight minutes' less sleep at night.

So on the one hand we have pockets of evidence across different areas of research which suggest that using digital technology in the evening can have some fairly negative effects on our ability to rest: the spectral profile of light that screens emit has the potential to interrupt basic biological processes involved in sleep, teenagers report feeling pressures to use social media late into the evening, and, depending on the type of digital technology we're talking about, evening use can translate into later bedtimes, difficulties getting to sleep and less overall time spent sleeping. On the other hand, the magnitude of these effects doesn't seem to be particularly burdensome – we're talking about a few minutes' less sleep per night, not hours. How do we reconcile these two seemingly conflicting lines of evidence?

The answer, I think, lies in how we frame the relationship. We often consider the link between sleep and technology use before bedtime to be a critical one, perhaps the most critical one, because it represents a relatively contained system that's easy to get our heads around. And, like many aspects of the debate about screen time effects, when a few studies come along that support the belief that digital technology is bad, they reinforce a world view that coalesces around the idea that screens directly cause problems with sleep, and big problems at that. And here's the thing: that might, to some extent, be true. We can't say for certain that screens do or do not have a meaningful negative impact on sleep, because the research evidence isn't fully there yet. Nevertheless, it's very likely that, given what we currently know, any changes we make to our evening technology use will only result in, at best, small gains with regard to sleep.

If what we really care about is getting a better night's rest there are other, much more impactful things that we need to focus on. As I write, there is a war going on in Ukraine which, quite apart from its horrors, is causing shockwaves around the world in terms of food and energy security. Closer to home, we are experiencing unprecedented price increases across the board coupled with stalling wage growth, high inflation and an embarrassment of a government either unwilling or unable to do anything meaningful about this crisis in the cost of living. The backdrop to all of this is a climate catastrophe driving irreparable damage to the planet we will be leaving to our kids. These are the worries that keep us awake. If we want to fix sleep, it would probably be a good idea to stop the world from burning, both literally and metaphorically. That, and make school start times later so that teenagers have a half-decent chance of getting some rest.

But small changes can be easy changes, and small gains over time can still have a meaningful effect. So perhaps a better way of framing the relationship, at least for now, is that while emerging lines of research suggest that, yes, there is a link between screen use and sleep, it's worth bearing in mind that screens are not the most important cause of bad sleep. If we're worried about the effects writ large, or we have concerns about our own technology use or that of our kids, then rather than hit the panic button and instigate all-out bans before bed, instead we can take a smarter approach and think about how best to make our screens work for us, instead of against us. For example, one aspect of night-time technology use we can all relate to is as a distraction activity. You've had a stressful day at work, there are lots of things on your mind. When you go to bed you can't sleep because you're anxious about something that's happened during the day, or something that's going to happen tomorrow, or (if you're like me) you're just anxious generally. So you pick up your phone and watch a YouTube video, or play a game for a bit, or read. Sometimes it helps but sometimes it doesn't, and before you know it you've spent the last forty-five minutes working your way through a few irritating levels of Candy Crush instead of getting that much-needed sleep. So now you're anxious it's late, and that's forty-five potential minutes of precious sleep you're not going to get back. Do this again and again over time, and essentially you're conditioning yourself to be awake and anxious when you're trying to sleep. 'We need to think about stimulus control,' explains Brant Hasler. 'Doing anything besides sleep in bed – with the exception of sex – carries the risk of developing conditioned associations with whatever that activity is. And if it's anything that can contribute to arousal in any way, then you're risking conditioned arousal with your bed.' Simply put, conditioned arousal is the phenomenon whereby you inadvertently learn, over time, to be awake and alert when you're in bed. If you go to bed worried and you use your phone to try to offset that worry, then what you're doing is tossing a coin. For some people the distraction works; they calm down and get to sleep. For others the act of being awake and doing something stimulating, however slight, has the effect of training their bodies to associate being in bed with not being asleep. 'I have patients all the time who will say "Yeah, I walk past my bed, and I just look at it with dread. I'm really sleepy, I go to bed, and the sleepiness is gone." That's a red flag for conditioned arousal,' Brant explains.

The trick is to try to spot those associations and do something about them if you feel they're starting to become a problem. If you're the kind of person who can happily unwind using your phone in bed before sleep, then great. But if you catch yourself screen-surfing and it's not helping your anxiety levels, then it's time to change things up. That can be something as simple as switching the thing you're doing on your phone – remember, not all screen time is the same. Try reading a book instead of doomscrolling through your chosen text-based social media app, or playing a word puzzle game instead of cycling through Instagram or TikTok videos. Or get up, do something else for a bit until you feel sleepy and then try going back to bed. Over time you can break that association, and in turn hopefully get a better night's sleep. Stick Night Shift mode on while you're at it – sure, the research so far suggests that it doesn't do anything, but it definitely doesn't hurt to use it, and if we're talking about something as simple as flicking on a digital switch, it's worth a try.

Fifteen across. Once in Berlin House, Edward was knocked out. Nine letters.

Small changes, small gains. My son slept through for the first time a few nights ago. It was just the one night, mind you. Nevertheless it was a breakthrough: a small glimmer of hope that things can get better on that particular nocturnal battlefront. I'm still doing the crosswords, though – just not in the middle of the night. Brightness down, glasses on, the ones with the blue filters. I still have Brant's voice ringing in my ears, telling me that they don't do anything, but at least I can actually read the screen with them on. The crosswords have gone from a way to keep me awake and semi-functional when I really shouldn't be to something that acts as a decompression chamber for my brain, a way to dampen down the bustle of the day and clear a space for a decent chance of rest. For now, they seem to be doing a pretty good job of that. And the moment I catch myself staying on the app for Just One More Game, I'll know it's time to move on to something else.

Twenty-three down. Combination of gin and hot dog to make you sleep well. Nine letters.

5

Attention

'Mg plus O_2 equals ...'

The dull thud of a rather hefty chemistry textbook on the desk at the front of the lab snaps me out of a glassy-eyed daydream.

'*ETCHELLS*, what's the answer?'

I look up at my chemistry teacher, Mr Sharples. DJ Ray, we used to call him – although not to his face, obviously. He was a larger-than-life character like many teachers are, with a look that vacillated somewhere between a 1980s glam rock guitarist and a wedding DJ, hence the nickname. He also had an amazing way of bringing chemistry to life in the classroom, on the unspoken condition that you turn up, ready to learn, and that you bloody well pay attention when you're there.

On this occasion, I'm not *quite* paying attention.

He is well aware that I'm not *quite* paying attention. Everyone in the room knows the scenario that's currently playing out. Whatever my answer now, it is a no-win situation for me. I already lost the moment he saw that my mind was elsewhere.

'Um ... Mg ...'

Before I have chance to blurt anything else out, he interrupts, erupting in faux hysterics.

'Mg plus O_2 equals MgO_2! These are easy, *gimme some more!*'

He looks across the class at a sea of quiet faces – some smirking – before explaining the correct way to balance the equation, for the umpteenth time, in an equally sarcastic fashion. By a curious coincidence I am picked on for the next few examples, all of which I nail, providing some small modicum of redemption for myself in the process.

I wasn't paying attention because I was thinking about the internet. To be more specific, I was thinking about my friends on the internet. To be more specific still, I was thinking about a coterie of friends I was talking to, in a game, on the internet. I was sixteen, it was the turn of the millennium, and while I did have a mobile phone it was switched off, in my bag, because at that moment in time no one really saw any need for a teenager to be able to take a phone call or a text message in the middle of the school day. Smartphones, and their constant connectivity, were still the exclusive realm of science fiction. And so, with no means of managing my online social life during the day, I was left only with the option of excited anticipation, of watching the clock tick slowly, inexorably towards home time.

For a long time during that teenage period, for a few precious hours in the evening, social media – or at least the protoapplications that laid the groundwork for the modern-day phenomena – would consume my world. It was multitasking at its finest: AOL Instant Messenger in one corner of the screen, MSN Messenger just below. ICQ floating around somewhere, usually next to a newly skinned Winamp window running a playlist of forty-to-fifty-second mp3s, because my 56k dialup internet connection wasn't up to downloading songs in their entirety. Overlaying all of this was Internet Explorer, where I was logged into an online role-playing game called Vampire: The Masquerade. Vampire was a pen-and-paper RPG akin to Dungeons & Dragons, designed to be played over long hours and in person. The online version that I took part in, lacking a group of friends at home who were willing to go through the slog of a live campaign, was essentially a glorified chatroom. All of these windows – save Winamp – were there to achieve one thing: to connect with people. Some of those people were friends from school, some were friends halfway across the world who I'd never met in real life, and yet more were people with who I shared the nerdy joy of role-playing games.

The Vampire RPG chatroom, in all its clunky, glitchy, JavaScript glory, felt like a home away from home. Yes, we played games, but more often than not, in the small group of close friends I had formed there, we would simply chat for hours about everything and nothing. We'd share crackly, hastily ripped WAV files from our favourite albums with each other. We'd try to cheer each other up when we felt low. We spent a lot of time creating fantastical player characters for the game, coming up with intricate back stories for avatars that we would never actually end up using. We'd talk about meeting up with each other for real someday – and in some cases we did. There was a fairly even split between those of us who lived in the UK and those in the US, and the British contingent would daydream about organising a trip across the ocean for the grandest of meet-ups. What an adventure that would be! I would sometimes hear my mum downstairs, fretting vocally to her partner about what I was doing online, what sort of monsters I was talking to. I ignored all that because these monsters were my friends, the people who knew me best in the world.

These were the things that I was thinking about in the chemistry class that day. I wanted to be home, talking to my mates. I didn't care about balancing chemical equations. Connection, that was what was important – those friendships were infinitely more essential, more valuable to my life than magnesium ions. I guess, from Mr Sharples' point of view, the opposite was true; all he saw was an idle student, not engaging with the class. What was important for him, then and there, was the teachable moment. And to be fair, it's a moment that has stuck with me my entire life – I've learned to pay attention when it's right and respectful to do so, and that however it might feel at the time, teachers don't actually hate you or want to show you up. They just want to give you the best possible chance of developing and thriving so that you can make it out there in the world.

Attention. It's taken me about three days to write about that story. Not because it was a particularly difficult one to write or remember, but just because there are *so many distractions*. Whether it's a politician resigning, someone saying something infuriating or thought-provoking in today's must-read article, my daughter barging into the room to see what I'm doing, emails, WhatsApp messages from work, home ... It feels as though we live in an always-on culture where everyone and everything is constantly vying for our attention. It seems impossible to concentrate on work, to focus on, well, *anything* meaningful for more than tens of minutes at a time. The obvious scapegoat for this apparent collective collapse is, of course, screens, and over the past few years we've seen a few high-profile clarion calls alerting us to the insidious damage that tech companies are inflicting on our conscious ability to pay attention. Perhaps the most recent example of this comes from journalist and noted Wikipedia editor Johann Hari.

In early 2022, Hari published a book called *Stolen Focus*, boosted by a high-profile excerpt in the *Guardian* newspaper titled 'Your attention didn't collapse. It was stolen.' In it, Hari explains that it's not just me, or him, or you who feels as if our ability to concentrate on anything meaningful has been eroded. It's happening on a mammoth scale, to everyone. There are, by Hari's estimation, twelve reasons that have been 'proven' to undermine our collective attention, but it's clear from both the book and the *Guardian* excerpt that social media is a frontrunner. Throughout Hari's account, anecdotes of situations in which he becomes increasingly alarmed at either his own fixation on digital technology, that of someone close to him, or just random people in his vicinity are peppered among a series of interviews with researchers, clinicians and tech gurus, with the odd study thrown in here and there for good measure. There's no doubt that Hari is an accomplished storyteller, and in many ways *Stolen Focus* is a compelling, if terrifying read that leaves you feeling ever so slightly unnerved about picking your phone up to check any message ever again. But the book suffers in the same way that so many offerings of its ilk do. You know the sort: the Petersonian or Gladwellian kinds of books that prioritise the story, the narrative, over a rigorous look at the relevant science in all its messy, complex, fascinating glory. And if you do start to do a deep dive into that science, you end up finding a very different picture emerging, one that I'm sure will feel all too familiar by now: that there haven't been any thorough long-term studies showing that our attention has declined over time; that some studies show attentional benefits to social media use, some show disadvantages and others show nothing at all; and that, as with many stories about the science of screens, there is no consensus about how to even talk about the relevant factors. In fact, in psychology more broadly, attention itself is a hotly contested concept.

The problem with taking a surface-level approach in the service of a more easily digestible and engrossing story is that important facts are inevitably missed or misconstrued along the way. Some of these are excruciatingly obvious: Hari spends a fair amount of one particular chapter chastising Facebook for not having a feature that allows you to check whether any of your friends are nearby, so that you can use an online app to facilitate offline connection. The reason for this, he suggests, is in part because Facebook want to maximise the amount of time that you're on their app or website because that's how they make money: either through advertisements or, more insidiously, through data-harvesting. It seems scary and depressing, until you realise that between 2014 and 2022 Facebook *did* have a built-in feature that let you see which of your friends were in the local area. It was literally called 'Nearby Friends'. It showed you who was close by and allowed you to share your precise location with them for a short period of time,* all to make it easier to meet people offline.

But there are other, less overt issues that relate to the evidence base cited. In a series of tweets following the publication of the book, cultural historian Dr Matthew Sweet noted that where some studies are drawn on by Hari as evidence of our collective inability to pay attention, a closer look reveals a very different picture. For example, one of the arguments put forward early on in *Stolen Focus* is that our capacity to concentrate is being eroded because we're constantly multitasking: when we're trying to get on with something

---

* Facebook shut down this feature in late May 2022, likely due to relatively low usage, or being outcompeted by other apps which do the same thing but better.

important, whether it's playing with our kids or chipping away at a work task, having a phone nearby that pings us notifications about new messages inevitably distracts us away from the thing we want to do. And because task-switching comes with a cognitive cost – it takes time and effort to try to do more than one thing at once – over the course of tens or hundreds of phone notifications popping up per day we become much slower and more error-prone at more complex tasks we're trying to focus on. In the book's endnotes, Hari cites a number of sources to support this idea (and in a broad sense, the notion of a cognitive cost associated with task-switching is well researched in psychological science), but instead of a deep dive into this fascinating research area, the spotlight is shone on one particular study from Carnegie Mellon University. In it, 136 students were asked to take a test during which one group had their phones switched off and the other group had their phones switched on, and were periodically interrupted with text messages. The phones-switched-on group, we are told, performed about 20 per cent worse than the phones-switched-off group. 'Other studies in similar scenarios have found even worse outcomes of 30 per cent,' Hari tells us. 'It seems to me that almost all of us with a smartphone are losing that 20 to 30 per cent, almost all the time. That's a lot of brainpower for a species to lose.'

There are a couple of problems here, aside from the obvious fact that no one worth paying attention to would ever seriously suggest that the human species, collectively, has lost nearly a third of its cognitive capacity in recent years. The first is, as Matthew Sweet has pointed out, that the Carnegie Mellon experiment was never actually published as a bona fide scientific study – it was commissioned by authors Bob Sullivan and Hugh Thompson for their book *Getting Unstuck: Break Free of the Plateau Effect* (2014). While that doesn't mean we should completely ignore the findings, it does mean that it's harder to assess the study for methodological rigour. The second problem is that if you read the description of the experiment in *Getting Unstuck*, you learn that there were three experimental conditions, not two, and that the test was conducted twice, not once. The control group had their phones switched off throughout but, critically, the other two groups were told that they 'might be contacted for further instructions' via text – that they might get a phone notification containing information *important to the test they were doing*. One of those groups, the 'interrupted' group, were sent text messages twice in both iterations of the test. The other, called the 'on-high-alert' group, were sent messages in the first test, but not in the second – in other words, they were anticipating a notification which never came. In the first test – billed as a standard cognitive skill test, although we don't know which one – both groups answered correctly 20 per cent less often than the control group. But the results from the second test paint a very different picture. The control group didn't show any differences compared with the first test, but the 'interrupted' group improved by 14 per cent, almost reaching the same level of performance as the controls. The 'on-high-alert' group *outperformed* the control group the second time round, improving by 43 per cent. Sullivan and Thompson tantalisingly suggest that the study was to be published in an upcoming paper, but to date I haven't been able to find anything, which means we can't drill down into the results with any more precision. At any rate, it's difficult to reconcile what results we are able to glean with the notion that we're losing 20–30 per cent of our collective brainpower because of smartphones.

As straightforward as it is to debunk some of the arguments claiming that our collective attention has disintegrated, we're still left with the feeling that something isn't quite right about our ability to concentrate. Understanding why we feel that way is never going to be explained with a simple, straightforward story, no matter how elegantly it is presented. That's simply not how science works, and psychologists have the often unenviable task of studying ephemeral and elusive phenomena that are extremely hard to isolate in the laboratory. Sometimes that means research teams produce results which contradict other research findings. Sometimes – well, often, in fact – we spend years inadvertently using inexact methods, thinking that we have found out something meaningful about the world, only for that notion to be completely upended with the arrival of more robust and rigorous studies. Sometimes scientists make mistakes. We're only human, after all. And sometimes we even struggle to figure out what it is that we're actually trying to study in the first place. As it happens, attention is an excellent example of this.

Attention is one of those foundational topics that every undergraduate psychology student comes across sooner or later (usually sooner) in their university studies. I have very fond memories of sitting in the lecture theatre in my early foray into introductory psychology, enthralled as we learned about things like the cocktail party effect and the invisible gorilla test. The cocktail party effect, originally described by Scottish philosopher Dugald Stewart in the late 1700s but later made famous in a classic study by Colin Cherry in 1953, is the phenomenon whereby we are able to focus our attention on one particular stimulus or signal while simultaneously filtering out other irrelevant things going on around us. Imagine we're talking to each other at a cocktail party. From an auditory point of view, that situation is a mess: multiple conversations, all happening at the same time, glasses clinking, music playing. Nevertheless, we can, seemingly effortlessly, ignore all that noise and have a coherent* conversation with each other. Given the vast amount of information that bombards our senses, we have the ability to sift the signal from the noise – to pick and choose what we pay attention to, and what we ignore. Sometimes, though, we're too good at this, and the invisible gorilla test is a neat example of what is known as 'inattentional blindness'. Psychologists Dan Simons and Christopher Chabris demonstrated the effect in a surprising experiment in 1999. Participants were shown a series of videos of two small teams of players passing a ball to each other in front of a set of lift doors. They were told to pay attention to one of the teams, and silently count either how many times the ball was passed by one of their players or how many times that team made a bounce or aerial pass. In some versions of the videos, about forty-five seconds in, a woman wearing a gorilla suit walked across the scene. Afterwards the participants were asked if they spotted anything odd happening, and on average just over half *didn't* report seeing the gorilla walk directly through their field of view. Their attention was so focused on one particular task that they simply didn't notice something completely out of the ordinary happening right in front of their eyes. And these two effects are just a small part of the vast array of research that has been conducted on attention more broadly; it is a very deeply, extensively studied concept (at the time of writing, the invisible gorilla experiment alone has been cited nearly 4,000 times).

Despite being one of the cornerstones of modern-day experimental psychology, and a topic of interest dating at least as far back as the days of Aristotle, some fundamental questions about attention still remain unanswered. Perhaps

---

*   Well, depending on how many cocktails we've had.

first and foremost among these, as I've alluded to, is that no one really knows what 'attention' actually means. In fact, there is literally a paper that was published in the journal *Attention, Perception and Psychophysics* in 2019 titled 'No one knows what attention is'.* In that paper, a team led by Bernhard Hommel at the Leiden Institute for Brain and Cognition argued that attention, as a term, has been overused and misused to the point that it now covers so many potential phenomena it is essentially meaningless. We've already come across two of these uses – the idea of 'selective' attention, as highlighted in the cocktail party effect, and 'inattentional blindness' in the invisible gorilla experiment. To that list they added 'focused' attention, 'involuntary' attention, 'spatial' attention, 'divided' attention, 'sustained' attention and more. The upshot of all this, they argued, is that in using the same term for everything we risk viewing attention as a unitary concept, when it's rather unlikely that these different forms of attention are all the same process governed by a single set of neural mechanisms.

Perhaps more of a problem, Hommel's team suggest, is that there is a tendency throughout the research literature to reify attention: attention is an abstraction, but one that has become implicitly assumed to be a concrete entity that has a causal impact on other things – for example, a quick Google Scholar search for the term 'attention affects the' brings up over 2,500 research papers ('attention affects the processing of tactile stimuli', 'attention affects the recognition of briefly presented visual stimuli in infants', and so on). But because

---

*   It followed a 2011 paper in *Frontiers in Psychology* titled 'There is no such thing as attention', written by Britt Anderson at the University of Waterloo. Anderson went on to write a paper titled 'Stop paying attention to "attention"' in 2021. Then there was 'Attention is a sterile concept', published in 2018. One can't help but feel that there is something of an existential crisis in attention research at the moment.

attention doesn't exist as a unitary 'thing' in the brain, it therefore can't have any causal impact on, well, anything. And so, despite a vast amount of research on attention over the decades, it's not clear any more what the phenomenon that we're researching actually is. Is it the case, for example, that attention is a limited resource within the brain, and therefore acts as a sort of cognitive bottleneck for processing information? Or is it the case that because we have so much incoming sensory information to process, attention is a way of dealing with that bottleneck, allowing us to focus in on important or relevant details? Without a clear rethink as to what we really mean by attention, the risk is that we end up getting stuck in a loop of developing circular arguments (attention is both the cause of, and solution to, all of life's problems), and miss out on the opportunity to gain a deeper understanding of the processes involved in guiding our perception and actions.

One concept that has dominated research in the area, and particularly research on visual attention, is that of the spotlight metaphor. The modern formulation of this is to imagine that you're at a music concert. Once everyone has filtered into the venue, got their drinks and found their favourite spot on the floor, the lights go down and the crowd goes silent. Then, in the inky blackness, a single spotlight blazes to life, into which steps your favourite music act!* (Or whichever artist *du jour* it would give you some cultural capital to name-drop here;† you can take your pick.) Anyway, everyone in the audience stares, enrapt, as if there's nothing or no one else around them. You are entirely focused on that person or that band lit up on the stage. That, basically, is your attentional spotlight.

Spotlight theories of attention, at least in the realm of visual attention, lean heavily on two fundamental aspects of

---

*   Foo Fighters for me. Rest in power chords, Taylor.

†   Still the Foo Fighters.

human visual perception. The first is that not all incoming sensory information through the eyes has the same level of detail: in essence, we have a central area in our field of view, called the fovea, where visual information is at its highest resolution, which gets increasingly worse as you move out into the peripheral field. We don't consciously perceive this, but you can get a sense of it by focusing on a single word in this sentence. Try to hold your gaze on the word 'fovea' above, and without moving your eyes see if you can read the words at either end of the sentence, or two or three sentences above – you might be able to see that there are words there, but it will be virtually impossible to make out what they are. The technical name for this phenomenon is inhomogeneity of the retina, and rather than being a failing in the system, it is a form of built-in efficiency: if we were to resolve all incoming information across the visual field to the same level of detail that we can in the fovea, we would need a huge amount of neural machinery in order to process that information, which in turn would jack up the energy needs of an already power-hungry organ by orders of magnitude. The second fundamental aspect effectively compensates for this variation in resolution by employing a specific form of eye movement called a saccade. Saccades are extremely fast, jerk-like movements that our eyes make in order to direct our central region of vision – our fovea – to whatever it is that we're interested in. In other words, our visual system has its own built-in spotlight, directing the small portion of our visual field in which we can see things in detail on to objects of interest, quickly and frequently.*

---

* Very quickly and frequently, in fact; saccades are the fastest movements that the human body makes, with a peak angular speed of around 700 degrees per second. We make about three or four of them each second. Although we don't notice it, we don't take much information in when a saccade is being generated; if we did, the world would be a blur of colour and light.

It's easy to see, then, why spotlight theories have been so dominant in the popular discourse about attention for so long. They make intuitive sense (we filter out irrelevant information and 'focus our attention' on pockets of high-priority information, because otherwise we would get overwhelmed very quickly), and we know that there are biological correlates of such spotlights – I've focused on vision as one example here, but there is a vast literature which argues for similar correlates in other cognitive domains.* But, convenient though it is in structuring our instincts about attention – that we have a single focal point to deal with a resource limitation – in recent years a number of lines of evidence have argued that modelling attention in this way doesn't provide us with the complete picture. For our present purposes, one of the ways in which spotlight theories start to waver is that they don't do a great job of explaining results from studies which show that, far from being a unitary focal point, attention can sometimes be distributed across a number of things at the same time. This therefore has important consequences in trying to understand our ability to multitask. When public commentators decry a societal collapse in attention because of things like social media, if you start to dig into the details you invariably end up looking at multitasking as a focal issue: humans are bad at attending to more than one thing at once, social media distracts us from more important things that we're doing, and therefore we can't concentrate on important things any more. I don't think that this is an easy or convincing line to

---

*   Although it's worth noting here that attentional spotlights do work independently of our eye movements. In fact, most experimental studies of attention require participants to keep their gaze as fixed as possible, in order to control for what you might call 'overt' shifts of attention (that is, explicitly moving your eyes to focus on something of interest). These sorts of studies instead focus on 'covert' attention, where you try to concentrate on something happening that you're not directly looking at.

take if you follow the research evidence though. We'll get back to that in a minute, but let me quickly bring you up to speed on some of the latest thinking about how attention might be modelled, and how it impacts our understanding of the nature of multitasking.

As we encountered earlier, a predominant (if implicit) line of thinking in cognitive science is that attention is a causal agent. Following the spirit of criticisms such as those laid out by Bernhard Hommel and others, though, it might instead be better to think of attention as an epiphenomenon – rather than being a direct influence, attention is a by-product of a system that's trying to process incoming sensory information in as coherent a way as possible. This sort of approach has spurred researchers to instead redefine attention as involving a 'priority map' system. A priority map can be thought of as a neural representation of the space around us, akin to a topographic map, wherein peaks of activity on the map correspond to locations or objects in our environment that we're more likely to pay attention to. Where previous frameworks characterise attention as being driven either by 'top-down' processes (that is, voluntarily directing our attention based on our current goals) or 'bottom-up' processes (in other words, our attention is grabbed by salient features in our sensory environment), priority map models integrate both of these alongside learned or motivational signals.

To try to break that idea down a little bit, we can think of it this way: spotlight models assume that we have a singular focus point for our attention, which we move around our environment. Sometimes it's directed to things we want to do or objects we're interested in, and sometimes it's pulled away because something has grabbed our attention that we might not have anticipated. So, for example, my attentional spotlight is currently focused on my computer screen, because I want to write as much as I can today before my daughter comes back from nursery. A colleague has just sent me a message on WhatsApp, though, and the ping from my phone – just off to one side on my desk – grabs my attention for a moment. I was doing one important, goal-driven thing but suddenly I'm looking at my messages, and maybe I risk staying there for a while, because that's where my attentional spotlight is now focused.

Priority maps characterise this process differently, though. Overlaid on the spatial map of my environment is a topographical representation of 'what am I interested in right now' – where that map is flat, there is nothing of interest to me (at least, currently), and where there are peaks my attention is more likely to be focused. In the area corresponding to my computer screen, there's a fairly large peak. There's also a peak, but not quite as large, corresponding to my second monitor – that's where some of the research on attention which I'm digesting is located. The map is flat where my phone is, but when that WhatsApp notification comes through a peak appears. Is that peak large enough to draw my attention away from the computer screen? Well, that depends on more than the basic pull of a stimulus appearing in my environment. Right now I would say that that peak is pretty small, because I've got a strong motivation to carry on writing before I run out of time today; I said to myself earlier that I would try to ignore any incoming messages for at least an hour or so, and I know from previous experience that if I look at my messages, I'm also more likely to lose my line of thinking. In other words, my attentional priority map has integrated bottom-up information (my phone pinging), top-down information (I really want to write while I have time), and learned motivational information (I want to keep on track while I have a clear line of thinking in my mind), producing a small peak where my phone is. That doesn't match or exceed the peak corresponding to my computer screen, so I don't look at my phone – or rather I do, but I quickly snap back to the more important task at hand. Has my attention been focused on a single thing during that time? No, it has been spread over multiple areas, proportionally allocated depending on a number of complex and interacting factors. This is quite a simplistic overview of how priority maps work, and I've necessarily glazed over a lot of details here. Suffice to say, research based in this sort of framework has suggested that priority maps can be found not just at the early stages of attentional processing in the brain, but throughout our neural architecture – maps on top of maps on top of maps, as it were – and therefore the sum output of these processes can guide quite high-level, complex behaviours.

Right, with all this in mind, let's focus on media multitasking. Research in this area was kick-started in 2009 with an influential paper by Eyal Ophir and colleagues at Stanford University. Across a combination of media-use questionnaires and cognitive experiments, Ophir's team showed that, compared with light media multitaskers, heavy multitaskers exhibited greater difficulties in filtering out extraneous stimuli and took longer to respond to, and made more mistakes in, task-switching situations.* The results, Ophir's team argued, suggested that people classified as heavy media multitaskers

---

* How media multitasking is defined here is not simple to explain, and is in fact a matter of considerable debate in the research literature. The definition that Ophir's team used involved an equation that takes into account how many other media streams someone is using while using a primary medium, the number of hours per week they report spending using that primary medium, and the total number of hours per week spent with all media. In essence, it arguably provides a snapshot of how much multitasking is going on per hour spent on a given medium, but doesn't do a good job of distinguishing between, for example, someone who is using just two media streams but constantly and someone who is spreading their attention across lots of media but for shorter amounts of time. As always, we need to be cautious in our interpretation.

tend to be more distracted by the vast amount of digital media they are taking in and are more driven by bottom-up attentional processes than light multitaskers, who tend towards greater levels of top-down attentional control. Now, I don't think we should buy too much into the results because it was a small study – between thirty and forty-one participants took part in the experimental portions – and therefore likely to be statistically underpowered. The measure of media multitasking also included whether or not participants used print media, so you could be defined as a light multitasker if you reported that you read books and used computers at the same time – and given that the participant pool was sampled from Stanford University students, I would wager that most would define themselves in this way. And the task-switching experiment – in which participants had to flip-flop between classifying a series of numbers and letters according to a cue on each trial – defined the 'switch cost' as the difference in mean reaction times between trials in which participants had to switch classification category compared with the previous trial, versus those where they carried on using the same category. For heavy multitaskers, the switch cost was 167 milliseconds longer than that for light multitaskers – perhaps of importance from a statistical point of view, but not a cost that translates easily into everyday activity. Nevertheless, it represented one of the first published efforts to scientifically study the potential effects of media multitasking on cognitive behaviours. It also reinforced one of our common worries about screens: that if you flick your attention between lots of digital media in parallel, you become more distractible and make more mistakes in more important tasks at hand.

Flash forward some ten years, though, and the state of the research literature hasn't appreciably moved on. In a 2018 review, Melina Uncapher and Anthony Wagner, also at Stanford University, looked at twenty-one studies that had been conducted in the area since Ophir's paper. On balance they concluded that heavy, as compared with light, media multitaskers showed poorer abilities across a range of cognitive abilities, but this was by no means consistent or conclusive. Some studies, for example, show a greater switch cost for heavy multitaskers, others show smaller costs, and some show no differences at all. Then, in 2021, Doug Parry and Daniel le Roux at Stellenbosch University published a meta-analysis specifically focusing on the ten years of research following Ophir's original paper. While the results indicated that there was some support for the idea that heavier media multitaskers showed more problems with distractibility, the actual size of the effect was quite small and 'likely to be of minimal practical significance'. They noted that while small associations were found between media multitasking and sustained attention, that link was mainly driven by studies which focused on self-reported outcomes, and we've already covered the potential problems with those. On the basis of their analysis, Parry and le Roux concluded that the current evidence doesn't support the idea that media multitasking improves our ability to task-switch – but nor is it the case that there are any appreciable reductions in our ability to manage such tasks. They end by stating that ten years down the line from Ophir's study, we've not really made any headway in understanding how media multitasking impacts on cognitive control.

Further research is needed, then, as always. Of course, absence of evidence does not mean evidence of absence, but it's hard to square what research has shown us so far with the notion that digital technology is inexorably eroding our attention. 'Whenever people say attention, especially in pop science, really what they mean is self-control – particularly the ability to feel like you're in control of your own focus,' explains Dr Jacob Fisher, an Assistant Professor at the University of Illinois Urbana-Champaign. Jacob's research focuses on the interplay between digital technology, attention and decision-making. 'That's only one aspect of what attention is, and it's also an aspect that is extremely difficult, if not impossible, to measure,' he adds. In fact, you could go further than this and say that equating attention with self-control is just a fundamentally incorrect thing to do. Certainly, in terms of psychological science the two things are conceptually different, each with their own colossal fields of research publications. Jacob explains that, in part due to the fluid definition of attention in the research literature, but also because that definition is somewhat ephemeral in common parlance, what we're really talking about is the phenomenological experience of being able to focus, rather than a specific behaviour. Our lived experience is of course important, but as to whether there's any objective evidentiary basis supporting the idea of declining attention? 'I don't know. I've yet to see anything that's actually convincing,' he tells me. Professor Chris Chambers, Head of Brain Stimulation at Cardiff University, agrees: 'It would be obvious if there was a decline. It would be easy to look at the last, say, fifteen years of research on attentional-cueing and look at whether reorientation costs are getting higher,' he says. 'My virtually certain prediction is that you would get no effect whatsoever. If our cognitive system was so fragile to changes in the environment, we wouldn't be here. We'd have been selected for extinction a very long time ago.'

Perhaps part of the reason for this is because of our evolving understanding of what attention actually is. Recent shifts in characterising attention not as a spotlight but as a topographic priority map of interest spread across our environment have only recently started to gain traction in the context of media multitasking. Under this assumption, our attentional resources are distributed across everything that we're doing or could do at a particular moment in time, with our direct focus allocated according to how rewarding a particular task is, how much effort it takes to complete it, how much we need to prioritise doing that thing, and to what extent it aligns with our goals and desires. Perhaps, rather than thinking of digital technology as a simple form of sense-based distraction that moves our focus away from more cerebral (and therefore more important) endeavours, it's better to think of our smartphones and social media as one part of our attentional ecosystem. Sometimes these things have a high priority, because it's *perfectly fine* to want to connect with people. At other times they have a lower priority because there are other things to do, other ways of connecting with each other. And sometimes they have a higher priority than we think they should do (or want them to) because we're stressed out, or stuck on a difficult problem, and we get a bit of relief from the distraction. But it's early days for this line of theorising.

So one of the problems of having an inconsistent literature, hampered by inconsistent operational definitions, is that it leaves us with a gap in our understanding of the real-world effects of digital technology on attention. Our best guess right now is that there may be some positive effects, some negative effects, but it depends on the type of attention we're talking about and the specific type of attentional task we assess. Even then, if there are any effects, they don't look to be very big. It doesn't make for a particularly exciting story, but such is the way with many complex topics in psychological science. This wouldn't be so much of a worry if that messy reality was reflected in the broader public discourse. But all it takes is for the odd scare story to come along, confidently and convincingly delivered, and suddenly attention becomes a significant worry.

It's not a new phenomenon – as Matthew Sweet eloquently puts it, 'Technologies of pleasure always acquire enemies.' I ask him why this is the case, and he explains using an example from the mid-nineteenth century. 'When the paper tax gets repealed at the beginning of the 1860s, a new litera-ture emerges for a young readership. It's very sensational, and that produces a panic about what boys are reading.' In the nineteenth-century UK there were a number of so-called 'taxes on knowledge' including, among other things, excise duties on paper, pamphlets and newspapers. This effectively put access to the daily news out of financial reach for many people, and for the working class in particular. 'While it's imposed, news-papers, magazines, books are all very expensive, to the point that there's an effect on the kinds of things that get written,' explains Matthew. Over a thirty-year stretch in the mid-1800s and following lengthy campaigns, these duties were gradually reduced or repealed, with the last of them – the paper duty – ended by William Gladstone in 1861. 'One of the consequences of this is that suddenly all these cheap newspapers appear, and books get longer and more widely circulated,' Matthew points out. 'Coupled with rising literacy levels, it creates this sense that there are all these people who had nothing to read before, except maybe the Bible, and now they can read stories about highwaymen and boys committing crimes.' The result is that a general sense of panic and concern hits British society. 'You get descriptions in newspapers in remembrance of a woman who's neglecting her children because her new box of books has arrived,' Matthew adds. 'The image is of somebody who can't keep away from the gin bottle – there's this pile of books that must be read, and the children are all crying in the corner.' The underlying sentiment was that the kind of literature that was developing wasn't particularly erudite – it instead spoke to our base nerves and instincts. For the most part, most people weren't paying attention to this narrative and weren't participating in the almost ritualistic anxiety about it. They were just reading and enjoying books. 'I think what makes some want to pursue that ritual is that it's about something that other people are doing,' Matthew tells me. In other words, when a shift in the way that society consumes or has access to knowledge occurs, it drives a sort of high-level anxiety that this must be wrong in some way, and therefore should be regulated in a misplaced need to 'protect' those who are perceived to be oblivious to the looming disaster.

It's definitely the case that I feel it's harder to concentrate on things nowadays than when I was younger. I'm also convinced that I probably felt the same way ten, fifteen years ago. Is that because screens are a more prominent part of my everyday life, and actually driving that loss of focus? Or is it that when I was younger I had less stuff going on? No kids, no mortgage to worry about, climate change was less of an immediate threat, energy prices didn't cost a small fortune, so it was just easier to focus on things. Or have I always been as distractible as I am now, but I just never noticed it before because it wasn't something that people kept banging on about in the news? I'm sure many of us feel this way, and it's not always immediately clear what the reality of the situation is. That gap in our knowledge becomes a problem if it gets filled by apocryphal nonsense that plays into our fears about everything getting worse. A few years ago, for example, we saw a slew of headlines claiming that research from Microsoft had shown that as a result of our increasingly digital lifestyles, our attention spans had dropped from an average of twelve seconds at the turn of the millennium to eight seconds by 2013, a full second worse than that of a goldfish.

Nothing about this story was correct. Our attention span wasn't eight seconds in 2013, and it wasn't twelve seconds in 2000. Goldfish don't have a nine-second attention span. Microsoft didn't conduct that research – their consumer insights team simply mentioned it in a 2015 marketing report which cites, rather elusively, 'Statistic Brain' as the originator. If you search for that source you end up at a website for the 'Statistic Brain Research Institute', which does apparently have data on attention-span statistics, but it costs $18 a month to access it, which my disposable income doesn't currently stretch to, unfortunately. As it happens, though, there are multiple archived captures of the website on the Internet Archive, tracing back to 2012, and prior to sticking their data behind a paywall the SBRI did share some summary statistics year on year – one of which was that our average attention span is eight seconds.

Just when you think you're getting somewhere, another hurdle crops up: as journalist Simon Maybin reported for BBC's *More or Less* in 2017, the SBRI don't, in fact, seem to be the original inventors of the eight-second statistic. On the 2014 version of the website, the SBRI cite the National Center for Biotechnology Information and the Associated Press as the sources, but Maybin was unable to find any records of such research having been conducted when he made enquiries with both. Even more confusingly, if you go back further on the Internet Archive, in 2012 (average attention span also eight seconds), they just cite the Associated Press. But then a 2015 archived version of the site puts the average attention span at 8.25 seconds, not eight, which seems to persist until the data get locked behind a paywall mid-2018. In other words, it's a zombie statistic with no obvious or convincing origin – from a scientific point of view there's no such thing as an 'average attention span', but even if we take the concept at face value the statistic suggests that since 2012 our attention spans have basically been stable.

Like all good zombie statistics, it's one that will simply not die. *Time* reported on it in 2015, the *Guardian* mentioned it in relation to the US election in 2016 ('Can Hillary Clinton convince in the age of the goldfish?'), and even though Simon Maybin admirably debunked it in 2017, it returns from the dead that same year in *USA Today* ('NBA will consider shortening games due to millennial attention spans'). It appears again on CNBC's website in 2018 ('A 2015 study pegged the average attention span at eight seconds. That's shorter than a goldfish's.'), and on the *i* newspaper's website in 2022 ('Pop songs are getting shorter, but it's about a lot more than shorter attention spans'), and so on, ad nauseam. When we're persistently bombarded with this sort of mythology, it's no small wonder that we end up worrying so much that something's going wrong with our attention: it's simply impossible to get away from media pundits forcing that concern on us. Of course it might well be the case that, zombie statistics aside, the reason why we see these sorts of stories crop up in the media so much is because *things are actually getting worse*, and those reports are simply reflective of the realities of modern-day digital life. But there is some broad evidence on digital technology effects that may suggest a different explanation, and it's one we've already come across.

In Chapter 1 we looked at research led by Heather Shaw at Lancaster University which showed that, when it comes to the relationship between screen use and wellbeing, subjective measures of smartphone use produced larger correlations with mental health than more objective measures of actual screen time. To put it another way, people who worry that their technology use is bad for them tend to report larger correlations between screen time and wellbeing than people who don't think that their digital tech use is that bad. 'It's a sort of self-fulfilling chicken-and-egg problem,' explains Jacob Fisher. In their write-up, Shaw's team allude to this as well, suggesting that if we want to see improvements in wellbeing, helping people to manage the way they feel about their smartphone use might do more good than trying to reduce that use itself. In some ways, I appreciate that this might seem like a tenuous argument to make – we're talking about broad-stroke measures of tech usage and 'wellbeing' here, not attention specifically, and we know the potential pitfalls that come with that way of thinking. But in my conversation with Jacob, I get the sense that there's a comparable line of emerging evidence when it comes to our ability to focus. 'My hopefully as-unbiased-as-possible assessment of the literature right now is that when it comes to social media, or media multitasking, or media habits as your independent variable, and attention-related variables as your dependent variable, there's a pretty clear correlation self-report to self-report,' he tells me. 'But when you start studying actual cognitive performance differences in the lab – like differences in grades or differences in doing an attention-inhibition task – those effects basically completely evaporate.'

Let's try to pull all of this together. There isn't any particularly strong or convincing scientific evidence to suggest that our attention is collapsing, or that digital technology is the root cause of such a collapse. Where commentators argue that it is all going to pot the evidence base tends to be a bit shaky, using arguments that rely on anecdote, nonsense statistics that simply will not die, or a cursory view of an extremely complex research literature. And yet for many of us, our lived experience is that it *does* feel harder to concentrate on important things now more than ever, and I'm sure you can think of instances where you felt guilty about using your phone when maybe you should have been focusing on other things. A 2022 survey by researchers Bobby Duffy and Marion Thain, based at the Policy Institute and Centre for Attention Studies at King's College London, showed just this, finding that nearly 50 per cent of those who were canvassed were more likely than not to say that they felt their attention span was shorter now than it had been before. Half of the survey sample also thought that the eight-second attention span trope was true (around 25 per cent correctly identified it as false), and two-thirds believed that media multitasking has a harmful effect on our ability to complete even simple tasks. But how we feel things are going as opposed to how they *are* actually going can often be very different things.

We feel as though we can't concentrate, and that this is impacting our ability to be productive, but this isn't reflected in the data we see; for example, if we quantify productivity* at national level as gross domestic product per hour of work, then between 2000 and 2019 the US saw a 34 per cent increase in productivity, the UK a 21 per cent increase, Ireland a whopping 172 per cent increase and China a 232 per cent increase. In fact, most countries across the world saw a net increase in productivity during that time. Couple this with the fact that there really isn't any convincing evidence objectively showing a drop in attention spans during that period, and it's difficult not to come to the conclusion that the reason we're all worrying about attention is because we're incessantly bombarded with media stories telling us to do so.

I don't want to come across as too dismissive here, because that's not my intention. I also don't think the relative dearth of scientific evidence that digital technology is shrinking our attention span gives tech companies a free pass, for reasons

---

* The data here are from Our World In Data, and are adjusted for inflation and cost of living differences between countries.

I'll explain in a moment. I do think that the story of how digital technology impacts on attention is like many others about screens, though: a complicated one that has been overly simplified and muddied to the point of uselessness by shrill public commentators, people who often paint a very pessimistic picture about the apparently inevitable negative impact of that relationship. One of the implicit assumptions we see throughout these narratives is that we, as users, lack agency. Like the women, children and working classes who needed to be patronisingly 'protected' from an influx of trash literature following the paper tax repeal in 1861, our attention has been somehow stolen from us in a way that we were unable to notice and were powerless to stop from happening. It's a form of technological determinism, and one that provides a rich environment for moral panic about screens to thrive. But we have more control over our digital lifestyles than some would have us believe. If the public narrative – and our own attitudes – towards screens starts to shift and acknowledge this fact, then there are at least three useful things that I can see coming out of it.

The first is that we will start to perceive the positive impacts of our own technology use more clearly. Thankfully, there is some evidence to suggest that a decent chunk of people can see these. For example, in Duffy and Thain's attention survey mentioned earlier, although some 50 per cent thought screens were ruining our attention span, roughly the same proportion believed that the reason some people got easily distracted had nothing to do with technology but was simply a facet of their personality. Moreover, many of the respondents could see the potential benefits of our seemingly divided attention: six out of ten people surveyed said that having access to near-instantaneous information helped them to overcome problems both at work and at home, with just 12 per cent disagreeing.

Around 45 per cent agreed that social media offered a useful source of viewpoints and information that otherwise wouldn't be available from more traditional forms of media, and 43 per cent agreed that using social media at the same time as watching TV or listening to radio made the experience more enjoyable, because it allowed them to connect with other people. Access to digital technology can be a potential boon, then, but only if we're well placed to use it in a beneficial way.

If we can start to move away from generalised narratives about screens and attention, we can also start to see where there are outcomes that aren't so beneficial for us and where we do need to focus our energies. When we're not getting positives out of our own digital technology use but we feel empowered to do something about it, that's when we can start to see meaningful change. Let's try to understand, for example, that our attention isn't merely going to get passively distracted by our smartphones but that our goals and motivations, desires and needs can drive moments of focus; this will allow us to prioritise tasks when we need to and not get distraught when we spend an idle moment talking to friends or checking the news. And if we realise that the way we're interacting with screens isn't working for us, that's the point at which we can do something about it. This could be something as basic as switching off notifications on our phone to stop them from distracting us when we need to focus on something, or experimenting with different computer set-ups at home and at work; or it could mean more complex decisions being made about our screen time routine throughout the day. Like many solutions we've talked about so far, often it's the little changes to our behaviours that can make the big differences in the long run. Those changes are really hard to effect – or even see as possibilities – if all we're doing is panicking about a misperceived lack of control.

Doing both these things – acknowledging the positives of our own tech use, while being mindful of the activities and behaviours that don't work for us so much – means we can pinpoint apps, or features in apps, that are causing consternation. And if we can do that, we can start meaningfully doing one of the most important things to change our relationship with screens: we can hold technology companies to task and demand change where it's needed. In an article for *The Conversation* about their attention survey, Marion Thain closes by saying: 'There is no question that we need to figure out how to live better with the "attention economy", and that the monetisation of our attention is challenging us in fundamental ways.' As much as I hate the term 'attention economy' – whatever this ultimately refers to may not actually have anything to do with attention itself – I do agree with the sentiment here, and while the scientific evidence for a general erosion in attention simply isn't there, that doesn't mean digital technology companies aren't interested in our time and focus.

Part of what infuriates me here is that if you read any digital-marketing book or blog that talks about attention or engagement, you will inevitably find a comment along the lines of 'Digital technology is ruining attention spans, and you should care about this because it means it's harder to get your customer's attention.' There's no reflection here as to whether attention is really becoming limited, or whether engaging in a race to the bottom, to grasp every last morsel of our focus before it disappears for ever, is a responsible way to approach digital design. There doesn't seem to be any compassionate or critical thinking about what any of this actually means in practice; and because we're lost in a miasma of scare stories based on easily dismissible nonsense statistics, no one with any part to play in this story has a particularly vested interest in improving the situation. 'There's a certain sense in which our technologies do often divert us from what we wish we could be doing. So how do you think about technology design in a way that helps us do things that we find important?' Jacob Fisher asks. 'Like, if I sit down and plot out my ideal day, and then I look back at the end of the day, how do we design technologies that make those two things line up more?'

With that thought in mind, let's now turn to some specific examples of aspects of our digital lives where I think technology companies have really dropped the ball, and how we might go about fixing them.

6

Ghouls in the machine

I'm sure we've all had the feeling that our phones are listening to us. We all have stories where we've been talking to someone about the next holiday we're thinking about planning, or the latest movie we want to go and see, and then a few hours later, when we're scrolling through our phone, we get a bit unnerved when we start seeing loads of adverts encouraging us to book some cheap flights to Florida or tickets for the seventeenth *Avengers* movie. It's hard, when that happens, not to feel as though we've been spied on, as though our phones, rather than being there to make life a bit easier or more efficient, are in fact there to control what we do.

Digital technologies are listening to us, but not in the overt way that we often worry about. They're not literally eavesdropping in on our conversations (with Alexa-like speakers being a notable exception); rather, they draw on the tremendous amount of information that we provide about ourselves in other ways – through our search histories, spending behaviours, browsing habits and more – to build up a picture of things they think we might like to see, do or buy. We vastly underappreciate the sheer extent to which we reveal information about ourselves online, and it's this nescience which often translates into the feeling that our phones are spying on us. But at the same time, the information we do give away is often imperfect and incomplete, and therefore leads to slip-ups in the recommendation process. This can be as innocuous as being presented with adverts for things we have absolutely no interest in, but in extreme cases it can go wrong in the direst of ways. In 2023, for example, the *Guardian* reported on how unsuspecting TikTok users could be bombarded with self-harm content within a few minutes of signing up to the app, and there are horrific stories about the knock-on effect that being exposed to this sort of content can have on children. For many of us, while the consequences are much less extreme than this, they can nevertheless make for exhausting, and sometimes painful, experiences.

Social media, search engines and news platforms often rely on what I'm broadly going to call 'recommender systems' to filter and curate the content that you're presented with. Sometimes this is overt – for example, Netflix uses a combination of information based on, among other things, your previous viewing history, the ratings you've given shows and movies, how long you watch programmes for, and other people who have similar viewing habits to yours in order to present you with a list of programmes you might be more likely to watch. The benefit to you, ostensibly, is that you're told about programmes which you might have a genuine interest in watching, but which you might not otherwise come across. The benefit to Netflix is that you're more likely to keep using their app, and therefore maintain your subscription.

While it's fairly obvious what Netflix is doing in this instance, the same sort of curated experience happens all over the place, and often much less visibly. And sometimes what you want to see (or even what you need to see at that particular moment) comes into direct conflict with the recommender system, which is trying to show you what *it thinks* you want. In 2018, *Washington Post* writer Gillian Brockell wrote an open letter to the technology industry titled 'Dear tech companies, I don't want to see pregnancy ads after my child was stillborn'. In the letter, she details how her online activity during her pregnancy would have provided a very clear signal to recommender algorithms that she was expecting a baby:

I know you knew I was pregnant. It's my fault, I just couldn't resist those Instagram hashtags – #30weekspregnant, #babybump. And, silly me! I even clicked once or twice on the maternity-wear ads Facebook served up. What can I say, I am your ideal 'engaged' user.

You surely saw my heartfelt thank-you post to all the girlfriends who came to my baby shower, and the sister-in-law who flew in from Arizona for said shower tagging me in her photos. You probably saw me googling 'holiday dress maternity plaid' and 'babysafe crib paint.' And I bet Amazon.com even told you my due date, Jan. 24, when I created that Prime registry.

Like many people who lose a child during pregnancy, Brockell's heartbreak and pain were prolonged and intensified because of the recommended content she was bombarded with following her loss. It's something my wife and I have had similar experience of. As quickly as the algorithms are to learn that you're expecting, they appear to be agonisingly slow to get the message that you don't want to see baby-related content any more. UK-based charity Tommy's, which funds research into the causes of miscarriage and stillbirth, has a page on its website devoted to providing advice on what you can do to try to block pregnancy-related adverts if your pregnancy has ended in loss. This is a hugely useful resource, but we shouldn't be in the position where it is needed in the first place. It is not good enough that pregnancy-loss charities and grieving parents are having to do the hard work because the likes of Meta and Amazon have a blind spot with their algorithm systems.

Recommender systems are therefore a double-edged sword. On the one hand, there's an idealised view that they are there to make life that little bit easier for the end user: by pulling together a picture of who we are and what we like, they offer us personalised suggestions – be they for products, services or media content – that speak to our interests, habits and quirks. On the other hand, one of the goals of using recommender systems is to keep you engaged with a particular app or digital platform. Those two purposes are not necessarily at odds with each other; if you're getting something genuinely positive out of an app, in part because you're being presented with interesting and relevant content, then that's a good thing. It also so happens that the tech company behind the app gets something desirable out of it too. But recommender systems aren't perfect. They are largely retrospective in nature: by relying heavily and primarily on what you've done in the past they are unable to take into account present contextual factors in order to make accurate, relevant or in some cases even desirable suggestions. It's also often not entirely transparent how such systems actually work in any sort of detail. Among other things, this means that it's not clear how, and on the basis of what data, recommendations are actually made. Moreover, the algorithms they employ can often be biased, either towards certain types of content or towards certain demographics. If you put all these things together, it means that when recommender systems are implemented irresponsibly, with the *sole* goal of keeping people engaged on a digital platform, then they run the risk of doing more harm than good. It is this sort of situation that results in such systems emphasising extreme, harmful or polarising content – simply because more people engage with it, in spite of its negative impact on our wellbeing.

Ultimately, then, because recommender systems and the algorithms upon which they are built are designed by humans, and humans are fallible beings, they are prone to all sorts of intentional and unintentional biases and misuse. This means that however much we would like to think that algorithms are objective pieces of computer code, the combination of errors or technical limitations in the system, a lack of deep understanding as to what populations will use them (and in what situations), pre-existing cultural or social biases held by the coders themselves, and, ultimately, the corporate pressures driving their reason for existence mean that they can very quickly and very easily become unintended sources of bias. A particularly egregious example of this was highlighted in a 1988 commentary in the *British Medical Journal*. In the article, editorial team members Stella Lowry and Gordon MacPherson detail the story of systematic race and sexual discrimination in the admissions policy for a London medical school. In an effort to reduce the workload of selecting potential students, in the last years of the 1970s St George's Hospital Medical School developed a computer programme to assist in the process, which would extract data from a central university admission form and assign a weighted score accordingly, with the lowest-scoring (and therefore top-ranking) candidates then being invited to interview. An early form of 'recommender system', in a way. The data the software extracted focused on two areas: academic performance and personal information, which included factors such as age, hobbies, parental occupation and, critically, gender and race, with candidates being classed as either 'Caucasian' or 'non-Caucasian'. These categorisations were then used to apply a weighting to a candidate's overall score, and both the 'non-Caucasian' and 'female' categories specifically carried detrimental weightings. The result of this was that candidates who were assumed to be female and/or non-Caucasian had a lower chance of making it through to interview stage at the school, completely independently of their academic ability. They were being discriminated against in the most bizarre and idiotic of ways – the application form didn't have a 'race' category, so whether a candidate was flagged as either Caucasian or non-Caucasian was based on guesswork using their name or place of birth. A resulting 1988 report by the Commission for Racial Equality (CRE) into the incident reproduces actual scores versus race and sex-weighted percentile scores from St George's admission data, and shows, for example, that a male Caucasian scoring 1.6 on this system would have been ranked at the 25th percentile, whereas a male non-Caucasian with the same score would have been ranked at the 42nd percentile. For female candidates, that same score resulted in ranks at the 28th and 44th percentiles for Caucasians and non-Caucasians respectively.

The program was written by a member of staff at St George's, one Dr Franglen, with the seemingly good intention of reducing staff workload and making for a more consistent interview process, but ultimately it ended up with the medical school being found guilty of racial and sexual discrimination. The CRE's report estimated that for nearly a decade, as many as sixty applicants per year may have missed an interview place, not because of their academic performance but because of their sex and ethnic origin. Critical to that report was understanding why this situation arose in the first place, which is a crucial step in apprehending any sort of bias that computer algorithms display. Over the course of a number of years of the program's development, Franglen aimed not to come up with a new system of candidate selection but to mimic, as closely as possible, the decision-making process within the existing system. He did this by closely observing the selection process over time, and then building the factors and criteria that the human selection panel used into the algorithm. The result was that by around 1979, after six or so years of refinement, the algorithm was generating selection gradings that had around a 95 per cent correlation with those of the human selection panel. In other words, there wasn't a bug in the algorithm, and the bias didn't arise spontaneously as a result of computer error. The bias arose because it was *already present in the system*. The algorithm just did an excellent job of replicating it, and ultimately exposing it in the starkest light.

Algorithmic bias can sometimes happen because of an honest error in the system, or because an algorithm is being used or applied in an unintended way. But biases also often arise because those algorithms are coded by humans, who are prone to all sorts of cultural, social and systemic partialities. How accurate, or useful, a particular algorithm or recommender system can be is therefore reliant on a number of decisions that are made offline, about how best to train that algorithm, what the primary purpose for implementing it is, and what systemic structural problems exist that might be filtered and amplified through the system. Aside from recommendations, one of the most important jobs algorithms can be used for on social media is in moderating content – given the vast amount of messages generated on these platforms, it's simply impossible for human moderators alone to sift through and filter out malicious or illegal material. Automated systems are therefore essential to keeping on top of the sheer mass of information we collectively produce on a daily basis. But algorithms are by no means perfect in this regard; even with the best will in the world, they will struggle with nuance and being able to place messages in an appropriate context. Algorithms don't do satire. And when coupled with endemic coding biases, the systems that are used to try to make social media a nicer place for everyone can instead end up reinforcing and amplifying existing structural inequalities.

For example, in its efforts to police and remove hate speech on its platform, for a number of years Facebook operated a 'race-blind' policy, essentially treating all hateful language as equal. At face value this might seem like a reasonable approach to take, but in 2020 the *Washington Post* reported that, according to internal company documents, Facebook was revisiting the moderation algorithms because they were disproportionally removing content, some of which was fairly innocuous, from marginalised communities. Because the algorithm focused on protected characteristics like race or sex, messages that contained the words 'white men' would effectively be prioritised over messages with the phrase 'women drivers' or 'Black children', even though women and Black users are more likely to be the target of hateful and harmful posts. And because explanations and descriptions of systemic racism often necessarily involve talking about the role of white people, in an over-zealous attempt to be impartial the content moderation algorithms would regularly flag or remove those descriptions. In trying to be race-blind, the algorithm was suppressing the ability for marginalised groups to be able to talk about the racism that they had experienced. Facebook's attempt to improve this state of affairs has been labelled the 'worst of the worst' or WoW project, but to date there is little public data as to whether things have improved.

If there's anything positive to be taken here, it's that these sorts of faults with recommender systems and moderation algorithms – these seemingly innocent, but quietly devastating faults – can begin to empower us with the knowledge and understanding that we need to fix them. They show us that algorithms are always looking at the past, learning about how things used to be, what we used to like, or want, or hope for. They know nothing about the present and, importantly, don't tell us anything about what the future will or ought to look like. They pick up on patterns in our digital history and magnify them so that they're impossible to ignore. The problem at the moment is that, as fast as digital technology companies are at getting these sorts of systems out into the open, they are simply not doing so in a sufficiently ethical or responsible manner, or with user wellbeing – our wellbeing – at heart. That algorithms do such a spectacular and overt job of amplifying inequalities and injustices isn't necessarily a failure in the system so long as we do something useful and positive with that information. This is where we're currently getting stuck.

Some of the solutions here require huge structural and societal changes, the potential payoffs of which go beyond improving our interactions with digital technology. But at a more fundamental level, tech companies need to get better at both coding and training algorithms, which involves being aware of the potential biases that can creep in and inoculating against them. This isn't a simple task, though, and has to go beyond statements of good intention and sticking-plaster workshops. Raising awareness of such biases is one thing, but actual behavioural (and in this case, technological) change takes much more effort. As an example, in 2020 the Behavioural Insights Team, an organisation that provides advice to, among others, the UK government, produced a fairly damning report into the evidence base for unconscious bias and diversity training initiatives of the sort that feature in many professional development schemes, and are often touted as an essential part of improving inclusivity. At best, the evidence suggests that such training schemes result in a broad-strokes increase in awareness that diversity issues exist, but only in the short term. To date, there is no convincing evidence that they change people's behaviour based on an awareness of their own implicit biases or actually improve the state of the workplace. The report suggests that in some cases the opposite can happen, citing sources which claim that mandatory diversity training can reduce the number of women in management positions, for example.

Part of the problem here is that such workshops are often seen as a solution in themselves: a 'quick fix' to show that senior management have done something positive. Instead they should be seen as a useful, but basic, first step. Research published in the journal *Psychological Bulletin* in 2016 showed that the attitudinal effects of diversity training drop off over time, so if you want to enact real change, training needs to happen more than once, over a considerable period, and ideally be combined with other forms of more targeted training. In other words, overcoming algorithmic bias involves overcoming pre-existing systemic biases, and that requires a commitment at all levels to decide what changes need to be made, set concrete goals to aim for and work towards them.

I'm not saying that any of this is easy and can happen overnight. But when it comes to algorithm bias, we've had enough high-profile examples of when things go wrong to see where priorities need to be set. It's fairly obvious, for instance, that any tech company with interests in face detection algorithms needs to have a diverse group of software engineers, or at the very least work with population-relevant training stimulus sets – if you train your algorithms just on white, Western datasets, of course it's inevitable that you're going to end up with a racist face detection system.* You want to keep people engaged on your platform? Fine, but not at the cost of their emotional or mental wellbeing – aside from the ethical vacuity of pushing dangerous content for the sake of it, once enough people realise what you're doing you won't have a viable product any more. You want to target ads to potential parents? Great. Talk to parent groups about what the pitfalls are there. Talk to charities like Tommy's. When your algorithm does throw up a bias, do something about it quickly – something that goes beyond removing a certain sort of search result or asking the user to block the service. Think hard, think quickly and think compassionately about what's needed to fix the algorithm. In short, be a responsible developer.

Responsible development is something that I think often takes a back seat in new digital technologies. Not because it isn't valued, but because in the absence of hard data, or a wider understanding of the potential societal impact of the technology you're developing, it's difficult to see what model responsibility towards user wellbeing looks like. That only comes with introspection and collaboration with researchers, policymakers and the very people you view as end users of the product. It especially becomes a problem when that responsibility might be overshadowed by new technologies which do a pretty good job of increasing profits. There is one particular example from my own area of research that I think neatly

---

*   Back in 2009, reports emerged that the face detection software onboard some of Nikon's digital cameras asked 'Did someone blink?' when photos of people with Asian features were being taken. A few years later, Google's 'Photos' app hit the news following complaints that it had automatically tagged a Black couple as 'gorillas'. Google were quick to apologise, noting that the company was working on some long-term fixes to the image recognition algorithms. In 2018, *WIRED* magazine tested the app on 40,000 images of animals, showing that while it did a pretty good job of classifying most, it would simply announce that there were 'no results' if search terms like 'gorilla' or 'monkey' were used. The long-term solution, it would appear, was simply to censor problematic search terms at the cost of further inaccuracy.

encapsulates this, while at the same time drawing together many of the issues around the way we engage with, worry about and ultimately try to regulate new technologies.

I do research on video games – their effects on our behaviour, on our wellbeing, and to what extent they can, as an entertainment medium, provide benefits to those things. For almost as long as they've been around, people have been worried about the deleterious effects that games might have on us. Are they addictive? Do they make us violent, or less sociable? But as research in this area has improved and matured, scientists have come to the realisation that it's not particularly useful to ask questions about how video games, generally, affect us – much in the same way that it's not particularly useful to ask a broad question about whether eating food is good for our waistlines. Over time, researchers become more focused not on video games as a category but on the specific mechanisms that games are built up from.

One mechanism that I've become increasingly interested in over the past few years involves how video games are monetised. When I was younger, as always seems to be the case, things were simpler – a game would be released, you would pay something like £30–£40 up front for the cartridge or disc, and that's where the transaction would end. For players, this was great – you paid once and you got a fully encapsulated gaming experience. For games developers, though, the model wasn't perfect. They would lose a certain percentage of the revenue to the retailer, and would have to soak up significant costs in terms of a physical game needing to be manufactured, packaged and distributed. As we shifted into the digital era in the first decade of the 2000s, though, advances in storage capabilities and internet connectivity meant that developers could start to sell their games online at the same price as a physical copy, while simultaneously removing the need to fork out for packaging (and the discs themselves). The move to digital distribution also meant that developers could explore new revenue streams in the form of extended content. Players could now buy a nearly complete game for an up-front price, and then be offered additional downloadable content (or DLC) a little bit later down the line for a little extra money. According to some estimates, in 2011 the worldwide market for physical video games was worth $22 billion, with the DLC market trailing at $5 billion. By 2021 there was a complete turnaround – the DLC market was now worth nearly $30 billion, whereas the physical market had dropped to just over $8 billion. It was clearly a more lucrative route for the games industry, but the trade-off was, arguably, a less satisfying experience for the player. No longer could they buy a complete game in one go, but instead had to pay repeatedly through a gated experience. And if your friends had bought the DLC but you hadn't, you wouldn't be able to play with them unless you followed suit.

The shift to digital distribution and gated content also offered another possibility: developers could sell in-game add-ons. For a small price you could now buy a new outfit for your character, or a pack of power-up items to help you through a particularly tricky level, or a whole new set of characters or equipment. In-game microtransactions of this kind have been around for a while – their existence dates back at least to 1990, when the coin-operated arcade game Double Dragon 3 allowed players to buy various items that offered in-game 'advantages' (actually necessities if you wanted to make any meaningful progress) for twenty-five cents a pop. But the relative ease with which they could be delivered, coupled with the possibility that there are potentially endless possibilities for generating new in-game content, meant that microtransaction mechanisms skyrocketed in the latter half of the 2010s, with one in particular coming to the fore: loot boxes.

'Loot box' is a fairly generic term that covers a wide variety of specific systems that are implemented in different ways, but they all share similar characteristics. Every so often, say after you've completed a level or upgraded your character, or even after a pre-specified time limit, you're given the option to open a box of digital spoils – depending on the game, it might be character costumes, or new abilities, or power-ups, or collectible artwork, or something else. Or, if you don't want to wait, you can spend money to get access to a box straight away – say, £1 for one box, or £35 for fifty boxes. Critically, the contents of the box are randomised, and subject to varying levels of rarity. For example, in the 2016 first-person shooter Overwatch, 'common' items would be found in 99 per cent of loot boxes (meaning that most of the time you'd receive one of these, and you'd likely get the same item repeatedly), 'rare' items would be found in 94 per cent of loot boxes, 'epic' items in 18.5 per cent, and 'legendary' items in 7.5 per cent, or once every thirteen to fourteen openings. Because we tend to value rarer things more highly, and legendary items tend to be a little flashier, they therefore become more desirable, regardless of any actual utility or inherent worth. In their simplest terms, loot box systems offer you a random chance of getting something you really want, and the more money you spend, the more likely you are to eventually get it.

If that all sounds a bit like gambling to you, then you're not alone. In 2018, the Belgian Gaming Commission published the findings of an extensive investigation into loot box systems within games, singling out three in particular – Overwatch, FIFA '18 and Counter Strike: Global Offensive – as being in violation of national gambling laws. The argument essentially boiled down to the particular implementations of loot box systems within these games being chance-based, and therefore involving placing a monetary bet on a specific, desired outcome. A number of other countries have also pursued regulatory routes in the past few years, albeit with varying outcomes. In the Netherlands, a €10 million fine was imposed on games publisher Electronic Arts in 2019, after EA refused to redesign the loot box system they had implemented in FIFA Ultimate Team so as to comply with the country's gambling laws. This was overturned in early 2022, with the courts ruling that the way in which they had been implemented didn't constitute a form of gambling; nevertheless, it spurred a political drive to develop more stringent regulations. In the UK the government is currently taking a 'watch and wait' approach, opting not to include loot boxes in existing gambling regulation but to review the state of affairs following recommendations that the games industry self-regulate such systems. Similar legislation discussions are ongoing in Australia and New Zealand, although in the US they have largely faltered.

Following a prolonged consultation process, the UK government's Department for Culture, Media and Sport (DCMS) published a document in mid-2022 detailing why they had opted not to pursue a regulatory route (or at least, not immediately). At the centre of their rationale was, perhaps unsurprisingly, the state of the research evidence base linking loot box spending with potential harm. Psychological research on loot boxes started in earnest around 2018, most notably kick-started by Dr David Zendle's lab at York St John University. Zendle's work, consisting of questionnaire-based surveys of gamers, has consistently shown clear correlational associations between spending money on loot boxes and problematic gambling behaviours, regardless of how loot box systems are implemented. The strength of that correlation varies depending on how the system works: for instance, if loot box contents are just cosmetic and don't confer any sort of in-game advantage there's a weaker correlation, whereas if players are shown what they could have won after opening a box – what you might call a 'near-miss' strategy – there's a stronger association. This finding has been repeated in a number of different studies since, and while correlations don't imply causal effects, an argument has emerged that, in a way, this doesn't matter. If spending money on loot boxes drives increases in problem gambling, then you could argue that they are a sort of 'gateway mechanism' that could lead to serious financial harm somewhere down the road. Alternatively, if people who already have problems regulating their own gambling have an increased likelihood of spending more money on loot boxes, then there's a sense in which games developers who implement these sorts of mechanisms are exploiting vulnerable people to make money. Research trying to tease this relationship apart is extremely sparse, with at least some preliminary evidence for a gateway effect. But either way, it looks bad.

Loot box research is an outlier in video games research, and in that of digital technology effects more generally, in that it's an area of study where scientists are doing a pretty good job of adhering to the best-practice principles of open science. The vast majority of studies in this area tend to be pre-registered, meaning that the methods by which data are collected and later analysed are written down and published in advance, so as to keep the process more honest. And very often, perhaps more often than in most areas of psychology, researchers make their datasets and analysis code freely available for others to use or audit. And it is clear that the correlation between loot box spending and problem gambling behaviours is definitely there – research from my own lab has

shown that it is about 1.85×10^{52} times more likely that there
is some sort of positive correlation between the two than
none at all.*

Nevertheless, loot box research suffers from many of the
same sorts of problems that dog the wider digital effects
literature. As we discovered when we looked at the evidence
base for the relationship between screen time and mental
health, if an area of study lacks a sound theoretical base it
can end up getting stuck in a reactive mode and not moving
our understanding forward particularly quickly. There is
relatively little discussion of theory in loot box studies, and
the entire research area essentially appeared in rapid reaction
to public concerns that a new, unregulated form of gambling
(and one that could be targeted at children at that) had
seemingly appeared overnight. The result of this is that the
research area at large seems to have become stuck in a loop
of finding the same correlation with problem gambling over
and over again, without looking more deeply into what that
relationship actually is or why it exists. But, perhaps more
perniciously, some commentators have started to argue that
the fact that we keep finding that same correlation, repeatedly across different studies and different research groups, is
in itself sufficient evidence that loot boxes are problematic
and should therefore be banned or regulated. After all, there's
no smoke without fire, right?

One of the problems that I have with this approach is
that it falls into the same sort of trap we've seen with other
areas of research into the effects of digital technology, in
that because 'harm' is poorly defined (if at all), a correlation

---

* That's $1.85 \times 10 \times 10 \times 10 \ldots 52$ times. Which is 185 followed by fifty
zeroes, a number larger than the estimated total number of atoms in the
world (back-of-the envelope calculations from Fermilab put this at around
10^{49} to 10^{50} atoms). It's also approximately the number of times every day my
daughter asks me a question.

with one potential form of harm – in this case, problem gambling – is implicitly taken as evidence of an impact on other forms. In fact, most quantitative studies of loot box harms focus just on problem gambling and nothing else, meaning that when I say we keep finding the same correlation over and over again I mean that we *literally* keep finding it. To the best of my knowledge, at the time of writing there are three published studies that have taken the next step and investigated the potential relationship between loot box spending and mental wellbeing. Two of them looked at this in the context of psychological distress, showing weak positive correlations (that is, as loot box spending goes up, so too does psychological distress). I was the lead author of the third study, which looked at both psychological distress and mental wellbeing. Our data suggested that in terms of psychological distress, there was moderate evidence in favour of the null hypothesis (that is, no relationship with loot box spending), and stronger evidence in the same direction in terms of mental wellbeing*.

So while it's clear that spending money on loot boxes is related, in some way, to a person's propensity to engage in problematic gambling behaviours, what we're currently less certain about is the extent to which this translates into a clear impact on wellbeing, if at all. Understandably, then, this makes it very difficult to come up with an objective,

---

* For the stats nerds, we used a Bayesian hypothesis-testing framework in this study, which is why the way I've phrased our findings might seem a little odd. Using this sort of framework, you look at two competing hypotheses (so in this case, 'there is a correlation' versus 'there is no correlation') and see which one the data are more likely to support. So when I say 'moderate' evidence regarding the relationships with psychological distress, more specifically I mean that it was about three times more likely that there was no correlation than some correlation. When I say 'stronger' evidence for mental wellbeing, it was about ten times more likely that there was no correlation than some.

evidence-based rationale for implementing broad-strokes legislation because it's not clear why, specifically, loot boxes are being regulated. As is the case in other realms of the debate around the effects of digital technology, some people argue that because it *seems* bad we shouldn't hang around for science to catch up, because people are being harmed right now. I'm sympathetic to that viewpoint to a certain extent, and it's certainly the case that some individuals have suffered tremendous financial distress as a result of coming into contact with loot box mechanisms. Stories abound in the news of gamers spending thousands of pounds on them, often at breathtaking speed. And it's hard not to see games publishers as either malicious or completely ignorant of the potential issues when they often implement them in such seemingly avaricious ways: not long after Blizzard Activision's much-anticipated (and equally controversial) mobile game Diablo Immortal was released in 2022, some players estimated that to guarantee obtaining the best character upgrades in the game, it could cost them upwards of *half a million* dollars. But I'm also aware that, without a clear-sighted understanding of how and why players engage with loot box mechanics, the real underlying problems might be missed in favour of a quick fix. Regulating or banning loot boxes because they look and feel bad, or because gamers don't really like them (and boy, do gamers *not* like them*) might stop people from suffering direct harm from loot boxes themselves, but that doesn't do anything to help our understanding of why that

---

*   Following the release of *Star Wars: Battlefront II* in 2017, droves of players voiced complaints about the game's loot box mechanics, as well as the amount of effort it would take to earn enough in-game currency to unlock new characters – over forty hours per character, by some estimates. When representatives from the games publisher EA posted a message on Reddit to defend the controversial system it generated over 650,000 down-votes, making it quantifiably the most unpopular comment in the history of the site and earning a dubious Guinness World Record in 2019.

harmful behaviour arose in the first place. So when the next digital monetisation technique comes along, we're still stuck at square one in terms of figuring out what sort of effect it might have.

Let's try to unpack that a bit. In the study I mentioned earlier, my research team and I found that, generally speaking, there was a correlation between problematic gambling behaviours and spending money on loot boxes. More specifically, when you categorise people based on the severity of their problem gambling, you essentially get a dose response relationship – that is, as you move from 'non-gamblers' through to low-risk, moderate-risk and problem gamblers, you see a clear increase in the amount of money that each group, successively, spends on loot boxes. We also asked our participants about other types of digital spending – how much they spend on game-related content that isn't gambling-related, as well as digital music, apps, ebooks and other computer software. Here we found some weak evidence that those categorised as problem gamblers spent more on these sorts of purchases than non-gamblers. Finally, a good number of our participants reported that although they played games containing loot box mechanics, they didn't actually spend money on them. When we compared that group with those who did buy them, we found that people who spent more money on loot boxes were also spending more across a range of digital products. To my mind, this raises a question as to whether loot boxes can or should be considered a unique category of spending that causes problems in and of itself, or whether they are instead just one particular product on which people who find it harder to regulate their financial decisions can spend money. If the former is true, regulation will help. If the latter is more representative of reality, though, then regulating loot boxes – which might well have the effect of getting rid of them if they're no longer seen by the gaming industry as a viable monetisation route – will 'fix' that particular problem but it won't do anything to help people struggling with their general spending behaviours. It just removes one outlet via which those problems can manifest.

Nevertheless, it's clear that loot boxes are a deeply problematic aspect of video games. From a scientific perspective, it's not yet clear how, or to what meaningful extent, they're harmful, but at the very least loot box mechanisms undermine the potential for video games to be a positive force in our lives. Play is one of the most fundamentally important activities that we can engage in, regardless of our age. For children it has a critical role in development by improving cognitive, social and emotional skills, as well as confidence and general wellbeing. As an activity, play is just as important for adults: it provides a vehicle for social cohesion, improves our mental and physical wellbeing and can reduce stress. In this regard video games are one of the most important entertainment media of the twenty-first century, not least because of the sheer power they have in bringing people together with a common interest. Stick a loot box mechanism in a game, though, and suddenly it's not about getting people to have a good time any more. It's about getting them to persistently, repetitively, spend money to maintain an illusion that they're having fun. There are echoes here of the issues with social media recommender systems. Social media, in its basic form, has an altruistic goal in that it's all about bringing people together. Stick the wrong sort of recommender algorithm in there, though, and very quickly it becomes a toxic nightmare that can do untold damage to people's lives.

The debate around loot boxes therefore exemplifies many of the public concerns, research difficulties and policy pitfalls that plague digital technology effects more generally, and not least because the focus on them has the potential to take oxygen away from deeper underlying issues. In a way, loot boxes are the low-hanging fruit of questionable monetisation practices: they're relatively well known, and while the science is still out as to whether they cause direct harm, they look so much like slot machines that *of course* everyone is going to worry about them, especially when we find them in products aimed at children. And whether or not they turn out to be truly psychologically akin to gambling, because they look and feel like gambling it's relatively easy to focus efforts on restricting them in the context of gambling regulation. But to do so risks losing sight of other features of video game monetisation that are potentially much more problematic. To date, for example, relatively little research effort has been directed at the effects of what I would call predatory 'gated delivery', a feature which dominates a notable proportion of mobile games.

Perhaps counter-intuitively, many of the most profitable mobile games don't cost anything up front: you can download and play them for free. Or at least, you might be able to play the first few levels, or play for a certain amount of time, without having to pay anything. At some point, though, players of these kinds of games will find it increasingly harder and slower to work through content at the pace they would like to. There are a number of different ways in which this sort of gating works, but one example is through allocating players a certain number of 'lives' or level attempts. In early levels lives aren't easily lost, so you can progress fairly quickly and with relative ease. As the game content gets harder, each level might take more than one attempt to get through. When a life is lost you will be able to replenish it for free, but you'll have to wait, perhaps as little as fifteen minutes, maybe up to twenty-four hours. Or you can pay a small amount of money to replenish your lives immediately.* Or you can opt to watch a short in-game advertisement to get the life back – usually these are around thirty seconds long and are promoting another game that works on the same principles. It's a remarkably lucrative business model. One of the best-known games that gates content behind a limited number of lives is Candy Crush Saga, which generated $306 million in revenue in the first quarter of 2022. It's also completely off the radar of most legislation efforts at the moment because it has nothing to do with gambling. There is no game of chance involved in this mechanism, nor do you need to wager any bets. You just have a set number of attempts at a particular level, and if you require more you must either wait a while or pay some money. And because there isn't any particular public panic about it right now, it's a low priority for research in the area.

It might sound like a fairly innocuous way of generating revenue, but you have to remember that the key to this sort of model working is to create a game environment which encourages players to spend money, little and often. And because of that, it's a model that's prone to misuse and abuse. I highlighted the issues with this kind of monetisation system in my previous book, *Lost in a Good Game*. There I explained that the crux of the problem is that games which employ this sort of download-now, pay-later system often rely on well-known psychological vulnerabilities to encourage people to keep playing. For example, although it might sound

---

* It's usually a little more complicated, in that you typically first have to use real money to purchase a fictitious in-game currency and then use that currency to replenish your lives. Of course, that itself is problematic – it adds a further level of detachment between the thing that you're 'buying' and real money, with the implication that it increases the likelihood of players spending more than they would otherwise want to.

sensible to limit the amount of time people can play a game by imposing a delay on replenishing lives, work from behavioural psychology has shown that this can ultimately make you want to play more. The technical term for this effect is 'hedonic adaptation': if you are given completely unfettered access to something you enjoy or want, then over time your enjoyment of it wanes. Alternatively, if you restrict access to that thing your enjoyment of it remains high. Let's say you really enjoy eating pizza. If you were to eat it for dinner every day for a month, I think it's fairly reasonable to assume that you'll be sick of eating it by day thirty; if I give you the choice to either carry on or eat salad on day thirty-one, you'll probably go for the salad. But if you're only allowed to eat pizza once a week as a Friday night treat, then you'll enjoy it much more each time, and if you're anything like me, really look forward to Friday nights. So temporally gating a player's ability to enjoy a game risks leaving them craving more later down the line. While they might not play for very long in one particular gaming session, they will ultimately play much more over an extended period of time, and the more they play the more likely they are to spend money in-game.

Or, as I mentioned, you can both skip the wait period and not spend any money by watching an advertisement. Most in-game ads for other games are usually interactive: they let you play a sample for around thirty seconds, so at face value it feels like a 'try before you buy' sort of deal. These are often hugely frustrating and borderline predatory experiences, though. Very often, the 'sample' game bears absolutely no resemblance to the advertised game at all. Moreover, the samples are largely designed to encourage you to repeatedly tap the screen, meaning that when the advert abruptly finishes with a download link you end up inadvertently being taken to the App Store page for that game. Many of these ads that

I've seen recently are for what look suspiciously like casino games, offering free spins on slot machines if you download them and use a special code that you've been lucky enough to be given during the same thirty-second advert that everyone else on the platform has seen.

I'm generally an optimist when it comes to video games. I think that they can be a force for good. And the games developers I've talked to over the years don't typically come across as evil capitalists: they're nerds, like me, who grew up with them and found careers in which they get to do something they love. But to be honest, at the moment they're also doing a pretty good job of making it look like all they're interested in is money. Loot boxes look and feel grubby. So too do gated delivery mechanisms. The same for in-game advertisements. This perception isn't helped by instances where, given the opportunity to have honest conversations about whether questionable in-game mechanics have the potential to cause problems for players, senior games executives instead appear at best to be completely out of touch with the zeitgeist, at worst disparagingly dismissive. When Kerry Hopkins, the Vice President of Legal and Government Affairs at games publisher EA, was questioned about the ethics of loot boxes during a UK government committee hearing on immersive and addictive technologies in 2019, she explained that the company doesn't actually call them loot boxes. They instead view them as 'surprise mechanics'. 'If you go to … a store that sells a lot of toys and do a search for surprise toys, you will find that this is something people enjoy,' she explained. 'They enjoy surprises.' It was an utterly bizarre and tone-deaf response to a line of questioning around ethics codes in games publishing, but one, I think, that was inadvertently very telling. It reveals a focus, however unintended, on technology companies protecting revenue streams to the detriment of their core philosophies. To continue with EA as an example, the company's website states that 'Everything we do is designed to inspire the world to play, and we believe we're at our best when we listen, learn, and empower each other. We celebrate openness and curiosity and are committed to making a positive impact in the world.' These are laudable goals, and I would expect no less from a games publisher. But it's hard to square favourable outcomes of this sort of ethos, such as the company's 'positive play charter', with the darker side of questionable monetisation practices.

Again, the answer comes back to the question of responsible development and innovation in digital technology. In the same committee hearing that we heard about 'surprise mechanics', other senior games executives noted that their companies neither work with nor employ any psychologists to provide input into the design of their games. While I don't think that would be a panacea for problems in responsible development, it does speak to the same need we keep coming back to time and again: the digital technology industry must engage more seriously with independent researchers in human psychology, mental health and wellbeing, and researchers with the expertise to provide meaningful input require clearer pathways through which to effect positive change. At the very least, digital tech companies – whether they're involved in video games, social media, retail apps or otherwise – can learn from the frameworks that are used in publicly funded research to nurture ethical and accountable developments. For example UK Research and Innovation, which is the UK's principal public body for funding science, encourages the use of the AREA model (Anticipate, Reflect, Engage, Act) when considering the potential social and ethical impact of funded research projects. Such frameworks are based on the idea that responsible innovation necessarily involves acknowledging that neither science nor technology exist in a social (or even political) void, however much we would like them to. It's highly likely, therefore, that with any sort of research there will be unanticipated or unintended consequences. Some of these may be hugely beneficial, whereas others may cause considerable harm. Responsibility in research thus comes in trying to understand and anticipate what those knock-on effects might be, and in developing responsive approaches to addressing them if and when they arise. Responsible innovation in digital technology development is no different: it requires companies to understand what society is concerned about and interested in, and embed reflective assessments of these in their design processes.

I appreciate that, in some ways, I'm probably being naive here. At the core of any problem with digital technology there is invariably a deeply embedded societal issue, and therefore the fix is never going to be as simple as tweaking a particular algorithm or removing a particular feature. Likewise, I appreciate that the 'solution' of getting digital technology companies to stop and reflect on the potential impact of their products during a design process which can happen at dizzying speed is not as simple as saying 'just do it'. But just because something is difficult to accomplish, just because it might not induce observable benefits in the short term, doesn't mean that it isn't right or necessary to do it. As I write, a 2010 video clip of the then UK Liberal Democrat Party leader (and subsequent Deputy Prime Minister) Nick Clegg is doing the rounds on social media; in it he shoots down the introduction of new nuclear power stations because they wouldn't come into effect until around 2022. What was then seen as something with no immediate benefit would, had it been enacted, gone a decent way to protecting the country against the unprecedented energy crisis it now finds itself in. Clegg is currently President of Global Affairs at Meta, which sees him focusing on the increasing regulatory scrutiny that the digital technology industry faces across the globe. We can but hope that Clegg's lack of foresight when it came to nuclear power has been a lesson learned, but there's a very real risk that we'll just see the same old story play out. Writing about his promotion, Meta founder Mark Zuckerberg noted that 'Nick will now lead our company on all our policy matters ... as well as how we make the case publicly for our products and our work.' This doesn't scream to me that Meta are interested in rethinking their design process; it seems more like a high-level way of closing ranks and digging in with a defensive footing.

In some respects, digital technology is reaching a crisis point. At some point soon, a number of core aspects of the way in which tech companies develop their products is going to have to change. Either that change will arise organically from within the companies themselves, or they will drag their heels for so long that government regulation will fill the void. I don't hold out much hope that the industry will do a good job of self-regulation, because as it stands there's very little to motivate it to do so. Likewise, I worry that attempts to enact genuinely practical legislation will be hampered by a lack of deep understanding of the issues involved, coupled with a scientific evidence base that always feels like it's playing catch-up.

In the absence of a clear overarching solution, and whether we like it or not, if we want to see change we, as the end users, have the power to drive it. Just as we are the ones who are impacted by those unintended or unforeseen consequences of things like algorithm biases, so too are we the ones who can thrust them into the cold light of day, who can force their developers to confront those problems. Remember, you are not enthralled by your smartphone, or social media, or whatever new digital technology comes next. These things are created to ease, improve or augment our lives, and we have the power to change them if they are no longer working for us in that way. So if we want to make effective and positive advances, we need to know, specifically and precisely, what it is that we're dealing with, and not get stuck in an endless cycle of panics about digital monsters that don't really exist. We've already come across a few instances where common sense tells us to worry, but where the best science suggests that our concerns might be better focused elsewhere. We've also now begun to uncover some of the real issues with digital technology that have the potential to impact us in negative ways. We're starting to gain knowledge, and knowledge is the means by which progress is realised. But if we want to go all the way, if we want to figure out how to truly make a difference in our digital lives, then there is at least one huge misconception that we first need to clear up.

Digital addiction

You are not addicted to your smartphone.

I know that's a big statement to make, and I'm going to spend this chapter unpacking it, but I think it's important to just flat out say it. You are not addicted to your smartphone. We are constantly told otherwise: that digital technology turns us all into dopamine junkies, unable to resist mindlessly swiping and jabbing at our screens. On a number of different levels this is wrong. But aside from anything else, the subtext to these sorts of comments is this: that because digital technology is addictive, and perhaps even addicting by design, we, as the poor suckers using it, haven't got a cat's chance in hell of doing anything about it. It's already too late. I don't think this is a helpful position to take though, and I find it a bit patronising. With that in mind, let's try to figure out how we've got into this state of affairs, and whether there's a better way of thinking about what happens when our relationship with screens feels as though it's going wrong.

For most of the year, the *BMJ* (formerly the *British Medical Journal*) is a serious academic journal, publishing important and timely research on the pressing medical concerns of our time. Then, every Christmas, it brings out a special issue of light-hearted satirical research that inevitably becomes fodder for journalists in need of something to fill the festive void. These aren't hoax or fake studies so much as real research on silly topics. In 2012 we had a study of nasal microcirculation in reindeer, in an attempt to shed light on why Rudolph's nose might be red (it turns out that reindeer have a nasal vascular density that's 25 per cent higher than that in humans). In 2013 there was an analysis of James Bond's alcohol consumption over the course of Ian Fleming's fourteen novels, with a view to figuring out whether Bond's drinks were shaken (not stirred) as a result of alcohol-induced tremor. That sort of thing.

While it's fine to give scientists the chance to let off a bit of steam at the end of the year, they are not a group known for impeccable comedic timing, and the problem with publishing satirical work in an otherwise serious journal is that the joke can fall flat if it's taken seriously by the mainstream press. In 2017, for instance, a tongue-in-cheek literature review of 'man flu' in the *BMJ* Christmas issue was picked up fairly uncritically across the press as new evidence that the phenomenon actually existed. Depressingly few outlets made any sort of attempt to emphasise that the paper was meant as a joke. The reason I point all this out is not to be a killjoy – I love a cringeworthy attempt at a science joke as much as the next nerd. It's more that sometimes, if a scientist's attempts at satire are a little too near the knuckle, what starts off as a bit of fun can end up having long-lasting ramifications for actual proper research. I can think of no better example of this than in the case of internet addiction.

The debate around whether digital technology is addictive or not is probably the biggest battlefront in the war on screens. It is rife with misunderstandings and misrepresentations of the relevant science. And, like many arguments about our digital lives, it is also one that is highly emotionally charged, underpinned by our collective lived experience that there's something about screens which – sometimes at least – feels a little bit unnatural. When everyone around us seems to be glued to their phones, it is entirely understandable to wonder whether it's all gone a bit wrong, that this shouldn't be the way technology influences our lives. Couple this with a persistent cycle of pundits in the news bemoaning screens as 'digital heroin', and it becomes very easy to fall into the trap of thinking that digital technology is necessarily and inevitably addictive for the vast majority of people who use it. That's not to say that there won't be anyone out there who experiences harm or distress as a result of their technology use – there are such cases, and it would be churlish, dismissive and ultimately incorrect to suggest otherwise. But the key point to remember is this: addiction is not the inescapable end point for the overwhelming majority of people who use digital technology, and when it comes to most forms of what you might consider digital addiction, barring one exception, there is no such formally described clinical disorder.

In the mid-1990s, the internet was a heady mix of clunky user interfaces, Usenet newsgroups, rotating pixelated gifs and endless loading times. If you had a hobby or a passion, chances are there was a bulletin board forum dedicated to it – or if not, you could just start one up yourself. For Dr Ivan K. Goldberg the forum of choice was PsyCom.Net, a board which he had set up some nine years earlier as a virtual gathering place for fellow psychiatrists. That forum, and Goldberg himself, would gain notoriety in 1995 when, in an attempt to send up the *Diagnostic and Statistical Manual of Mental Disorders* (or *DSM* – psychiatry's go-to text for listing the diagnosis criteria for a range of mental health issues), he posted a description of an emerging illness which he termed

'Internet addiction disorder', or IAD. The original bulletin board, and therefore Goldberg's post, no longer exist, but an article in the *New Yorker* published in 1997 stated that the proposed symptoms of this new disorder included things such as 'important social or occupational activities that are given up or reduced because of the internet', 'fantasies or dreams about the internet' and, perhaps most tellingly of Goldberg's intent, 'voluntary or involuntary typing movements of the fingers'. Goldberg's aim was not really to propose the existence of a new mental illness. Instead, he was poking fun at the *DSM* itself; although a powerful guidebook (and one which plays a critical role in providing treatment recommendations in the US, and therefore influencing the ability for patients to get financial support), it is often criticised for being overly specific and rigid, to the point where it has the potential to pathologise otherwise normal and healthy behaviours.

The joke backfired spectacularly. Rather than generate a discussion of the relative pros and cons of the *DSM*, instead Goldberg found himself inundated with requests for help from colleagues worried that they were suffering from a disorder that he had seemingly made up. From the *New Yorker*'s account, discussions and worries about internet addiction quickly started to appear elsewhere, particularly across universities. 'IAD makes it sound as if one were dealing with heroin, a truly addicting substance,' he told the magazine. 'To medicalise every behaviour by putting it into psychiatric nomenclature is ridiculous. If you expand the concept of addiction to include everything people can overdo, then you must talk about people being addicted to books, etc.' And yet, just as Goldberg's parody took off, other researchers were seriously considering whether some forms of internet use could indeed be considered pathologic-al or addictive. In 1998, clinical psychologist Dr Kimberley

Young published a paper titled 'Internet addiction: The emergence of a new clinical disorder'. In it, Young noted that because there were an increasing number of anecdotal accounts of people describing themselves as 'addicted' to the internet, the problem needed to be formally described so as to spur further research and to understand what it actually entailed. Young's study involved the development of a new diagnostic questionnaire based on a set of criteria that were adapted from those used in the *DSM* for pathological gambling. The questionnaire was then administered to some 600 individuals, through university flyers, newspaper adverts and posts on online self-described internet addiction support groups. Amazingly, the questionnaire was also set up on a website, so that people who used a search engine to look for 'internet' or 'addiction' would find it in their results list. Unsurprisingly, out of around 500 valid responses to the survey, 80 per cent of respondents were classified as internet-dependent, meeting five out of eight criteria devised by Young. The age of the internet addict was born.

Over the past twenty-five years research on this phenomenon has rumbled on in earnest, while at the same time sprouting an ever-increasing number of new branches as novel technologies come to the fore. Alongside academic debates about the existence and nature of internet addiction, we have similar discussions (and the associated public worries) about smartphone addiction, video game addiction, social media addiction, online shopping addiction, and so on. None of these are classified as formal disorders save for video game addiction, which the World Health Organisation controversially recognised in the eleventh edition of its *International Classification of Diseases* (*ICD-11*) in 2018. However, research on these potential disorders suffers from the same general set of issues. All the above can be broadly considered as behavioural addictions – assuming they actually do exist, they can generally be defined as a type of addiction that, unlike substance use disorders, doesn't involve an individual consuming a drug that directly modifies how the brain works or causes a change in feelings, thoughts or mood. Instead, a behavioural addiction means that a person engages in an activity on which they become dependent and which, over time, causes enough harm or distress to functionally impair their normal day-to-day life. Currently, the latest edition of the *DSM*, published in 2013, only lists one such behavioural addiction, namely gambling disorder. Internet gaming disorder is included in a special section, reserved for conditions which require further study; and I think that's a good place to start understanding why, I would argue, we've got the whole academic debate about digital addictions wrong.

In the same way that worries about internet addiction have been around as long as the internet has had a tangible impact on our lives, so too have the concerns that video games might be addictive overshadowed their mainstream popularity. Back in 1981, Scottish MP George Foulkes proposed legislation called the Control of Space Invaders (and Other Electronic Games) Bill in response to growing public panic that video games were harming the youth of the day. 'I have seen reports from all over the country of young people becoming so addicted to these machines that they resort to theft, blackmail and vice to obtain money to satisfy their addiction,' he told Parliament. 'They play truant, miss meals, and give up other normal activity to play "space invaders". They become crazed, with eyes glazed, oblivious to everything around them, as they play the machines.' The Bill was defeated – narrowly, mind you, by 114 to 94 votes – but nevertheless it provides a useful example of how anecdotal concerns (Foulkes was prompted to suggest the Bill by a head teacher in his constituency) can quickly snowball into having a tangible and potentially far-reaching impact on our digital lives.

We've already come across some of the problems that research faces when it takes a reactive approach to public panics, and studies of video game addiction provides a particularly good example of the end result of those problems. Early work on gaming addiction took a similar approach to Young's in the mid-1990s, in that because there were anecdotal accounts of people struggling with their video game play which used the word 'addiction', researchers started off with the base assumption that the addiction actually existed. Little attempt was made, at least in the early days, to stop and consider what the unique characteristics of such an addiction might be, why they occur, or even whether it can be considered a disorder at all. Instead, research very quickly became confirmatory in nature: that is, it wasn't concerned so much with developing a solid theoretical foundation for understanding gaming addiction as with determining how many people were suffering from it. And because of a lack of curiosity about what the distinctive features of gaming addiction might be, instead scientists took the same sort of Frankenstein approach that is often used in digital addiction research, developing 'new' questionnaires and diagnostic criteria by cobbling together pre-existing scales that had been constructed to measure other disorders which have a similar look and feel – namely, gambling and substance addiction. In some cases, the adaptation could be as basic as using the same questionnaire items but simply replacing the word 'gambling' with 'gaming'. Research which took this approach inevitably led to a situation in which some video game players, because they reached a certain threshold or because they met a certain number of criteria, were classed as addicted to games, because the symptoms they reported or exhibited were the same as those which you might see in other more established and formalised addictions.

Over time, these sorts of questionnaires are modified, tweaked and tested in multiple populations, leading to a slew of studies which all appear to use slightly different methods of testing for gaming addiction but argue that some people score highly enough to be classed as addicted (for a given definition of addicted). Eventually, when a critical mass of fundamentally indistinguishable papers is published, we end up in a situation where the sheer volume of papers claiming to show the existence of gaming addiction is taken as evidence per se that it does indeed exist. There's no smoke without fire, after all. When the American Psychological Association included Internet Gaming Disorder in the fifth edition of the *DSM*, not as a formal disorder but as a condition that required further study before it would be considered, the aim was reasonable; there seemed to be an understanding that, despite countless studies of the proposed disorder, we still weren't really getting anywhere near understanding its unique characteristics. By flagging it as a potential disorder of interest, then, the hope was that this would spur exploratory research which would seek to address that gap in our knowledge.

This didn't happen. Instead, the research field took this as further evidence that gaming addiction *did* actually exist, and that the *DSM*'s proposed criteria were the correct ones to use. Over the course of the next five years or so, our understanding of gaming addiction didn't move on in any meaningful way, while the published research base continued to swell with incremental confirmatory studies. As a result, in 2018 the World Health Organisation decided to formally include the addiction, under the guise of 'gaming disorder', in what is effectively the international version of the *DSM*, the *ICD-11*. At no point has the research community come up with a satisfactory conceptualisation of gaming disorder, nor does it even have any clear idea of its prevalence. In a 2020 systematic review and meta-analysis, for example, researchers at the University of Adelaide found that across fifty-three studies published over a ten-year period, eighteen different questionnaire measures were used, with twenty-six different cut-off criteria, resulting in estimates that anywhere between 0 and 22 per cent of the gaming population met the benchmark for gaming disorder. Other research has put this estimate as high as 46 per cent. In other words, although gaming addiction is considered a genuine clinical disorder, currently it's not clear how we should responsibly or reasonably categorise it, how many people might be affected by it, how we distinguish between harmful and non-harmful behaviour and, ultimately, how we might best treat it.

In the absence of both a valid definition and a coherent evidence base which discernibly explains and delineates the disorder, public-facing discussions about digital addiction inevitably fall back on what psychologist Jesper Aagaard characterises as neurobehaviourist discourse. That is, because the word 'addiction' is used, there is a tendency to compare digital technology use to drug use, and therefore contextualise its effects in biological terms. It is often claimed that screen time – be it binge-watching *Only Murders in the Building* on Disney+, or scrolling through Instagram, or playing Fortnite – leads to a surge in a neurotransmitter called dopamine in our brains. And because dopamine is characterised as a 'pleasure chemical', if we get a neural kick from doing something, we're more likely to do it repeatedly, and therefore we can become addicted to it. These sorts of arguments find their basis in a combination of vague references to famed behaviourist B.F. Skinner's work on operant conditioning and classic biological psychology research from the 1950s. At that time two psychologists, James Olds and Peter Milner, were interested in whether it would be possible to influence the way a rat moves through a typical laboratory T-maze by inserting an electrode to stimulate a specific section of the brain called the reticular formation. Due to a lack of experience on Olds's part, though – he was a young psychologist who had only just mastered the techniques involved in such procedures – the electrode missed its mark, instead landing in an area called the septum. Rather than having the intended effect on navigation, and to the duo's surprise, when the rat received electrical stimulation it reacted as if something pleasurable had just happened. In subsequent research, Olds set up an experiment in which rats were placed in boxes and presented with a lever which, if pressed, would deliver a jolt of electricity through an implanted electrode and into their brain. When the electrodes were placed in the septum and other associated areas, sometimes the rats would press the lever thousands of times per hour, and would even carry on doing so until they were on the verge of death from exhaustion. Later work showed that all these brain areas had something in common: either directly or indirectly, they stimulated the release of dopamine. In referring to these areas as 'pleasure centres in the brain', Olds kick-started the modern scientific race to understand the neurological basis of why we enjoy things, and why, sometimes, we might enjoy things a little too much.

Dopamine is a neurotransmitter – a type of chemical messenger that has a variety of effects throughout the brain – involved in everything from movement and attention control through to stimulating breast milk production. In the context of addiction, though, it's usually dopamine's role in something called the mesolimbic pathway, and in particular an area of the brain called the nucleus accumbens, which forms the focus of attention. As the common-sense story goes, stimulant drugs like amphetamine and cocaine, which cause increases in excitement, alertness and mood, have the biological effect of both increasing and prolonging the presence of dopamine in the nucleus accumbens, an area central to reinforcing various types of behaviours. The dopamine theory of addiction suggests that if something causes a dopamine release in the mesolimbic pathway, we find that thing more pleasurable or more rewarding.

Because they result in a much more intense release of dopamine in this pathway, drugs like cocaine become so motivationally rewarding that it quickly becomes impossible to control their use. As with the lever-mashing rats in Olds and Milner's experiment, other activities become so banal by comparison that we will do anything to get the euphoric rush from taking a drug, even if it comes at the cost of other essential aspects of life.* It's not difficult, then, to make a slight logical jump and wonder if the same is true of *any* sort of pleasurable activity. If you find something – say, playing video games or scrolling through social media – really enjoyable, it's likely that it causes a huge surge in dopamine, and so of course there's a risk that addiction may soon follow. Alternatively, if digital technologies are coded to try to hijack the brain's pleasure systems in some way, it is clear that they are addictive by design.

It is this line of reasoning that has, for decades, pervaded most public-facing discussions about the negative effects of using digital technology. There's no nuance here, though, and the apparent neurological link between drug use and screens is often flagrantly and unabashedly pushed. Elsewhere

---

* Although a word of caution here: in the case of true addiction, it's not an inevitable chronic disorder based on these sorts of biological mechanisms alone. Addiction is hugely complicated, and both social and environmental factors play an important role in its development, particularly in humans.

the rhetoric is a little less frenzied, but nevertheless makes a clear association between screens and drug use. Books like Susan Greenfield's *Mind Change* (2014) and Adam Alter's *Irresistible* (2017) make the clear insinuation that dopamine is the root to understanding our addiction to technology. In turn, we hear of 'dopamine detoxes', 'dopamine fasting', even 'dopamine fashion' as a way to reboot our brains and make us happier. One of my favourite examples comes from 2020, when noted UK chef Tom Kerridge published *The Dopamine Diet*, a cookbook purporting to be a way of both losing weight and being happier by increasing our 'happy hormone' levels. The problem is that this line of reasoning only makes any sort of scientific sense if it relies on a number of fundamental misunderstandings of what dopamine is, and how it actually works.

Following Olds and Milner's pioneering work, research through the 1970s and 1980s firmly placed dopamine as the target chemical of interest in trying to understand addiction. Various studies showed, for example, that blocking the effects of dopamine within the brain also disrupted the reinforcing effects that stimulant drugs could have. In the late 1980s, further research found that a range of addictive drugs beyond those classed as stimulants also had the effect of increasing the effects of dopamine in the reward pathways in the brain, whereas other types of psychoactive substances, which weren't considered addictive, didn't. By the 1990s, neuroimaging techniques had advanced to such a stage that it was possible to show that the extent to which stimulant drugs caused dopamine release predicted the levels of self-reported feelings of euphoria that those drugs created. Such findings led to a generalised theory which suggested that any substance which caused any sort of release in dopamine carried with it a risk of being addictive. Research gradually shifted away from trying to critically understand the specifics of the proposed theory, and instead turned towards a progression of studies which attempted to show that if a particular activity was considered pleasurable, then it must be associated in some way with dopamine being released.

Studies looking at a wide range of everyday fun activities – anything from playing video games, to meditation, to simply eating – have reported associated increases in dopamine release. And as this line of thinking has been translated to popular science stories in the mainstream, the dopamine theory of addiction has been distilled into a simple, compelling and somewhat scary idea: *anything* which can be considered pleasurable or rewarding must necessarily be mediated by the effects of dopamine. The higher the dopamine rush, the more pleasurable that thing is – and also the more addictive it can potentially be. There are countless examples in the media of where this line of thinking has gone awry, but one that has always stuck in my mind comes from an article on *Forbes*'s website in 2013, which ran with the somewhat breathtaking headline 'Why Oreos are as addictive as cocaine to your brain'.*

As noted neuropsychopharmacologist Professor David Nutt and colleagues explain in a 2015 review, as research efforts shifted towards figuring out whether the rewarding activity *du jour* could be linked to increases in dopamine, scientists became focused on attempts to 'prove' that the dopamine theory was correct, rather than addressing research findings which appear to undermine the basics of the theory itself. The theory quickly became universal in nature, suggesting that because dopamine is critical in the experience of reward, any substance – any behaviour, even – which creates feelings

---

*   They're not.

of pleasure or euphoria must therefore have a direct impact on dopamine levels in the brain. And because dopamine also has an important role to play in addiction, anything which we find pleasurable therefore comes with a risk of abuse. But the link between dopamine, pleasure and addiction isn't a straightforward one.

Dopamine has different effects throughout the brain because, although it is a single chemical, there are numerous disparate ways in which it can interact with our neural architecture. Neurotransmitters are detected, and in turn have some sort of effect, through their interactions with receptors on neurons. You can think of these as a sort of lock-and-key mechanism; when a neurotransmitter like dopamine (the key) collides with the surface of a neuron, if it happens upon a dopamine receptor (the correct lock) it will bind to it, triggering some sort of action to occur in the neuron itself. There are at least five subcategories of dopamine receptors, each of which have different effects. This goes some way to explaining why dopamine has roles to play in behaviours beyond addiction, but even in that case the story isn't so simple.

For example, a logical assumption of the dopamine theory would be that if surges in dopamine can be correlated with pleasurable feelings (and ultimately, therefore, addictive tendencies), then if we were to chemically block dopamine receptors we would see concurrent reductions in the feelings of euphoria that addictive drugs create. And yet a number of studies since the mid-1980s have shown that this doesn't consistently happen. Nor is it the case that drug-induced highs are necessarily diminished if dopamine production is artificially dampened in the first place. Elsewhere, studies have discovered that interfering with mesolimbic dopamine transmission, rather than disrupting pleasurable responses to food, leaves some fundamental aspects of that behaviour intact. And in some cases, researchers have found evidence that dopamine is also involved in motivational responses that push us to avoid things that are unpleasant. For example, work with rats by Frédéric Brischoux and colleagues at Imperial College London has shown that while some dopamine-related neurons are inhibited by electrical shocks to the feet, others demonstrate a surge in response to the same event. Along similar lines, work by Israel Liberzon has revealed that war veterans dealing with post-traumatic stress disorder show increased activity in the nucleus accumbens in response to combat noise, such as helicopter sounds or gunfire. That is, there seems to be an uptick in dopamine activity in response to highly *aversive* stimuli.

None of this is to say that dopamine isn't involved in addiction, but simply that neuroscientists no longer consider it the sole or universal culprit. It certainly has an important role to play in addiction to stimulant drugs, but for other substances and behaviours its role isn't as clear-cut, and there are other neurotransmitter systems, and other parts of the brain, that are going to be involved. This means that any talk of 'surges' in dopamine driving addiction, particularly in the context of behaviours like digital technology use, doesn't really hold up when we properly attempt to understand what dopamine actually is or what it does. Which is inevitable, in a way – it's a complex chemical, and not many people can lay claim to fully comprehending its intricacies, at least not enough to communicate accurately, at large, the job that it does. This is true even when people try to push back against some of the more scaremongering claims about digital addiction. For instance, one common counterclaim is to argue that even if it were truly the case that there was a simple correlation between dopamine levels and addictiveness, the evidence for dopamine's role in driving digital addictions isn't particularly compelling. The evidence typically cited here is that studies have shown that, for example, playing video games increases dopamine levels by about 100 per cent, which is on a par with eating food or having sex. Methamphetamine use, on the other hand, results in a dopamine increase to somewhere around 1,200 per cent of normal levels, and so video game play isn't really comparable to recreational drug use. It's a compelling argument, but one which finds itself on a shaky footing.

On the digital side of things, the evidence comes from a 1998 study which used a novel brain-scanning method to apparently demonstrate that playing video games roughly doubles the levels of extracellular dopamine in the brain – which, incidentally, has also been used as evidence that video games *are* addictive. In fact, the study doesn't quite show this. Eight participants were asked to play a video game for fifty minutes, and stare at a blank screen for the same amount of time (either condition could come first), while undergoing a PET brain scan. Dopamine levels therefore weren't directly measured, but inferred from the extent to which a radioactive tracer binded to dopamine receptors. It was a fascinating study, and an important one for demonstrating how neurotransmitter levels might be estimated during real-time behavioural tasks in a brain scanner; however, it doesn't provide particularly convincing or conclusive information about dopamine-level variability after playing a game – this is not reasonably comparable, after all, with staring at nothing for nearly an hour. On the drug side of things, it appears as though the 'meth results in a 1,200 per cent increase in dopamine' argument comes primarily from a 2003 study on rats, which isn't really useful if we're trying to claim comparisons in humans.

Biological allusions to digital addictions therefore fall flat because they often rely on a limited understanding of the underlying neuroscience, and because that evidence itself is frequently disparate and conflicting. And it becomes easy to see how ridiculous the analogies between screen use and recreational drug use are when it comes to the suggested solutions, which regularly fall back on vague discussions around limiting exposure to screens, either by age or by amount of time. In the same 2016 *New York Post* article which claimed that 'iPads, smartphones and Xboxes are a form of digital drug' we were also told that the solution wasn't to go for an all-out ban, but instead to 'demand that your child's school not give them a tablet or Chromebook until they are at least ten years old'. That is, if you truly, honestly, believe that giving children access to screens is like giving them unrestricted access to recreational drugs, then it seems laughable to suggest that the answer is to let them have some, but just, you know, not very much. In reality, of course, I would wager that no one actually believes this. It's just a shock tactic used to scare us into accepting a certain point of view.

What is hopefully starting to become clear is that, despite the many and frequent concerns about digital addictions that are flagged in the mainstream media, from a scientific perspective it still isn't clear whether these actually exist, how many people could be affected, and who those people might be. In recent years, numerous scholars have suggested that we've reached this sort of impasse because everyone has become hooked on the term addiction, and the unhelpful cycles of questionnaire development which inevitably follow, without first considering whether there might be alternative ways in which to consider the problem. Do digital addictions exist? That depends on what we mean by addiction in this instance, and what it is about digital technology use that we're specifically worried about. Critically, in answering that question we need to be extremely careful that we don't, as Ivan K.

Goldberg warned, end up inadvertently pathologising normal, everyday behaviours in a misplaced crusade to exhaustively medicalise every problem we ever come across.

A crucial 2017 paper written by an international team of researchers led by Dr Daniel Kardefelt-Winther attempted to make some positive headway on this issue by providing a much more formal and detailed operational definition of behavioural addiction. The definition is straightforward in and of itself: behavioural addiction, they argued, could be considered as 'a repeated behaviour leading to significant harm or distress. The behaviour is not reduced by the person and persists over a significant period of time,' and 'the harm or distress is of a functionally impairing nature'. Critically, though, Kardefelt-Winther's team argued that if a problem behaviour was to be considered an addiction, not only did it have to fit the definition thereof, but a number of additional exclusion criteria needed to be met. For example, is there another, underlying disorder that better explains the behaviour? Is it happening as a result of a coping strategy? Is the individual heavily engaging in the behaviour, but not becoming distressed as a result? And even if it is potentially harmful, is it the result of intentional choice? Those criteria, although not necessarily exhaustive, provide a useful starting point for researchers to consider more deeply what, exactly, it is about an observed behaviour that could be considered problematic, and whether it is truly leading to some sort of harm.

In the context of digital addictions, then, if we adopt a framework like that proposed by Kardefelt-Winther's team, it's not entirely clear that they exist – or rather, that if they do exist, we have a woefully inadequate understanding of what they might actually look like. Because research in the area is framed largely within the theoretical boundaries of substance abuse disorders, our understanding of digital addiction largely focuses on excessive use, repetitive use and irritability following withdrawal of the technology. These factors are insufficient, because they do not necessarily, consistently or systematically lead to functional impairment, nor do they do a good enough job of separating harmful overuse from high levels of engagement or simple enjoyment. For example, one of the *ICD-11* criteria used in the diagnosis of gaming disorder is that increasing priority is given to playing video games, to the extent that it starts to take precedence over other interests and activities. This assumes that high or intense use is inherently a bad thing, though, and that it is not an entirely normal part of day-to-day life that some hobbies can become favoured over others. In a similar vein, many measures of social media addiction tend to focus primarily on the motivations for what scientists call 'social information-seeking' – essentially, interacting with other people online and seeking companionship – intense levels of which are associated with a variety of negative outcomes and, ultimately, addiction. But again, per se this isn't necessarily a useful indicator.

In 2021, a research team led by Dr Liam Satchell at the University of Winchester published a tongue-in-cheek article highlighting this issue, in which they claimed to have developed a new 'offline friend' addiction questionnaire – pleasingly called the 'O-FAQ' for short. In the study, Satchell's team amalgamated a number of prominent social media addiction measures, replacing social media terms with other, offline-relevant phrases – so, for example, 'I spend a lot of time thinking about Facebook' would become 'I spend a lot of time thinking about spending time with friends.' The O-FAQ was administered to just over 800 participants, and using established cut-off criteria for determining addiction the research team argued that nearly 70 per cent of their sample could be classified as being addicted to offline friendships.

The point that they were trying to make was not that looking for support from our friends in 'real life' constitutes the next major public health issue. Rather, that it is worryingly easy to construct an evidence-based and apparently valid measure which, if not fully thought through, ends up warping our perception of a perfectly normal aspect of human behaviour. The research team noted that while it would be silly, on the basis of their findings, to foment public health concerns around making friends, that is precisely what has happened with the original social media measures on which their satirical study was based. The reason this happened, they argued, is that such research doesn't do a particularly good job of explaining how online social behaviour differs from parallel offline sociality and, critically, tends to forget that social-seeking behaviours are not inherently bad or maladaptive things. Much to the contrary, it's often the case that such behaviours point towards positive aspects of wellbeing. We are all fundamentally social creatures, after all.

Given the state of the research literature, then, over the past few years a number of scholars have made gentle, reasonable suggestions that we might do well to start considering whether there is another theoretical lens, one that isn't necessarily addiction-related, through which we can try to improve our understanding of problematic digital behaviours. I would argue that we need to go a step further and completely draw a line under the digital addictions debate. To be clear, I'm not saying that digital technology doesn't cause significant problems for some people in some situations. What I'm saying is that talking about technology addiction as though it means something concrete no longer serves a useful purpose – if indeed it ever did. If what we really want to do is figure out what those problems look like, how we might best overcome them and how we might meaningfully help people

who are truly struggling, then we need to consider alternative theories and concepts that might better encapsulate and
explain situations in which our relationship with screens goes
wrong. There are two broad concepts which I think can be
useful here.

The first is that it might be more helpful to instead consider problematic screen-related behaviours in the context
of coping strategies and escapism. For example, one of the
earliest studies in this area, published in 2000, used a modified substance-abuse disorder questionnaire, coupled with
measures of self-esteem and impulsivity, in an attempt to
determine the potential underlying risk factors for internet
addiction. The study's authors found that while impulsivity
didn't seem to have any sort of impact, lower self-esteem
accounted for a significant proportion of the amount of
time that participants said that they spent on the internet,
as well as about a fifth of the variability in the reported
internet addiction scale scores. The authors concluded that
the link with low self-esteem suggested that people who
used the internet more heavily were essentially doing so
as an escape from other difficulties in their lives. So while
the study was framed within an addiction perspective, the
conclusions from the study seemed to imply that a different
theoretical foundation better explained what was going on.
Assuming one state of affairs but then finding evidence that
points to a different explanation is a perfectly reasonable
thing to happen, and occurs naturally during the course of
scientific work. However, in this study there was no appre-
ciation of this possibility. Despite the brief nod to thinking
about heavy internet use as a type of coping strategy – for
example, that problems offline might drive a greater desire
or need to spend time online – the findings were nevertheless
still shoehorned into an addiction framework, where the

emphasis was on claims that internet overuse was driving other problems. It's a pattern that we see across the research field, and one which stifles meaningful theoretical advances in our understanding of how and why internet use might go awry. Critically, as some researchers have noted, using addiction as a frame of reference also results in a tendency to ignore two key factors that very likely have a significant impact on digital technology use, namely agency and motivation. Given that screens are such a ubiquitous part of our everyday lives now, we, as researchers, can no longer afford to overlook these sorts of core elements. We need to go back to basics and answer the fundamental questions of what compels people to use digital technology in the first place, how individual choice and volition impact that use, and whether the behaviours that we would consider to be problematic are really a manifestation or marker of deeper underlying 'real-world' issues.

The second, related concept that I think is helpful in reframing our approach is to reconsider our technology use in terms not of addiction but of habits. I should start off by saying that this isn't a particularly novel idea; even in the most stringent neurobehaviourist accounts of problematic digital technology use it's telling that the discourse, sooner or later, moves away from talking about full-blown addiction and towards breaking 'bad habits'. These are very different concepts, but they are often conflated both in the research literature and in the wider public debates about the relationships we have with our screens. Are people addicted to technology? It's extremely unlikely that this is the case. Do we *overuse* digital technology? Absolutely, and lots of us likely do – or at least, we feel as though we do from time to time. One of these seems inescapable – that if we're addicted to screens, this has happened to us without us realising and without us having any sort of ability to do anything about it without outside intervention. The other is something that, however uncomfortable it might feel, is within our power to change.

Habits are often conflated with the concept of automatic behaviours, but the two are not quite the same. One sense in which we can think of habits is as what Sartre might have called a pre-reflective process – they are an immediate response to something, or a tendency to behave in a certain manner, in part because we are familiar with that object or situation. Over time, we become so used to acting in that way that eventually our actions happen outside our conscious awareness. Or, as some researchers have put it, habits are not automatic behaviours in and of themselves, rather they are learned automatic responses that have specific features: they tend to be fast, efficient, inflexible and generally unaffected by moment-by-moment changes to our immediate goals.

Habits are developed over time and are best thought of as, in themselves, neutral. Developing an automatic response to something doesn't tell you whether your resulting behaviour is good or bad: eating a bag of M&Ms every day is a bad thing for your health, whereas locking your car after you've got out is a good habit. Checking your smartphone is perhaps a more useful example here, though. It takes time and conscious effort to learn how to use a new piece of technology, so when we first made the shift to iPhones and Androids, it's likely we weren't in much of a habit of checking them very often – perhaps only when we heard a message ping alert. But over time, as we add new apps, join social media networks, WhatsApp groups and the like, because we repeatedly end up reaching for our devices to check for new messages, this behaviour starts to become habitualised. Whether that habit is good or bad depends on the situation – checking for messages while we're driving a car is distractingly dangerous, whereas grabbing our phone to message a friend if we're at home and feeling a bit lonely is a positive thing to do.

In this frame of thinking, then, developing digital habits is not something that we should be intrinsically worried about, or particularly concerned about in the context of solely negative outcomes. We can cultivate healthy, positive digital habits, as well as those that are more problematic in nature. Where the tipping point between good and bad occurs depends, in essence, on a certain degree of self-regulation. In other words, the frequency with which we check our phones, to continue the example, is not inherently pathological or harmful to our wellbeing. But the more frequently we check our phones, the more chances we are creating to experience some sort of problematic outcome every now and again. Whether or not we *do experience* those problems depends on how good we are at reflecting on our technology use, and particularly how our technology use either aligns with or comes into conflict with our immediate goals. As researchers like Adrian Meier have argued, this sort of self-regulation is key, because if it isn't a well-practised habit, the more likely we are to be distracted by our devices when really, deep down, we don't want to be.

This sort of approach is much more helpful than an addiction framework, because it considers both positive and negative outcomes of digital technology use, rather than inherently framing it as an unhealthy behaviour to engage in. It also means that we don't end up getting overly focused on the sheer amounts of time we're spending on our screens in order to consider whether we're developing a problematic relationship with them. It's likely that we've all developed bad habits when it comes to our screen use, but we don't take any action because we've not really noticed them – or we have, but because we're thinking about them in terms of addiction, we feel less empowered to make positive changes. If we try to move beyond this binary, addicted-or-not-addicted way of thinking, then we allow ourselves the possibility of exerting control over our habits. We can boost the good ones and modify the bad.

That doesn't mean that it's easy, though. Or that it doesn't require some difficult conversations with ourselves.

'We call technology addictive, as opposed to calling it what it really is for the vast majority of people: it's a distraction,' explains Nir Eyal, author of two best-selling books on our relationship with digital technology, *Hooked* (2013) and *Indistractable* (2019). 'But when we call it a distraction, well, now we have to do something about it,' he adds. 'Shoot, now I have to ask myself: why can't I read a book as opposed to constantly watching the news? Why can't I do my work as opposed to checking email and Slack channels? Is it technology's fault? Or is it something inside of me that I don't know how to process or deal with?'

As uneasy as asking these sorts of questions of ourselves might feel, we're not talking about anything new here. Plato called it *akrasia*, or the tendency we have to do things that act against our best interests. 'It's not something that technology suddenly thrust upon us,' Nir tells me. 'Struggling with distraction is just something that's part of the human condition. But when we moralise and medicalise it, well, now it's not our problem any more, right?' But if we look at our technology use simply for what it is – a behaviour, and therefore something that we can regulate – then as hard as those conversations with ourselves might be, they allow us sway over what we're doing.

As Nir explains in *Indistractable*, this isn't a problem unique to digital technology use. Very often, if we find ourselves feeling overly engrossed in our smartphones or tablets there's something deeper going on, and people who try to cut down on their tech use often find themselves getting pre-occupied in other ways. For example, Nir recounts the story of how, in an effort to reduce his own digital technology use after he felt that it was infringing on the time he was spending with his daughter, he tried a sort of digital detox. He started to write on an old word processor from the 1990s instead of his computer. He subscribed to print editions of newspaper instead of scrolling through online articles. He bought a basic mobile phone to avoid email and social media. But none of these worked: the newspapers went unread while he con-sumed the news on TV instead; the dumbphone meant that he found it much harder to get around and plan his days; and when he sat down to write, he found himself getting side-tracked by reading books completely unrelated to what he was writing about. One distraction – the one that everyone thinks is the main problem – was simply replaced with others. Nir's example suggests that if we feel we have an unhealthy rela-tionship with digital technology, the solution probably needs to go beyond focusing on that relationship alone.

If we want to regain a sense of control over our own digital technology use, then, we first need to reframe and rethink the way we talk about tech use, both privately and in public. We need to move away from framing everything in terms of whether we're 'addicted' or 'hooked', or our brains being 'hacked' or 'hijacked'. As we have come to see, it's a type of rhetoric that removes individual agency from the equation, and in doing so mischaracterises digital technology as some-thing designed to exert control over our behaviour. Implying that we're victims of deliberately addictive technology is all a bit tinfoil hat, and sidesteps important questions about the complexities of the interactions that we have, need to have, and want to have with our screens. It also reveals a misunder-standing of what addiction truly means, and what we know about the science of addiction. And it also doesn't reflect the reality of what technology companies are trying to do. 'I can't think of any media that is looking to addict people,' explains Nir. 'Why? Because what happens when you addict people is that they tend to burn out. That's not the best business model.'

Instead, thinking about technology use – or, rather, technology use that we're not happy with – in terms of habit formation offers us a route out of the quagmire that not only does away with fundamental scientific misunderstandings about neurobiology, but also gives us a more productive roadmap towards a healthier relationship with our screens. We'll take a look at some of these tools and techniques in the last two chapters. But if nothing else, I think it's important that we really, in earnest, start to move away from the digital addiction perspective, because the most tangible solution it offers is one which causes more problems than it solves. I'm talking, of course, about the digital detox.

8

Detox and distraction

For a few heady years in the mid-2010s, I got to do something that no other academic has ever had the privilege of undertaking: I was the coordinator for the *Guardian* newspaper's science blog network. It was a unique position. Alongside my day job as a university lecturer, I was responsible for wrangling a group of bloggers drawn from all walks of scientific life, acting as a liaison between them and the newspaper's science desk. Aside from writing my own articles, I'd help in coordinating blog post timings, organising themed posts based around major scientific events in the news, training, recruiting new bloggers, surveying readers and more. We had an amazing team of writers – people who it was a genuine privilege to write alongside, like the noted particle physicist and CERN scientist Professor Jon Butterworth, comedian and neuroscientist Dr Dean Burnett, anthropological geneticist Dr Jennifer Raff,* cell biologist Dr Jenny Rohn and many others. At its peak, the network was drawing in millions of readers per month, and we were publishing articles on everything from cosmology and

---

* Jennifer's blog was called *The Past and The Curious*, which is one of my all-time, top-five most memorable science puns.

antimicrobial resistance to scientific political activism and glow-in-the-dark sharks.

The blog network was initially set up as an experiment in 2010, a way of broadening the breadth and depth of the *Guardian*'s science coverage by bringing in a select group of science communicators to write about anything for which they had a passion. And it really was one of a kind. Unlike the rest of the newspaper's content, there was no editorial control – while we had a production editor on hand to offer advice, we really could write and publish whatever we wanted to. It meant that the content we produced was distinct from anything ever seen on the websites of international newspapers, covering everything from the biggest scientific stories of the day from an inside perspective, right down to the most niche and nerdy pet interests or irritations. And while this resulted in some – many – genuinely incredible pieces of writing, it also meant that, on occasion, we missed the mark. For my own sins, I did so rather spectacularly early on in my writing career there, when I posted an article in 2014 about a 'scientist-invents-formula-for-X' PR stunt. You know the sort. Blue Monday is probably the best-known example, which started out as an advertising gimmick wherein a psychologist claimed to have devised a mathemagical formula to work out the most depressing day of the year. He hadn't; the nonsensical equation was a sham, paid for by a travel company in order to get people thinking that it was a good time to book a holiday. I'd written about pseudoscience of this type and others like it before, and it was the kind of thing that always irritated me enough to feel the need to pen a rebuttal.*

In advance of the World Cup that year, Irish gambling company Paddy Power held a press conference in collaboration with

---

* Which, on reflection, I realise was playing directly into the hands of any PR company wanting free exposure.

Professor Stephen Hawking, in which they unveiled a set of formulae that he had devised for working out England's chances of success in Brazil. It was all very light-hearted, but for some reason – whether it was the pressure I felt to write something that week, or some misplaced, entitled sense of feeling like the world's most famous physicist really shouldn't be doing some PR guff with a bookmaker – I ended up writing a blogpost about 'the fall of a childhood role model'. Oh God, it really was awful. I think that I'd originally intended it to be an obviously over-the-top, tongue-in-cheek response to what was clearly an over-the-top, tongue-in-cheek event: Stephen Hawking, his wheelchair emblazoned with Paddy Power stickers, in front of a screen showing Peter Crouch doing his robot dance while he explained how, mathematically speaking, bald players are more likely to score. I'd also meant there to be a poignant undercurrent in a way. My dad died as a result of motor neurone disease when I was in my early teens, so I had always felt a sense of connectedness to Hawking. The trouble is, none of this came out in the article I wrote. Instead, it just read as if some idiot without a sense of humour had completely misjudged the situation, got upset about it, and written a nonsensical opinion piece that managed to enrage fans of two sacred British institutions, Hawking and football, in one go.

I count that article as one of the worst, if not *the* worst I've ever written, and it's a moment that has featured in my mental cringe-reel of failures fairly consistently in the years since. I was somewhat naive, consumed by a misplaced sense of righteous indignation, and I wrote and published before I ever stopped to think whether it was a good idea. I have learned my lesson in that regard. The backlash to the article was fierce and vitriolic, which with the benefit of hindsight is, to some extent, understandable. At times it was also personal and insidious, though, and in the immediate aftermath I remember feeling nauseous and genuinely upset at some of the responses I was getting. Nobody likes being shouted at online, but when you're in that moment, when you're the Main Character* in that one particular social media storm, it can feel as though there's nowhere to turn, no way out of the abyss. For a while afterwards, I wondered whether I had been naive not only in writing the article, but also about the perceived benefits that an active online presence offered. It felt like maybe taking a digital break would be a good thing to do for a little while.

The idea that we can pause our online lives and go off the grid for a bit is one that carries with it a certain sense of romanticism. It's also an idea that is sold to us as a panacea of sorts: ditch your smartphone, we are told, and you can reap the benefits – you'll be less distracted, less stressed, and generally a nicer, happier person. You can find wonder in nature again. You can have real conversations – deep, meaningful conversations – with real people. There are countless advice columns, wellness services and 'digital detox' programmes around that extol the healthy virtues of disconnecting from our devices. Some people take this to extremes: in 2014, political blogger David Roberts wrote about his experiences in taking a year away from social media, blogging and job-related emails. He took a sabbatical from work, and, supported by his wife, kept his online life limited to a bit of shopping, gaming and the occasional use of Google Maps. In *Stolen Focus*, Johann Hari frames his thesis within the context of spending a few months off the digital grid in a quaint Massachusetts seaside town. But perhaps the most drastic example of this genre of storytelling comes from the writer Mark Boyle, who in late 2016 started living completely free of technology, in a cabin that he

---

*   A memetic axiom that cropped up in 2019 which states that 'Each day on Twitter there is one main character. The goal is to never be it.' Also applicable on most other social media platforms.

had built for himself in a rural part of Ireland on some land purchased from proceeds from his previous book, which was about not having any money. No laptops, no smartphones, no internet – but also no running water, gas, white goods and more. He chronicled the first year of his journey in a series of articles for the *Guardian*, writing columns by hand and posting them to his editor. Boyle was candid about the austerity he faced, noting that everything just took more time when it had to be done manually. 'Washing clothes by hand, before drying them with a mangle, is never an exciting task,' he wrote. 'I'm not going to pretend that working on wet days in the mud is always a joy.' He was also unabashedly fervent in his rejection of technological innovation, claiming that we were 'walking eyes half open, half asleep into a techno-dystopia even George Orwell couldn't imagine', and elsewhere calling smartphones, microwave ovens, electric toothbrushes and the like 'violent tech'. Contrasting with this view, there was a sense that reconnecting with a simpler life offered a certain kind of joyous freedom:

> I pick my own fruit and vegetables from the garden and hedge-rows, and eat them as fresh, raw and unwashed as is optimal. I cycle 120km each week to lakes and rivers, where I then spend three evenings of that week relaxing and catching the following day's dinner. I work outdoors, getting sweaty and dirty doing things I enjoy. I made the tough decision to live in the natural world so that I could breathe clean air, drink pure water and create life that allows others the same.

It's hard to read Boyle's musings and not come to the conclusion that he's a very lucky man. There's something tantalising about the idea of getting away from it all, going back to nature and leading what feels like a more natural, wholesome existence, and Boyle is living that dream. And while I bear no grudge or jealousy towards him, ultimately Boyle's experiment is just that: a dream. A fantasy. As admirable as it is to show the world that it's possible for one man to eschew the apparent trappings of modern-day life, there is no real practical message for the rest of us. 'I mean, this is why I wrote *Indistractable*,' Nir Eyal says. 'Like, I had this problem of distraction. And I read every book on the topic, and it was a bunch of professors with tenure telling me to stop using email and to stop checking social media.' As he was explaining this, I make a mental note, as a professor with tenure, to make sure I don't tell anybody to stop using email or to stop checking social media. 'My career and business depend on that! I can't just stop using these tools – it's not a practical solution,' he adds. 'Just like saying to someone "Well, if you're struggling in life, just go and live in a cabin in the woods or something." Well, thanks stupid, I can't!' Boyle's experience is at the hardcore end of the spectrum, but digital detox stories of this ilk all follow the same basic arc: tired of the daily grind, or feeling like something's missing in their lives, people (usually men) in a position to be able to do so take a week, a month, a year or more away from the trappings of digital technology, and inevitably come to the conclusion that they were better off without it in the first place. Most of the time, they then go back to digital life after the end of their escapade and find themselves missing their simpler, offline experience. Much as we all feel a bit of a comedown when we get back from holiday.

So rather than giving us any profound insights into the true impact of the technology we use in our lives, these types of stories fall flat because they represent an illusory escapism that is completely detached from our modern digital reality. The people who embark upon such journeys invariably have lifestyles that enable them to do so in the first place – they have the financial means to afford not doing any work for a bit, or the flexibility of a job that allows them to do just that, or they simply have the necessary friend and family support networks to help their lives carry on in the background while they're away. There is also often an undercurrent that the rest of us are idiots, that we're either too stupid to see what's happening to us or too lazy or set in our ways to do anything about it. These stories disregard the realities of many people for who digital technology is an essential part of staying healthy, maintaining social connections or a necessity for managing finances. And so in their conclusions they offer us little in the way of meaningful advice beyond the usual tropes of throttling our screen time and going for a walk in the woods now and again. In a sense that's understandable, because when it comes to the science behind digital detoxes – well, you know where we're going with this.

'Digital detox is anti-scientific, the whole notion of it,' explains Professor David Ellis, a behavioural scientist based in the Applied Digital Behaviour lab at the University of Bath. 'Yet it has this glimmer of hope that it *could* be scientific.' David's research has been instrumental in highlighting the myriad problems in which screen time is conceptualised, while taking the important next step of figuring out practical improvements to the way that we objectively and reliably measure digital technology use. But he's also conducted research on digital detox in the context of smartphone abstinence programmes; his research, with Thom Wilcockson at Loughborough University, has shown that in small samples at least, a twenty-four-hour phone detox results in participants missing their devices more, but doesn't have any effect on mood or anxiety levels. 'We know that most detoxes in the scientific community are known to be nonsense because our bodies are already very good at removing toxins,' David says. 'But the argument is very appealing from a marketing perspective – drink this, and you'll be "detoxed", you'll feel better. It sounds like it's a health thing, that there must be something to it.'

In a way, it's entirely unsurprising that digital detoxes have captured our imaginations. There are echoes of the fad diet industry and the general 'wellness' movement here. The promise is that if you do this one relatively simple thing – get rid of something unnatural or manufactured from your life, or shift your eating patterns or living behaviours towards a more primeval mindset – suddenly your mind, body and spirit will be enriched, and all of your medical woes will go way. And while it might often come across as a bit cantankerous to scoff at the notion – like you're mocking people who aren't doing anything apart from wanting to be healthier – the truth is that fad diets, bone broths, bee venom therapies or whatever else it is that wellness influencers happen to be currently hawking in the name of healthy living are all just pseudoscience: clever marketing, dressed up to look as if it's good for you, at a price. There's no real science behind them, no evidence that they actually do any good. Digital detoxes also have a puritanical undercurrent to them, in the same way that many attitudes towards our relationship with screens stray into censorious moralising. It feels as though we're not allowed to talk about the fact that, actually, most of us *enjoy* spending time using digital technology and find it a useful convenience from which we derive a lot of benefits. Instead, our screens are somehow fundamentally noxious to our being. And because they are inherently addictive, the only way to free ourselves from their grasp, we are told, is to renounce their use, fully and completely, or at least until such time as our spirit is revitalised.

The reality of the situation is that there is little convincing scientific evidence to suggest that digital detoxes have any long-lasting benefits. A 2021 systematic literature review of the area, for instance, showed that while some studies argued that there are positive effects and some that there are negative consequences, in the majority of cases no meaningful effects were detected. Drilling into the details paints an interesting picture, albeit one that we need to be cautious about over-interpreting. While the general take-home message was that there were no clear answers, in one or two cases the review argued that some consistent effects could be found: for example, the authors reported that a total of three studies looked at the effect of smartphone or social media abstinence on depression, and in all three cases there was, at face value, an apparent dampening of depressive symptoms.* On the flip side, there was a consistent *lack* of improvement across studies which looked at cognitive and physical performance.

---

* As a note of caution: one of these studies was an unpublished Master's thesis, and therefore not subject to the usual checks and balances as published research. The relevant section states that for participants who initially reported moderate depression levels, a two-week digital detox programme resulted in a four-point reduction in depression symptoms on a 0–60 scale. This is reported as statistically significant, but later as a non-significant difference when a more stringent analytical technique is applied. Whether or not it's a clinically meaningful difference is also a matter for debate.

Actually, while I'm here, one of the other reported studies didn't technically look at depression. The study by Morton Tromholt used a subsection of a depression scale which asked participants to reflect on their emotions. This was combined with measures from a different scale, called the Positive and Negative Affect Schedule (and incorrectly referred to in the paper), to create a sort of generic 'emotion' measure. Interesting, but not relevant to depression symptoms, and I think it's a bit naughty that the systematic review makes out that it's a depression study.

And yes, I'm fully aware of the irony of criticising a Master's thesis for not being peer-reviewed while at the same time noting that an actual peer-reviewed study gets some pretty basic things wrong. This aside is already longer than I had anticipated, though, and there are whole books dedicated to the problems in the way that psychological science is conducted, checked and published. If you're interested, I'd recommend Chris Chambers' *The Seven Deadly Sins of Psychology* (2017) and Stuart Ritchie's *Science Fictions* (2020) as excellent starting points. While you do that, I'm going to stop looking at broken studies and go and have a lie-down in a dark room.

For all other measures the results were contradictory – for example, in the context of life satisfaction, some studies saw an increase in this after taking a break from using social media, some no effect, and some a decrease. Inconsistencies were also found for sleep quality, anxiety and stress levels, and social connectedness. With regard to that last one, it's worth noting that one study (out of two reviewed) found that participants who were asked to stay off Facebook for forty-eight hours generally reported *lower* levels of connectedness, and that there was a rebound effect: people who reported feeling more disconnected ended up using Facebook much more post-detox. In the same way that fad diets don't do our waistlines any good in the long run, there aren't any quick fixes for our technology habits that do anything appreciably helpful for our mental health.

The authors of the review pointed out that the reason why we see such inconsistency in the research findings is, well, the same one we've encountered time and time again when we've talked about screen time research. They charitably noted that 'wide variety in the implementation of digital detox interventions was found', which is an admirably dispassionate way of saying that no one has ever bothered to be consistent in actually defining what they mean by digital detox. Some studies involved an abstinence period of a day, some two days, some weeks or more. Some focused on specific apps or social media sites, others looked at the effect of withholding smartphone use entirely. Some were prescriptive as to how the detox period should happen, others were more liberal, allowing participants to define and set their own goals. Different outcome measures were used. Different measures were used when looking at the *same outcome*. Few studies followed up long-term effects, post-detox. Sample sizes were all over the place – studies tested anywhere between fifteen and 1,095 participants. Brilliantly, most studies didn't actually check whether participants adhered to the abstinence regime through the detox or whether they just started using other devices or different forms of social media. The literature is a mess, but by and large it appears that digital detox programmes don't really do what we feel we want them to. 'As soon as you go towards bigger data, more transparency, there's no difference. It doesn't work,' David tells me.

Nevertheless, despite the evidence pointing towards digital detoxes being just another fad, I think there's something to be said about the fact that many of us still can't help but feel that we need to get away from our devices from time to time. And the thing is, there's absolutely nothing wrong with feeling like this, or actually taking a break for a while. It's simply that we don't have to frame it in terms of ditching something that's harmful to our bodies, or addictive for us, in order to get some benefit. Digital detoxes don't help in this way, because they don't offer us any depth of understanding as to what it is we're trying to get away from. Instead, they simplistically tell us that giving up digital technology is somehow just 'good for us'. The risk, therefore, is that in completely ditching tech for a bit, then yes, we might avoid things that aren't doing us any good. But we also throw out the benefits at the same time. And in doing so, we don't resolve any underlying issues that are driving the problematic side of our relationship with screens in the first place. So it's entirely unsurprising that when we finish our detox we just go back to our old habits and nothing changes.

'It's an unattainable ideal,' Nir Eyal tells me. 'It gives you no practical steps that the average person can take, right?' We've seen that same tiresome story play out time and again – if you read literally any account about a journalist going tech-free, nothing changes in the long term. They all, without exception, have a revelation that digital technology is apparently suffocating their lives, they go on holiday and have a nice time, and when they come back they return to the same old grind. These stories are presented with the implication that we've somehow been given some sort of great insight into how bad screens are for us, but we're not offered anything like a practical solution that really works.

Digital detox studies form a subcomponent of a much wider research area, one concerned with digital disconnection more broadly, and it's here that I think we can learn something useful about why we sometimes feel the need to take a break. Back in 2016, for instance, Ofcom, the UK's communications regulator, reported that just over 40 per cent of some 2,500 people surveyed said that they felt they spent too much time online. Interestingly, though, 34 per cent also said that they *wouldn't* like to do a digital detox – just 10 per cent said that they would. It seems as though, as unhappy as we sometimes are with how we spend our time online, we're pretty good at spotting fad diets, and perhaps we're after something that has more long-term benefits.

Recent research led by Professor Minh Hao Nguyen at the University of Zurich helps to shed further light on this. In November 2020, Nguyen's team surveyed a nationally representative sample of just over 1,100 people from Switzerland about their opinions on what constitutes a balanced digital media diet, reasons as to why people might wish to disconnect for a while, and what sorts of strategies they employ to manage their screen use. Nearly a third of the sample mentioned using digital media for an appropriate amount of time as being crucial – essentially, that it's important to find our own individual Goldilocks zones when it comes to the time we spend online. Perhaps surprisingly given the topic, the next most prevalent theme that arose was one of digital benefits. About a quarter of the participants sampled mentioned that there are so many positives when it comes to digital media use, full-on withdrawal wouldn't actually be helpful. Lower down the list, other themes which emerged were the importance of ensuring that our digital lives don't displace our offline lives, the need to develop skills in using digital technology critically and reflectively, and the importance of establishing 'offline moments' – understanding that in certain situations and places we need to set practices and expectations around whether or not it's acceptable to be on our screens. This is, I think, indicative of the broad feeling that participants appeared to have towards their digital diet – namely, that in times where we seek digital disconnection, it's not actually a total break that we want. Instead, what we're looking for is a realignment, a greater sense of equilibrium in our lives. We want to use digital technology when it can offer us useful information or a nice bit of downtime, but we don't want it to creep into those little moments of joy that we get offline – the chats around the dinner table about how our days have gone, say, or a shared joke with friends where you just had to be there to get it.

Nguyen's study next looked at the motivations that people report for taking a break from their digital devices. Using a statistical technique called Principal Components Analysis, the team mapped participant responses on to three core categories of reasons for disconnection. The first broadly related to what the team termed 'wellbeing and availability-related motivations': that is, sometimes participants reported that they would take a break from their screens because they wanted to focus on something important, they generally wanted to be more present in their offline life, or they strategically didn't want to be available for friends, family or work to contact them. The second category broadly encompassed what Nguyen's team termed 'content and privacy-related motivations'. In other words, sometimes people wished to disconnect or reduce their online presence because they were worried about the availability of information about them on the internet, they were worried what tech companies might be using their data for, they were finding the content that they were coming across upsetting, or they had simply lost interest in what they were doing online. The last category was socially motivated: where participants reported wanting to take a break when they were experiencing feeling overwhelmed with information or messages, or where friends and family were telling them they should cut down on their screen time. In terms of ranking, not wanting to be distracted from something important was the reason participants agreed with the most, whereas being told to cut down by friends and family or wanting to avoid FOMO were the least agreed-with. In their analysis, Nguyen and her team noted that there were important generational differences in terms of primary motivations to disconnect: Baby Boomers, the oldest generation sampled, were more likely to be driven by issues around content and data privacy, Generation Zers for social reasons. There were no generational differences with regard to wellbeing and availability motivations, but there were gender differences: female participants were more likely to agree with these as reasons for taking time away from their digital devices compared with men or individuals who identified as another gender.

Finally, Nguyen's team looked at the actual strategies that participants reported using in their drive to take a break from their online worlds, and here two overarching themes emerged: strategies based on setting rules, and ones based on digital device features. Rule-based strategies that participants reported included things like removing apps from their phones or actively deleting website accounts if they felt they were becoming too much of a time sink, deliberately restricting their digital media use to specific times of the day, or setting rules and expectations around when it's not appropriate to use digital technology, for example at the dinner table. Other rules included actively putting digital devices away and out of sight when participants wanted to do something else, or switching their phones into flight mode when they wished to focus on a particular task. People also reported that they just decided to spend less time on their devices from time to time, and did so without implementing any specific strategies. Feature-based strategies, on the other hand, included switching off notifications for 'nagging' apps like email, social media or news, muting group chats on messaging programs, or changing status updates to show they were away or offline and generally unavailable at that moment. More drastic tactics under this general theme included using programs that actively monitor and limit the amount of time they could spend on their devices, or strategically unfollowing or blocking accounts on messaging or social media apps. And again, there were generational differences in the types of strategies used: in general, older generations were more likely to report using rule-based ones, whereas younger generations opted more for feature-based ones. Female participants were more likely to report using rule-based strategies than anyone else, but otherwise there were no gender differences.

The results from Nguyen's study are interesting for a number of reasons. For one, the data show that we still often have a paradoxical way of thinking about our relationship with digital technology. If we're asked to consider our own digital consumption in the context of a 'balanced' diet, this seems to set us up to view it in terms of what constitutes an appropriate amount of screen time, as though it's a vice to be contrasted with our healthier 'real life'. Yet at the same time, we can readily see the benefits, the utility, of our screens – particularly when it comes to maintaining and reinforcing relationships with friends and family. Once again, then, it appears as though the way in which we frame our digital technology use has a meaningful impact on the effects we believe it has on us, and this in turn may drive people to feel the need to reduce their screen time. Or in other words, we're actually pretty good at spotting the benefits that digital technology can bring, but if we're primed to see it in terms of a contrast between our online and offline lives, we fall into a dichotomous way of thinking – that one (our offline life) has to be good, and so necessarily the other, our online world, has to be bad. But it's not just our beliefs about how screens affect us individually that guide us – perhaps just as important is what researchers Albert Gunther and J. Douglas Story have called the 'influence of presumed media influence'. This theory suggests that our opinions on the impact of (in this case) digital technology are not necessarily based on how we ourselves react to media content, but rather are more affected by our perceptions of its effects on other people. As we've seen countless times in this story, it's clear that we're persistently exposed to news articles, magazine stories, opinion pieces and even just general musings on social media that digital technology is harmful. The 'presumed influence' theory would therefore argue that it is exposure to this very strong message that our online lives are maladaptive which drives changes in our attitudes towards screens, over and above our own personal experiences. We're repeatedly told that digital technology is bad for us, so we start to feel bad about using it – not because it's actually causing us harm, but because there's an unfounded assumption that it might.

Second, the findings from Nguyen's study highlight the importance of looking at screen effects across different demographics. We know this already, but it's nice to see it in action. And don't get me wrong, it's not perfect – it's a broad-strokes attempt, grouping people largely by generation and gender. Nevertheless, the fact that we see clear differences across different age groups in terms of why people want to digitally disconnect and how they go about doing it suggests that there is never going to be a one-size-fits-all approach to managing our online lives. I mean, obviously that's the case. But while this is all well and good, and it's really useful to understand what people are doing about managing their online lives, we're still a bit stuck here. We now have a clearer idea of what people want out of a balanced digital life. We know what drives them to switch off when they want to. We know what people try to do. What works, though?

Now, it's at this point that we're at quite a significant risk of falling into the same trap that countless other pop psychology books fall into, which is to reveal, with a flourish, One Weird Psychological Trick that you can use to magically fix everything you find problematic about the way you use your phone. Hopefully, that's not what you were expecting, though: this isn't that kind of book, I'm not that kind of psychologist, and anyone trying to sell you One Weird Psychological Trick is actually hawking One Weird Psychological Trick That Only Works In Certain Situations For Certain People, Is Probably Based On One Quirky (Read: Poorly Designed) Tiny Study, And Probably Hasn't Been Replicated, So Is Actually One Useless Gimmick. There's no quick fix here. The best we've got is some educated guesses, coupled with some common-sense advice and a hefty dose of recalibrating the way we think and talk about screens. And do you know what? That will probably do us just fine.

*

Let's start with that recalibration. Framing our thinking in terms of technology addiction is entirely inadequate for the vast majority of people and interactions. It results in a focus on negative effects, but crucially does so in such a way that undermines our ability to overcome them. As we now see, this presents specific problems for advancing our scientific understanding, but it also poses difficulties for pretty much any discussion about screens. Technology addiction approaches have nothing helpful to say about the positive ways in which screens can influence our lives, over and above cursory nods to the fact that this might be a possibility. Instead, when we talk about screens in terms of addiction, we're often left with one solution: abstinence. And given that abstinence is largely impractical in most situations, what we're left with is a feeling of guilt that we can't do anything about the relationships we have with our devices. It's not so much a case of learned helplessness as an imposed helplessness.

Thinking about our technology habits, instead of technology addictions, offers us a number of advantages. First, technology use is no longer framed solely in terms of negative effects that are seen to be intrinsic to the device or app itself. Instead, technology habits can be both healthy and unhealthy; which category they fall into requires consideration of our behaviours beyond the screen. Earlier we came across the example of checking your smartphone, which I think serves as a useful illustration again here. Getting into the habit of frequently, almost passively, checking your phone is not in itself a bad thing. In fact, it can be quite a good thing in some instances – if you're doing it to chat to a friend when you're feeling lonely, or to make a note about something important that you've just thought of before you forget, there's nothing inherently sinister about that. In a different situation, though, those same automatic behaviours *can* be harmful – if you're expecting a message and keep looking for it while you're driving a car, say. Where framing our digital behaviour in terms of habits really starts to help is in that vast grey area in between those two scenarios.

I think about this a lot in the context of the relationship that I have with my daughter, and, as he has started to grow, my son. Patrick is now a little older than Matilda was in the story I related right at the start of the book: that moment, as an emerging toddler, when she found my iPhone and started playing with it, almost in an attempt to mimic how she'd seen me use it. And there's the crux of it: she was interested in my phone not because it was some sort of electronic siren that somehow emitted addiction rays and enthralled anyone who ventured too close. She was interested in it because *I* was interested in it. I use my phone to manage many different aspects of my life, which means that I check it *a lot*. At that age Matilda was a sponge, constantly absorbing everything going on around her, no matter how inconsequential it would seem to an adult. She saw me using my phone in what I thought were quiet moments when nothing was happening, and she logged that this was something to be interested in, something to use and play with. So *of course* she would see it as a prize to grab hold of whenever she was given the chance.

I'm fairly convinced that almost any story about the relationship we have with our screens, if it's written by someone who is a parent, will have a version of the situation above. Child plays with phone. Parent comes to realisation they're on their phone a lot. Parent wants to do something about it. Those stories will usually go on to diverge in terms of the solution they propose: digital detox tales will go for the nuclear remove-all-screens-or-maybe-even-ourselves option, whereas more moderate accounts will opt for more tempered disconnection approaches, the kind that most people already know about and might already practise. In all cases, though, you can usually detect an underlying commonality: that the moment of epiphany when we all realise that we're using our phones too much often comes with an undercurrent of shame, that we've somehow failed our kids and we need to atone and ensure that they don't follow us down the same murky path.

There's a different option here, though. After my own epiphany watching Matilda I didn't feel bad, or that I'd let her down. Instead, I acknowledged that this behaviour of mine, which I hadn't really ever been consciously aware of, was having an appreciable impact on the way she viewed the world. Whether it was having a positive or negative effect, overall, wasn't clear at that point. My decisions about what to do next might tip the scales one way or the other, though. My initial urge was to remove opportunities for her to get hold of my phone, which in turn meant that I would reduce my own use. But for what purpose? There's nothing intrinsically wrong with screens, and she's going to grow up in a world awash with them whether I like it or not. Better, then, to equip her with the skills necessary to navigate that digital world and to instigate rules – well, not rules per se, but rather expectations – from an early age about how we use digital technology at home. Screens aren't anathema in our house, but where possible and appropriate they are a shared experience. If I'm jotting a note on my phone, or responding to a message, and Matilda is in the room, she'll ask what I'm doing and I'll show and explain it to her. Usually she then wants to play with my phone to take some photos, so we'll end up doing that together. The streaks and flashes of light which she captured as a small toddler are now perfectly framed, if somewhat repetitious, masterpieces recording the gentle chaos of the playroom, or the kitchen, or wherever it was she happened to be pointing the camera. I think that they're lovely, though, and sometimes they take pride of place on the digital photo frame we have on our sideboard. And as Patrick has grown from an inert blob to a crawling, then tottering little human with a fledgling personality all of his own, he too has started taking an interest in the digital side of our lives. He doesn't find my phone anywhere near as fascinating as Matilda did at his age; nevertheless, he'll still take his chances at pilfering it from my pocket when he catches a glimpse of it. When he does manage to get his hands on it, Matilda is often quick to show him how it works. Or at least how to take a decent photo with it. And it becomes an opportunity, a chance to connect, when we can all share in the passing fun of the moment.

I don't want you to fall into the trap of thinking that we're having an easy time of it here. Parenting is really, really freaking hard, and as much as we want to make sure we share digital experiences with our daughter, sometimes we just need to stick the TV on so she can have some quiet time and we can catch our breath. My wife and I would often have conversations, when Matilda was younger, where we would fret over whether we were allowing Matilda too much TV time. And to be honest, we still do have those conversations – it's just that they're now framed differently in my mind. The fact that we're reflecting on the amount of TV she's watching is a *good* thing, because it shows that we're not just shoving her in front of a screen and forgetting about her. We're keeping tabs on what could become an automatic behaviour, and making sure that it serves a useful or positive purpose for us rather than being something that just happens.

Nevertheless, Matilda can be extremely good at building things into her daily routine without us realising. For example, for a time, whenever I washed her hair before bedtime, while I was drying it I'd sit her on my lap and she would ask if she could watch an episode of *Bluey*.* And I would give her my phone, because it meant she would sit still for the five minutes it would take to get the job done. Useful for me, sure, but if I'm honest with myself, not a particularly positive experience for Matilda – I was essentially distracting her with something shiny for a moment so I could accomplish something. It didn't take long for this to become an expected part of her routine, though, and when I then decided to decline the request, boy did I get it with both barrels. But we talked about it; as much as you're able to reason with a (then) two-and-a-half-year-old, I explained that it wasn't great to be watching cartoons at that point in the day because it meant that I'd miss watching it with her, and no one could really hear it over the sound of the hairdryer anyway. It took a couple of days to convince her, but we got there in the end. What was becoming an automatic behaviour, and not one I felt was all that helpful, was identified, explained and tweaked. Nowadays, whenever I'm drying her hair she rifles through a book, or has a look at whatever trinkets are lying around nearby for a little bit. And we still watch *Bluey* together on lazy weekend mornings.

Thinking about our technology use in terms of habits is a promising start, but it's really just the first step. Habits can be good, habits can be neutral, habits can be bad, and figuring out which category a particular technology habit falls into requires constant vigilance and self-reflection. It requires that we make a personal decision, not just to treat our relationship with screens differently, but to do so persistently, over the long term. And I get it, that's a hard thing, a daunting thing to suggest. But you *can* do it if you want to. There will be

---

* Easily the greatest children's cartoon of a generation. It's one of those rare gems of a TV show that's just as funny and interesting for the adults as it is for the kids, and I am of the fervent belief that everyone needs a bit of *Bluey* in their lives. There's even an episode about technology habits that absolutely nails a healthy and positive approach to screen routines.

stumbles, for sure – but the key is to be aware, and open to thinking about how you can use digital technology in a more constructive and less shameful way. I'm not going to be too prescriptive here, because how you personally go about doing that depends on so many factors: what you're actually doing, whether you should be doing something else at that moment, where you are, who you're with, how you're feeling and more. But when you do catch yourself checking your phone for a message that still hasn't come through (and maybe never will), or flicking through a social media feed, or watching that seventeenth YouTube recipe video, try not to be so hard on yourself. Don't just jump straight to the scorched-earth option of ditching your devices. Instead, appreciate the fact that you've identified a behaviour you're not happy about – this is a good thing! The next step is to figure out why it's made you unhappy. That requires looking at the bigger picture: should you have been doing something else? Did you *want* to be doing something else? Is this a one-off, or does it keep happening? If you engage in that process of self-reflection repeatedly, over time it will become less effortful, and itself more automatic.

Of course, there are specific things that you can do to give yourself an advantage when modifying your digital device use to work better for you. There are no big secrets here, and I should caveat that there's no hard science to support any claims that these strategies work in every situation. They're educated guesses, really, and in fact they're the same suggestions you see everywhere: switch your notifications off, stick your phone in airplane mode when you need to focus on something, delete apps that you're really not getting any enjoyment out of, that sort of thing. The key is to be smart about what you're trying, and why you're trying it. Think about what it is that you want to get out of the apps that you're using and do that, if you can, from the very first step. This is particularly true for social media: how many of us can remember why, or when, we first signed up to apps like Twitter, Instagram, WhatsApp, Facebook and TikTok? We can't really, because we tend to do these things in a spur-of-the-moment sort of way. We then spend most of the rest of our time on that app – which in some cases can literally be years – trying to figure out why we're using it and what we were doing there in the first place. Some people are extremely good at navigating this issue, expertly curating their social media feeds so that they're very specifically getting what they want out of it. For most of us, though, there's a little bit of utility mixed in with a lot of hot takes and angry people saying stupid things. We need to learn to better value the time we spend online, and to put more value in our online self-worth. If we want to maximise the chances of our time online being positive, we must make a conscious effort to set ground rules for how we operate. For example, after my ill-fated Stephen Hawking article and the subsequent abuse I got for it, I judiciously started muting or blocking any accounts that made me feel stressed out or annoyed. I still do, and my bar for muting or blocking someone is extremely low, because I've learned to value the time I spend online and I want to maximise my chances of that time being a positive experience. Likewise, I don't have notifications on, because there will be nothing happening on any social media platform that I will ever need to urgently attend to right that second. Seasons of repeatedly letting my feeds grow and then pruning them back eventually led to a place where I get exactly what I want out of my apps, and they work in the way I want them to. And when one of them stops serving a useful purpose for me I'll delete my account and move on to something else.

Now, this is all well and good, but I'm extremely conscious

that as a white middle-class male I will essentially be experiencing a lot of these apps on easy mode. So my point here isn't 'If you use social media like I use it, you'll have a great time too.' Instead, it's that figuring out what works for you takes time and necessary effort, but is an important thing to do if you want to try to get the best experience possible. It's very easy to fall into using something like Instagram just for the sake of it, or because everyone else is on it, or because someone suggested you should give it a go. But using any social media platform needs to have a purpose and *a benefit* for you. If you can't see what that benefit might be, then don't use it. If you can, then great – but it needs to be nurtured and protected. So use disconnection strategies to your advantage; not with the aim of achieving complete disconnection, but rather in order to give yourself the best chance of engineering positive, meaningful experiences while at the same time minimising the likelihood of encounters you might find stressful or harmful*. You know yourself best, so you know where your weaknesses might lie in this regard.

I know that this approach is potentially difficult, in part because it requires experimentation and an acceptance that in trying to figure out what works for you, things will inevitably go a bit wrong along the way. Often we don't feel like we have the time or head space to undertake such an exercise, so it's understandable that, in the pursuit of a healthier relationship with our screens, we often clamour for rule-based advice. If

---

*   From my own perspective, I know that I used to find it difficult to resist the urge to post sarcastic replies when Someone Has Said Something Wrong On The Internet. Having been on the receiving end of a pile-on, though, nowadays I always try to pause and reflect on the fact that there's another person behind that screen, someone with a life beyond that post, before I hit reply. Everyone has bad days, and regardless of whether or not their world view aligns with mine, they don't need or want some random person they've never met adding to the racket. Besides, no good ever comes from an onslaught of snark. My social media feeds are quieter as a result, and that's no bad thing.

someone could just suggest this particular strategy or that particular time limit, things would be easier. We know by now that this just isn't going to work, because screen time itself is such a useless concept, and the evidence to back up hard-and-fast rules – especially in the context of screen time limits – simply isn't there. But this doesn't mean that we can't think about more flexible rules – or rather, as I prefer to think of them, expectations – which can help frame our daily interactions with digital technology. And flexibility really is the key here: the moment we start trying to enact immutable edicts we're setting ourselves up for failure. This is particularly important to consider in the context of ground rules that we put in place for children and adolescents; it involves learning about the technology they use in order to establish a common language to discuss that use.

For example, if you have kids who are journeying into adolescence, chances are that you've had an argument about Fortnite at some point. Parents often come into conflict with their children over this when it's time to put the controller down and focus on homework, or have dinner, or get ready for bed, and very often these conflicts arise because of a disconnect between what parents want and how the game works. What feels like a simple, innocuous request – to pause or stop playing in order to come and do something else – runs counter to what is possible. In online games like Fortnite there is no pause button, and while you can literally stop playing it mid-match, doing so has the potential to impact the rest of the team you're playing with, and in some games can trigger penalties for players. To be honest, Fortnite is more of a glorified social network for kids than a game anyway; this was especially true during the pandemic, but even pre-Covid it was fast becoming a place to catch up with friends after school. To ask them suddenly to switch the game off is the modern-day equivalent of yanking your kid off the football pitch after twenty minutes, or telling them to hang up the phone in the middle of a conversation. So because we're primed to always think in terms of screen time and limits, we end up trying to enact rules based on abrupt restrictions, which often ends in failure. Instead, understanding both the way games like Fortnite work and the reasons why they're used allows for shifts in the language we use to better accommodate everyone's needs and wishes. 'Can you pause the game and come down now?', for example, becomes 'When you reach a point at which you can stop, or when the match finishes, can you come down?' Simple tweaks can often be the most effective.

The language we use in communicating expectations around our tech use can be important in other ways, too. Research from 2019 led by Professor Netta Weinstein at the University of Reading looked at this in the context of rule-framing. The study presented 1,000 British teenagers with scenarios in which parents were trying to regulate technology use through three different means: by talking in terms of threats of (or actual) punishment in order to enforce the rule; guilt-tripping teenagers into acquiescing; or guiding the conversation in what Weinstein called an 'autonomy supportive' way – that is, by paying attention to, and valuing, the teenagers' opinions while at the same time explaining the rationale for why the rule is there. After reading each scenario, the participants were asked to imagine how they might react if they themselves were in that situation. The authoritarian and guilt-focused approaches didn't fare so well: the teenagers said that they would be more likely to resist the rules and also, worryingly, that they would be more inclined to hide their tech use from their parents. In the autonomy supportive scenario, the participants said that they would still be likely to rebel against the rules – this is, after all, essentially the *raison d'être* of teenage life – but also that they were more likely to feel trusted, and less inclined to conceal their technology use. This is important, because setting rules and customs around our digital lives is only half of the equation: the way we talk to each other about how, why and when we use our screens is just as crucial in ensuring healthy behaviours. When kids start hiding what they're doing online, that's when the chances of them encountering harmful or dangerous content start ticking up. But it's also important for anyone, at any age. If we want to set up expectations about our screen use – whether that's having phone- or TV-free mealtimes, or creating ring-fenced portions of the weekend when everyone can play video games together – then we need to be perceptive, listen and understand what we each want and need out of both our shared and personal time, and do so with compassion and consideration.

Matilda is three years old now, going on four. Patrick is eighteen months old. It's terrifying how quickly time seems to pass – someone once told me that when you have kids, the days are long but the years are short. I'm starting to see – well, to feel really – the truth of that now. I'm also starting to see how different their world is, obviously compared with when I was their age, but even to the way things were even five, ten years ago. We were in the car the other day and she wanted some music on the radio. 'Echo!' she chirped up. 'Play *Paw Patrol* music!' It seemed silly at first, but then it occurred to me that the only way she's ever seen us play music at home is through a voice-activated speaker in our kitchen. Neither of them will ever know the world of cassettes and CDs and mixtapes. Scarily, they'll probably never know the world of ripping mp3s, or downloading songs into iTunes. But that's

OK. Theirs will be something new – something, that as I grow older, will start to feel increasingly scary and unwholesome. Douglas Adams already told us this, of course, in *The Salmon of Doubt*. 'Anything that is in the world when you're born is normal and ordinary and is just a natural part of the way the world works,' he wrote. 'Anything that's invented between when you're fifteen and thirty-five is new and exciting and revolutionary and you can probably get a career in it. Anything invented after you're thirty-five is against the natural order of things.'

I'm way past thirty-five now. But when I look at how Matilda is starting to involve Patrick in her fledgling digital world, the way she shares in the joy of taking a simple photo with one of the most complex and powerful devices in the history of humankind, I don't find it scary. The natural order of things is simply moving on to something different, bigger and hopefully better. Whether that last one comes to fruition or not is an open question, of course, but one that I am optimistic about. And for all the criticisms, issues and cul-de-sacs that we've talked about in this book, I'm also positive about the future of research in the area. I have a fundamental belief that, when it comes to the scientific understanding of how digital technology shapes our lives, regardless of how the studies, debates, arguments and news stories have turned out, everyone involved is trying to do the right thing: to figure out the right answers (or, perhaps more accurately, the least-wrong ones).

If we want to improve that process, if we want to move closer to the ultimate goal of teasing apart the good effects from the bad, we need to start making small changes. The science of screens, the public debates we have about them, the conversations we have with each other – they could all benefit from a refocus away from the persistent cycle of fearmongering and towards a more nuanced way of thinking about the little impacts, both positive and negative, on our lives. And of course, technology companies have a lot to do in this regard. We need to push them towards more ethical and responsible modes of development that place user wellbeing at their core. It's easy for them to ignore this, though, if the rest of us remain stuck in the same old arguments. If we want to change that story, the first steps start with the way we view our own relationships with screens – with embracing the idea that screens are not our enemy, not a dangerous master controlling our destinies, but a tool, useful for all sorts of things. But if you don't quite know how to use them properly, well, watch your fingers.

So don't let anyone ever tell you that you don't have a choice, that you can't change your approach to screens or your relationship with them. They are here to work for you, to make your life easier, more convenient, more enriched. Whether we want to admit it or not, digital technologies are not going away – they are a pervasive part of our lives now. But they are also a vital part. In accepting this, we begin to see the true opportunities, and risks, which they can afford. How they allow us to share precious moments of connection with those close to us and those far away. How they reveal and amplify divisions and inequalities. How they lend us a voice, let us speak truth to those who hold power and who, in times past, were never within earshot. How they act as a looking glass through which the best of us, and the worst of us, can be revealed.

In the end, the story of how digital technologies impact our lives was never so much about the machines themselves as about the complex web of human relationships they allow us to weave together. The science of screens is really the science of us – how we think, feel, communicate and interact with one another. If we want to make a positive difference to our relationship with screens, that revolution must come from within ourselves.

Coda

One of my favourite cities in the world is San Francisco. It's a beautiful place in its own right, but it holds special personal memories for me. The first time I went was the last time I ever got to go on holiday with my dad. We were visiting family out there, and I'd never been so far away from home. It felt as though every sight, sound and experience left an indelible print on my mind, not least because they would form some of the final happy, normal memories I have of spending time with him before he died. As time has passed, I've found myself returning there, once every decade or so, for conferences, research trips and the like. Whenever I do go, whether it's deliberate or not, I find myself retracing the steps of that first holiday, of those old memories and more innocent times. And in doing so I often end up being inexorably drawn towards 'Ripley's Believe It Or Not!' museum, a quirky collection of pop-culture memorabilia, artwork and interactive exhibits just off the Embarcadero, near Pier 45. Not far into the museum is a waxwork figure of a gurning man, J. T. Saylors, who was part of Ripley's shows in the 1930s and who was able to contort his face such that he could completely cover his nose with his bottom lip. The model of Saylors ushers you towards a large, semi-secluded mirror where you can try gurning, rolling your tongue or making other silly faces, safe in the knowledge that you can stop if you see someone coming up behind you. As you get towards the end of the exhibition, the trick is revealed, though: the mirror is actually two-way, displaying that private minute of silliness for all to see. I remember getting caught unawares by that mirror back when I was an awkward kid on the cusp of my teenage years, and the fleeting burn of embarrassment I felt as the true nature of the exhibit became apparent. My dad, wise to the ruse, chuckled and reassured me that it was just a passing thing, nothing to bother about. I watched as other hapless souls gurned away, just a few feet away, completely oblivious to my existence. The embarrassment ebbed and I grinned back at them – not because I was taking any pleasure in the igno-miny that was to come for them, but more in the realisation that we were, ultimately, all in this together. Every time I've been back to Ripley's museum since I've pulled a face in the mirror, just in case there was someone on the other side who needed that moment.

In one sense, the phone in your pocket is a two-way mirror. We can use it as a window on to the entirety of human knowledge, a means to understand, interact with and talk to the world; at the same time, the way we do so is often a reflection of our hopes, fears, strengths or weaknesses – of who we really are. At times, digital technologies can snare us unwittingly, when we're at our most vulnerable. And yet they can also bring us together, allow us to connect with other people and have an impact on someone's life, sometimes in ways we won't ever realise. My intention throughout this book has never been to say that there's nothing to worry or be vigilant about when it comes to our screen-based lives. That would be simplistic and wrong. What I do hope you've taken from it, though, is that we're now at a point where we need to break out of what Amy Orben calls the 'Sisyphean cycle of technology panics'. Just as the mythological king of Corinth was condemned for ever to push a boulder up a hill, only for it to be returned to the bottom every time he reached the top, so too we have found ourselves in a seemingly endless cycle of trying to understand and overcome fears about digital technologies, only for the panic to start afresh when the next new thing comes along. And if we want to break out of that pattern – if we really want to think differently about the relationship we have with our screens – here are a few steps I think we need to take.

1: We need to stop talking about screen time

Screen time is a dead-end concept – not just in terms of the way we talk about our digital technology use, but in terms of how we research it as well. If we want to improve the way we scientifically study digital technology, one of the first things we can do is move beyond attempts to encapsulate our behaviour online and on screens through a single, meaningless number. At the very least, we must demand objective measures of use. Simply asking people how long they think they've been on their phones, or Facebook, or Call of Duty, isn't good enough any more, and we already have the tools to do better. But in our own everyday conversations about screens, too, we need to start thinking in terms beyond the simple amount of time we spend using them. How much we use them isn't as helpful as considering both the content we consume and the context in which they play a part in our lives. It's in answering those questions that we'll be able to better understand where we're getting benefits, and where there are things which we would like to change.

2: We need to reframe our thinking in terms of screen habits

Considering our digital technology use in terms of questions around screen time invariably leads us to thinking about the issue through an addiction-like lens, whether we explicitly intend to or not. When we ask questions like 'How much screen time is too much?', not only do we end up viewing it in maladaptive terms, but the only solutions we're left with focus on abstinence, which is neither helpful nor practical. Instead, we need to recalibrate our approach to ask more nuanced questions around the habits we develop in using digital technologies. What does the landscape of our digital technology use look like? What are we actually *doing* when we use our screens? How are we using them? When? Where? With who? Are we using them intentionally, and are we getting something that we want out of the experience? Or have we dropped into less positive, perhaps more mindless habits? Reshaping our thinking in this way allows us to consider potential solutions beyond simple detox approaches and can empower us to make small changes, here and there, that can build up into meaningful improvements in our relationship with screens.

3: We need to interrogate and reflect on our screen habits, and we should do this often

Asking those sorts of questions about how we interact with digital technology won't result in meaningful change if we do it as a one-off exercise. Instead, we need to be more continually reflective of the role that it is taking in our day-to-day lives. This is probably the hardest thing to do, because it's very easy to fall into unhelpful habits without realising it. So it's a good idea to check in from time to time and talk with each other about how our tech use might be impacting our other relationships, whether for good or ill. Communication is key here: by reflecting, in small ways, on our own screen habits, as well as those of the people around us, we can start to get a better understanding of why we use screens in the way that we do. As we've come to see, framing those conversations in terms of understanding each other's needs and wants can lead to more positive outcomes than hard-and-fast rules. If we get better at figuring out why we have to play one more game, say, or why we have the urge to reply to that message right now this second, we can uncover deeper issues that might be at work. In that sense, what we first see as problematic screen use might instead come to be perceived as a marker for something else that we want to change in our lives. In the same way, we might come to an understanding of how those connections we're making through our digital devices are actually not the problem we first thought they were, and we can stop worrying about them. Regardless of whether the habits that we identify are ultimately good or bad, creating an environment in which we feel more comfortable sharing our experiences of digital technology is important if our goal is to maximise the benefits and reduce the drawbacks.

4: We need to build up a repertoire of strategies to tweak the habits that aren't working for us

If we do these things, it's inevitable that we will find elements of our digital diet that we're not happy with. Remember, this is a positive: identifying those issues is the first step in being able to do something about them. Once we've spotted our bad habits, we need to start experimenting with tweaks and adjustments to prevent them from turning into more serious problems. There's no foolproof scientific advice I can give you here, I'm afraid. But this doesn't mean that it's not worth taking the time, whenever we get the chance in an idle moment, to investigate potential strategies which are available. Part of this involves developing a deeper understanding of how the digital technologies that we use actually work, but also what kind of nudges might help us in that process of reflection. For example, even though there's scant research evidence to suggest that Night Shift mode on smartphones works, I still use it from time to time. Not because there's a vague possibility it might affect my melatonin production; I just prefer the warmer glow of a yellow screen at night, and having the conscious experience of seeing a shift in the colour tone of whatever it is that I'm doing helps to remind me that I will be wanting to go to sleep soon. So, experiment: whether that's with changing the way notifications work on your phone, or figuring out the parental controls on a games console, or curating your follower feed on whatever social media you use, making little adjustments, little choices over time can lead to bigger long-term changes than monumental, abrupt switches. It's always useful to have that knowledge in your back pocket, ready if, or when, you might need it somewhere down the line.

5: We need to be more critical – not just of our own tech use, but of what we're *told* about our tech use

It's important to understand that the impact digital technology has on us isn't just a product of how we use it, but comes in part as a result of the effects that we *assume* it has on us. This means that the broader narrative around screens that we see play out in the media has the potential to colour our interactions; and because that narrative, more often than not, is skewed towards the darker, scarier side of the story, we need to remain vigilant. News headlines tend to be geared towards sensationalism and hype, but to be fair to journalists, when it comes to science stories that over-exaggeration is just as likely to come from scientists, or their PR teams, as it is from the news desk. This means that we need to maintain a healthy level of critical thinking and scepticism when we read news reports about how screens can affect us. I'm not saying that you shouldn't believe anything you read in the news. Rather, I'm saying that it's important to ask reasonable questions, and follow the evidence, whenever you see a story come along about how a new study has shown a link between social media and mental health, or sleep, or video games and aggressive behaviours, or whatever. Don't just take the simple headline claim as a truism; instead, consider what new information we can glean over and above what previous research has already shown us, and in the likely context of that research being set within an area full of conflicting findings.

If you have the access and inclination, take a look at the study itself, if that's what is being reported. Do the claims match the findings reported? Do the findings still hold up in terms of the research methods used? What further information do we need in order to come to firmer conclusions? Does it make *sense*? And what do other scientists think about it?

There is, of course, a danger that in asking these questions we run the risk of falling into counterproductive contrarianism. As much as we want to avoid the trap of taking everything at face value, we also don't want to become immediately dismissive when new science comes along that aims to enrich our understanding of our screen-based lives. So the goal here is not to disregard those headlines out of hand – whether or not they are positive or negative – and neither is it to encourage a sort of pseudoscientific vigilantism. Asking reasonable and informed questions means doing more than a quick Google search to look for any old offcut of an argument to use as a counterpoint. Evidence-based reasoning is an intensive, slow process, and it often throws up as many questions and conundrums as it does answers. Rather than take a knee-jerk antagonistic approach to sensationalism about screens, then, we need to approach it with a sense of cautious curiosity. If you find yourself questioning a new study about digital technology that doesn't fit with your world view, then of course investigate, dig deeper – but do so constructively, with an open mind, and with the aim of understanding. In the same way, it is just as important to be critical of, and reflective about, stories and studies that *do* fit with your world view. I hope it's obvious to say that this goes for everything I've written over the course of this book, too.

Acknowledgements

This book has been a significant labour of love over the past few years, and there are a number of people who have helped me work through ideas, sanity-checked my writing, and generally been a brilliant support network throughout the writing process. In no particular order, my thanks go to: Scott Jones, Will Storr, Doug Parry, Chris Chambers, Linda Kaye, David Ellis, Tash Clarke, Kate Muir, Mirena Dimolareva, Naomi Heffer, Alex and Debbie Chong, Chris and Hayley Ware, Adam Smith, Lauren D'Rozario, Suzi Gage, Jermaine Ravalier, Dawn Albertson, Adam Rutherford and Kate Bevan. I am particularly indebted to Claire Weymouth and the team at UHBW for keeping my guts in check while I've been writing.

Thanks again go to my friend Tom Chivers for being a much-needed source of literary emotional support. For the second time, we've both ended up writing a book at the same time as each other, and I'm glad that we've been able to enjoy the journey together again.

Speaking of emotional support, special thanks go to my family on that front – to Mum, Tony and Christine, Maggie and Keith, Martin, Stuart, Meg, Annabelle and Clara. Thank you for all your continued guidance, wisdom and chats over many cups of tea. And to my constant canine companion, Willow, thank you for keeping me company through the entire process. Literally. I'm writing this now, your head is on my lap, and you're snoring away. Don't ever change.

I still consider myself incredibly lucky that Will Francis at Janklow & Nesbit saw fit to take me on board all those years ago. As ever, Will has been a font of all knowledge and an enduring source of support over the course of writing this book. I will always be thankful for his counsel and friendship.

My heartfelt thanks go to my editor, Holly Harley, as well as the wider editorial team at Piatkus and Little, Brown. Holly has been the best editor I could ask to work with, and this book is immeasurably better for her expert input and guidance. I can only apologise for all the WWE gifs I sent over direct messages during the many wobbles of doubt I had while writing.

It is a simple matter of fact that I would not have been able to write this book had it not been for the unwavering support and love of my wife, Frances. It goes without saying that I am eternally grateful for, and constantly in awe of, everything you do. This is all for you, and Matilda, and Patrick. My wonderful little family. I love you all.

About the author

Pete Etchells is a psychologist and science writer. He is Professor of Psychology and Science Communication at Bath Spa University, UK. This is his second book.

References

Chapter 1

Bigalke J. A., Greenlund I. M., Nicevski J. R., Carter J. R. 'Effect of evening blue light blocking glasses on subjective and objective sleep in healthy adults: A randomized control trial'. *Sleep Health*. 2021 Aug. 1;7(4):485–90.

Blum-Ross A., Livingstone S. 'The trouble with "screen time" rules'. In: *Digital Parenting: The Challenges for Families in the Digital Age*. Nordicom, University of Gothenburg, 2018.

Boyle M. 'Technology destroys people and places: I'm rejecting it'. The *Guardian*, 19 Dec. 2016. Retrieved 10 February 2023 from https://www.theguardian.com/commentisfree/2016/dec/19/life-without-technology-rejecting-technology

Haidt J., Lukianoff G. *The Coddling of the American Mind: How Good Intentions and Bad Ideas Are Setting Up a Generation for Failure*. Penguin UK, 2018.

Lee C., Kim H., Hong A. 'Ex-post evaluation of illegalizing juvenile online game after midnight: A case of shutdown policy in South Korea'. *Telematics and Informatics*. 2017 Dec. 1;34(8):1597–606.

Neuman S. B. 'The displacement effect: Assessing the relation between television viewing and reading performance'. *Reading Research Quarterly.* 1988 Oct. 1:414–40.

Orben A., Przybylski A. K. 'The association between adolescent well-being and digital technology use'. *Nature Human Behaviour.* 2019 Feb.;3(2):173–82.

Przybylski A. K. 'Digital screen time and pediatric sleep: Evidence from a preregistered cohort study'. *The Journal of Pediatrics.* 2019 Feb. 1;205:218–23.

Przybylski A. K., Orben A., Weinstein N. 'How much is too much? Examining the relationship between digital screen engagement and psychosocial functioning in a confirmatory cohort study'. *Journal of the American Academy of Child & Adolescent Psychiatry.* 2020 Sept. 1;59(9):1080–8.

Przybylski A. K., Weinstein N. 'A large-scale test of the goldilocks hypothesis: Quantifying the relations between digital-screen use and the mental well-being of adolescents'. *Psychological Science.* 2017 Feb.;28(2):204–15.

Radtke T., Apel T., Schenkel K., Keller J., von Lindern E. 'Digital detox: An effective solution in the smartphone era? A systematic literature review'. *Mobile Media & Communication.* 2022 May;10(2):190–215.

Reinecke L, Trepte S. 'Authenticity and well-being on social network sites: A two-wave longitudinal study on the effects of online authenticity and the positivity bias in SNS communication'. *Computers in Human Behavior.* 2014 Jan. 1;30:95–102.

Shaw H., Ellis D., Geyer K., Davidson B., Ziegler F., Smith A. 'Quantifying smartphone "use": Choice of measurement impacts relationships between "usage" and health'. *Technology, Mind, and Behavior.* 2020 Nov. 30;1(2).

Strouse G. A., Troseth G. L., O'Doherty K. D., Saylor M. M. 'Co-viewing supports toddlers' word learning from contingent and noncontingent video'. *Journal of Experimental Child Psychology.* 2018 Feb. 1;166:310–26.

Thomée S. 'Mobile phone use and mental health. A review of the research that takes a psychological perspective on exposure'. *International Journal of Environmental Research and Public Health.* 2018 Dec.;15(12):2692.

Torjesen I. 'Parents should decide when children's screen time is too high, says first UK guidance'. *BMJ.* 2019 Jan. 4;360:l60.

Twenge J. M. *iGen: Why Today's Super-connected Kids Are Growing Up Less Rebellious, More Tolerant, Less Happy – and Completely Unprepared for Adulthood – and What That Means for the Rest of Us.* Simon and Schuster, 2017.

Twenge J. M., Joiner T. E., Rogers M. L., Martin G. N. 'Increases in depressive symptoms, suicide-related outcomes, and suicide rates among US adolescents after 2010 and links to increased new media screen time'. *Clinical Psychological Science.* 2018 Jan.;6(1):3–17.

Van der Lely S., Frey S., Garbazza C., Wirz-Justice A., Jenni O. G., Steiner R., Wolf S., Cajochen C., Bromundt V., Schmidt C. 'Blue blocker glasses as a countermeasure for alerting effects of evening light-emitting diode screen exposure in male teenagers'. *Journal of Adolescent Health.* 2015 Jan. 1;56(1):113–19.

Vanman E. J., Baker R., Tobin S. J. 'The burden of online friends: The effects of giving up Facebook on stress and well-being'. *The Journal of Social Psychology.* 2018 Jul. 4;158(4):496–508.

Viner R., Davie M. 'The health impacts of screen time: A guide for clinicians and parents'. 2019. Retrieved 3

February 2023 from https://www.rcpch.ac.uk/resources/
health-impacts-screen-time-guide-clinicians-parents

Chapter 2

Bayer J. B., Triệu P., Ellison N. B. 'Social media elements,
ecologies, and effects'. *Annual Review of Psychology.*
2020 Jan. 4;71:471–97.

BBC Reality Check Team. Heatwave: 'Is there more crime
in hot weather?' BBC News, 19 July 2018. Retrieved
25 March 2022 from https://www.bbc.co.uk/news/
uk-44821796

Boer M., Stevens G. W., Finkenauer C., de Looze M. E.,
van den Eijnden R. J. 'Social media use intensity,
social media use problems, and mental health among
adolescents: Investigating directionality and mediating
processes'. *Computers in Human Behavior.* 2021 Mar.
1;116:106645.

Cavanagh S. R. 'No, smartphones have not destroyed a
generation', 6 August 2017. Retrieved 25 March 2022
from https://sarosecav.medium.com/no-smartphones-are-
not-destroying-a-generation-433cbb5e339

Corredor-Waldron A., Currie J. 'To what extent are trends
in teen mental health driven by changes in reporting?
The example of suicide-related hospital visits'. National
Bureau of Economic Research Working Paper 31493.
Retrieved 10 August 2023 from https://www.nber.org/
papers/w31493

Dolev-Cohen M., Barak A. 'Adolescents' use of Instant
Messaging as a means of emotional relief'. *Computers in
Human Behavior.* 2013 Jan. 1;29(1):58–63.

Etchells P. J. 'When it comes to claims about screen time

we need more sense and less hype'. The *Guardian*, 14 November 2017. Retrieved 25 March 2022 from https://www.theguardian.com/science/head-quarters/2017/nov/14/when-it-comes-to-claims-about-screen-time-we-need-more-sense-and-less-hype

Ferguson C. J., Kaye L. K., Branley-Bell D., Markey P., Ivory J. D., Klisanin D., Elson M., Smyth M., Hogg J. L., McDonnell D., Nichols D. 'Like this meta-analysis: Screen media and mental health'. *Professional Psychology: Research and Practice*. 2022 Apr.;53(2):205.

Glaeser E. L. 'Researcher incentives and empirical methods'. *NBER Technical Working Paper Series*. 2006. Retrieved 25 March 2022 from https://doi.org/10.3386/t0329

Gonzalez R. 'Why Apple can't tackle digital wellness in a vacuum'. *WIRED*, 5 June 2018. Retrieved 25 March 2022 from https://www.wired.com/story/apple-screen-time/

Gross E. F. 'Logging on, bouncing back: An experimental investigation of online communication following social exclusion'. *Developmental Psychology*. 2009 Nov.;45(6):1787.

Haidt J. 'The dangerous experiment on teen girls'. *The Atlantic*, 21 November 2021. Retrieved 24 March 2022 from https://www.theatlantic.com/ideas/archive/2021/11/facebooks-dangerous-experiment-teen-girls/620767/

House of Commons Science and Technology Committee. 'Impact of social media and screen-use on young people's health: Fourteenth report of session 2017–19', 2019. Retrieved 25 March 2022 from https://publications.parliament.uk/pa/cm201719/cmselect/cmsctech/822/822.pdf

Ioannidis J. P. 'Why most published research findings are false'. *PLoS Medicine*. 2005 Aug. 30;2(8):e124.

Jensen M., George M. J., Russell M. R., Odgers C. L. 'Young adolescents' digital technology use and mental health symptoms: Little evidence of longitudinal or daily linkages'. *Clinical Psychological Science*. 2019 Nov.;7(6):1416–33.

Kelley T. L. *Interpretation of Educational Measurements.* World Book Company, 1927. Retrieved 6 February 2023 from http://cda.psych.uiuc.edu/kelley_books/kelley_interpretation_1927.pdf.

Kreski N., Platt J., Rutherford C., Olfson M., Odgers C., Schulenberg J., Keyes K. M. 'Social media use and depressive symptoms among United States adolescents'. *Journal of Adolescent Health*. 2021 Mar. 1;68(3):572–9.

Kross E., Verduyn P., Sheppes G., Costello C. K., Jonides J., Ybarra O. 'Social media and well-being: Pitfalls, progress, and next steps'. *Trends in Cognitive Sciences*. 2021 Jan. 1;25(1):55–66.

Magnusson K. 'Interpreting correlations: An interactive visualisation'. 2021. Retrieved 25 March 2022 from https://rpsychologist.com/correlation/

Meier A., Reinecke L. 'Computer-mediated communication, social media, and mental health: A conceptual and empirical meta-review'. *Communication Research*. 2021 Dec.;48(8):1182–209.

Odgers C. L., Jensen M. R. 'Adolescent development and growing divides in the digital age'. *Dialogues in Clinical Neuroscience*. 2020 Jun. 1;22(2):143–9.

Odgers C. L., Jensen M. R. 'Annual research review: Adolescent mental health in the digital age: Facts, fears, and future directions'. *Journal of Child Psychology and Psychiatry*. 2020 Mar.;61(3):336–48.

Odgers C. L., Schueller S. M., Ito M. 'Screen time, social media use, and adolescent development'. *Annual Review of Developmental Psychology*. 2020 Dec. 15;2:485–502.

Ophir Y., Lipshits-Braziler Y., Rosenberg H. 'New-media screen time is not (necessarily) linked to depression: Comments on Twenge, Joiner, Rogers, and Martin (2018)'. *Clinical Psychological Science.* 2020 Mar.;8(2):374–8.

Orben A. 'Social media and suicide: A critical appraisal', 14 November 2017. Retrieved 25 March 2022 from https://medium.com/@OrbenAmy/social-media-and-suicide-a-critical-appraisal-f95e0bbd4660

Orben A. 'Teenagers, screens and social media: A narrative review of reviews and key studies'. *Social Psychiatry and Psychiatric Epidemiology.* 2020 Apr.;55(4):407–14.

Orben A., Przybylski A. K. 'Screens, teens, and psychological well-being: Evidence from three time-use-diary studies'. *Psychological Science.* 2019 May;30(5):682–96.

Orben A., Przybylski A. K. 'The association between adolescent well-being and digital technology use'. *Nature Human Behaviour.* 2019 Feb.;3(2):173–82.

Orben A., Przybylski A. K. 'Reply to: Underestimating digital media harm'. *Nature Human Behaviour.* 2020 Apr.;4(4):349–51.

Orben A., Dienlin T., Przybylski A. K. 'Social media's enduring effect on adolescent life satisfaction'. *Proceedings of the National Academy of Sciences.* 2019 May 21;116(21):10226–8.

Orben A., Weinstein N., Przybylski A. K. 'Only holistic and iterative change will fix digital technology research'. *Psychological Inquiry.* 2020 Jul. 2;31(3):235–41.

Peters J. 'When ice cream sales rise, so do homicides. Coincidence, or will your next cone murder you? *Slate,* 9 July 2013. Retrieved 25 March 2022 from https://slate.com/news-and-politics/2013/07/warm-weather-homicide-rates-when-ice-cream-sales-rise-homicides-rise-coincidence.html

Przybylski A. K., Weinstein N. 'A large-scale test of the goldilocks hypothesis: Quantifying the relations between digital-screen use and the mental well-being of adolescents'. *Psychological Science*. 2017 Feb.;28(2):204–15.

Rawlinson K. 'How TikTok's algorithm "exploits the vulnerability" of children'. The *Guardian*, 4 April 2023. Retrieved 16 May 2023 from https://www.theguardian.com/technology/2023/apr/04/how-tiktoks-algorithm-exploits-the-vulnerability-of-children

Rosenstein B., Sheehan A. 'Open letter from JANA partners and CalSTRS to Apple Inc', 2018. Retrieved 25 March 2022 from https://thinkdifferentlyaboutkids.com/letter/

Simmons J. P., Nelson L. D., Simonsohn U. 'False-positive psychology: Undisclosed flexibility in data collection and analysis allows presenting anything as significant'. *Psychological Science*. 2011;22(11):1359–66.

Simonsohn U., Simmons J. P., Nelson L. D. 'Specification curve analysis'. *Nature Human Behaviour*. 2020 Nov.;4(11):1208–14.

Thorndike E. L. *An Introduction to the Theory of Mental and Social Measurements*. Teacher's College, Columbia University, 1913. Retrieved 6 February 2023 from https://upload.wikimedia.org/wikipedia/commons/0/00/An_introduction_to_the_theory_of_mental_and_social_measurements_%28IA_theoryofmentalso00thor%29.pdf

Twenge J. 'With teen mental health deteriorating over five years, there's a likely culprit'. *The Conversation*, 14 November 2017. Retrieved 25 March 2022 from https://theconversation.com/with-teen-mental-health-deteriorating-over-five-years-theres-a-likely-culprit-86996

Twenge J. M. *iGen: Why Today's Super-connected Kids*

Are Growing Up Less Rebellious, More Tolerant, Less Happy – and Completely Unprepared for Adulthood – and What That Means for the Rest of Us. Simon and Schuster, 2017.

Twenge J. 'Have smartphones destroyed a generation?'. *The Atlantic*, September 2017. Retrieved 25 March 2022 from https://www.theatlantic.com/magazine/archive/2017/09/has-the-smartphone-destroyed-a-generation/534198/

Twenge J. M., Blake A. B., Haidt J., Campbell W. K. 'Commentary: Screens, teens, and psychological well-being: Evidence from three time-use-diary studies'. *Frontiers in Psychology.* 2020 Feb. 18;11:181.

Twenge J. M., Haidt J., Joiner T. E., Campbell W. K. 'Underestimating digital media harm'. *Nature Human Behaviour.* 2020 Apr.;4(4):346–8.

Twenge J. M., Haidt J., Lozano J., Cummins K. M. 'Specification curve analysis shows that social media use is linked to poor mental health, especially among girls'. *Acta Psychologica.* 2022 Apr. 1;224:103512.

Twenge J. M., Joiner T. E., Rogers M. L., Martin G. N. 'Increases in depressive symptoms, suicide-related outcomes, and suicide rates among US adolescents after 2010 and links to increased new media screen time'. *Clinical Psychological Science.* 2018 Jan.;6(1):3–17.

Twenge J., Haidt J., Cummins K. 'Opinion: Social media is riskier for kids than "screen time"'. The *Washington Post*, 16 February 2022. Retrieved 24 March 2022 from https://www.washingtonpost.com/opinions/2022/02/16/social-media-is-riskier-kids-than-screen-time/

Vuorre M., Orben A., Przybylski A. K. 'There is no evidence that associations between adolescents' digital technology engagement and mental health problems have increased'. *Clinical Psychological Science.* 2021 Sept.;9(5):823–35.

Whitelocks, S. 'Computer games leave children with "dementia", warns top neurologist'. The *Daily Mail*, 14 October 2011. Retrieved 25 March 2022 from https://www.dailymail.co.uk/health/article-2049040/Computer-games-leave-children-dementia-warns-neurologist.html

Williams K.D., Jarvis B. 'Cyberball: A program for use in research on interpersonal ostracism and acceptance'. *Behavior Research Methods*. 2006 Feb.;38:174–80.

Chapter 3

Au J., Gibson B. C., Bunarjo K., Buschkuehl M., Jaeggi S. M. 'Quantifying the difference between active and passive control groups in cognitive interventions using two meta-analytical approaches'. *Journal of Cognitive Enhancement*. 2020 Jun.;4(2):192–210.

Bach R. L., Wenz A. 'Studying health-related internet and mobile device use using web logs and smartphone records'. *PloS One*. 2020 Jun. 12;15(6):e0234663.

Boyd D., Hargittai E. 'Connected and concerned: Variation in parents' online safety concerns'. *Policy & Internet*. 2013 Sept.;5(3):245–69.

Buckels E. E., Trapnell P. D., Paulhus D. L. 'Trolls just want to have fun'. *Personality and Individual Differences*. 2014 Sept. 1;67:97–102.

Chen L. L., Magdy W., Wolters M. K. 'The effect of user psychology on the content of social media posts: Originality and transitions matter'. *Frontiers in Psychology*. 2020 Apr. 21;11:526.

Daine K., Hawton K., Singaravelu V., Stewart A., Simkin S., Montgomery P. 'The power of the web: A systematic review of studies of the influence of the internet on self-harm and suicide in young people'. *PloS One*. 2013 Oct. 30;8(10):e77555.

Dearden, C., Becker, S. *Young Carers in the UK: The 2004 Report*. Carers UK, 2004. Retrieved 16 May 2022 from https://www.lboro.ac.uk/microsites/socialsciences/ycrg/youngCarersDownload/YCReport2004%5b1%5d.pdf

El Asam A., Katz A. 'Vulnerable young people and their experience of online risks'. *Human–Computer Interaction*. 2018 Jul. 4;33(4):281–304.

George M. J., Odgers C. L. 'Seven fears and the science of how mobile technologies may be influencing adolescents in the digital age'. *Perspectives on Psychological Science*. 2015 Nov.;10(6):832–51.

Goldberg S. B., Lam S. U., Simonsson O., Torous J., Sun S. 'Mobile phone-based interventions for mental health: A systematic meta-review of 14 meta-analyses of randomized controlled trials'. *PLOS Digital Health*. 2022 Jan. 18;1(1):e0000002.

Hollis C., Falconer C. J., Martin J. L., Whittington C., Stockton S., Glazebrook C., Davies E. B. 'Annual research review: Digital health interventions for children and young people with mental health problems – a systematic and meta-review'. *Journal of Child Psychology and Psychiatry*. 2017 Apr.;58(4):474–503.

Jensen M., George M. J., Russell M. R., Odgers C. L. 'Young adolescents' digital technology use and mental health symptoms: Little evidence of longitudinal or daily linkages'. *Clinical Psychological Science*. 2019 Nov.;7(6):1416–33.

Jonsson U., Alaie I., Parling T., Arnberg F. K. 'Reporting of harms in randomized controlled trials of psychological interventions for mental and behavioral disorders: A review of current practice'. *Contemporary Clinical Trials*. 2014 May 1;38(1):1–8.

Kosinski M., Bachrach Y., Kohli P., Stillwell D., Graepel T. 'Manifestations of user personality in website choice and behaviour on online social networks'. *Machine Learning*. 2014 Jun.;95(3):357–80.

Kowalski R. M., Giumetti G. W., Schroeder A. N., Lattanner M. R. 'Bullying in the digital age: A critical review and meta-analysis of cyberbullying research among youth'. *Psychological Bulletin*. 2014 Jul.;140(4):1073.

Mascheroni G., Ólafsson K. 'Net children go mobile: Risks and opportunities'. Repr., 2nd edn, Educatt, 2014. Retrieved 16 May 2022 from https://netchildrengomobile. eu/ncgm/wp–content/uploads/2013/07/ NCGM_FullReport_2.0.pdf

Modecki K. L., Minchin J., Harbaugh A. G., Guerra N. G., Runions K. C. 'Bullying prevalence across contexts: A meta-analysis measuring cyber and traditional bullying'. *Journal of Adolescent Health*. 2014 Nov. 1;55(5):602–11.

Mohr D. C., Zhang M., Schueller S. M. 'Personal sensing: Understanding mental health using ubiquitous sensors and machine learning'. *Annual Review of Clinical Psychology*. 2017 May 8;13:23–47.

Odgers C., Robb M. B. 'Tweens, teens, tech, and mental health: Coming of age in an increasingly digital, uncertain, and unequal world'. Common Sense Media, 2020.

Odgers C. 'Smartphones are bad for some teens, not all'. *Nature*. 2018 Feb. 21;554:432–4.

Odgers C. L, Jensen M. R. 'Adolescent development and growing divides in the digital age'. *Dialogues in Clinical Neuroscience*. 2020 Jun; 22(2):143–9.

Odgers C. L., Jensen M. R. 'Annual research review: Adolescent mental health in the digital age: Facts, fears, and future directions'. *Journal of Child Psychology and Psychiatry.* 2020 Mar.;61(3):336–48.

Odgers C. L., Schueller S. M., Ito M. 'Screen time, social media use, and adolescent development'. *Annual Review of Developmental Psychology.* 2020 Dec. 15;2:485–502.

Olweus D. 'Cyberbullying: An overrated phenomenon?'. *European Journal of Developmental Psychology.* 2012; 9(5):520–38.10.1080/17405629.2012.682358.

Orben A. 'Teenagers, screens and social media: A narrative review of reviews and key studies'. *Social Psychiatry and Psychiatric Epidemiology.* 2020 Apr.;55(4):407–14.

Pratap A., Neto E. C., Snyder P., Stepnowsky C., Elhadad N., Grant D., Mohebbi M. H., Mooney S., Suver C., Wilbanks J., Mangravite L. 'Indicators of retention in remote digital health studies: A cross-study evaluation of 100,000 participants'. *NPJ Digital Medicine.* 2020 Feb. 17;3(1):1-0.

Przybylski A. K., Bowes L. 'Cyberbullying and adolescent well-being in England: A population-based cross-sectional study'. *The Lancet Child & Adolescent Health.* 2017 Sept. 1;1(1):19–26.

Quercia D., Kosinski M., Stillwell D., Crowcroft J. 'Our twitter profiles, our selves: Predicting personality with twitter'. In *2011 IEEE Third International Conference on Privacy, Security, Risk and Trust and 2011 IEEE Third International Conference on Social Computing,* Oct. 9 (pp. 180–5).

Rideout V., Robb M. *The Common Sense Census: Media Use by Tweens and Teens.* Common Sense Media, 2019. Retrieved 16 May 2021 from https://www.commonsensemedia.org/sites/default/files/research/report/2019-census-8-to-18-full-report-updated.pdf

Sempik J., Ward H., Darker I. 'Emotional and behavioural

difficulties of children and young people at entry into care'. *Clinical Child Psychology and Psychiatry.* 2008 Apr.;13(2):221–33.

Vuorre M., Przybylski A. K. 'Estimating the association between Facebook adoption and well-being in 72 countries'. *Royal Society Open Science.* 2023 Aug. 9;10(8):221451.

Waasdorp T. E., Bradshaw C. P. 'The overlap between cyberbullying and traditional bullying'. *Journal of Adolescent Health.* 2015 May 1;56(5):483–8.

Yau J. C., Reich S. M. 'Are the qualities of adolescents' offline friendships present in digital interactions?'. *Adolescent Research Review.* 2018 Sept.;3(3):339–55.

Zhu C., Huang S., Evans R., Zhang W. 'Cyberbullying among adolescents and children: A comprehensive review of the global situation, risk factors, and preventive measures'. *Frontiers in Public Health.* 2021:167.

Chapter 4

Altman, D. G., Royston, P. 'The cost of dichotomising continuous variables'. *BMJ.* 2006 332(7549):1080.

Arendt J., Skene D. J. 'Melatonin as a chronobiotic'. *Sleep Medicine Reviews.* 2005 Feb. 1;9(1):25–39.

Bigalke J. A., Greenlund I. M., Nicevski J. R., Carter J. R. 'Effect of evening blue light blocking glasses on subjective and objective sleep in healthy adults: A randomized control trial'. *Sleep Health.* 2021 Aug. 1;7(4):485–90.

Blume C., Garbazza C., Spitschan M. 'Effects of light on human circadian rhythms, sleep and mood'. *Somnologie.* 2019 Sept.;23(3):147–56.

Boivin D. B., Duffy J. F., Kronauer R. E., Czeisler

C. A. 'Dose-response relationships for resetting of human circadian clock by light'. *Nature*. 1996 Feb.;379(6565):540–2.

Brainard G. C., Hanifin J. P., Greeson J. M., Byrne B., Glickman G., Gerner E., Rollag M. D. 'Action spectrum for melatonin regulation in humans: Evidence for a novel circadian photoreceptor'. *Journal of Neuroscience*. 2001 Aug. 15;21(16):6405–12.

Brunetti V. C., O'Loughlin E. K., O'Loughlin J., Constantin E., Pigeon É. 'Screen and nonscreen sedentary behavior and sleep in adolescents'. *Sleep Health*. 2016 Dec. 1;2(4):335–40.

Calamaro C. J., Mason T., Ratcliffe S. J. 'Adolescents living the 24/7 lifestyle: Effects of caffeine and technology on sleep duration and daytime functioning'. *Pediatrics*. 2009 Jun. 1;123(6):e1005–10.

Carskadon M. A. 'Sleep in adolescents: The perfect storm'. *Pediatric Clinics*. 2011 Jun. 1;58(3):637–47.

Cespedes E. M., Gillman M. W., Kleinman K., Rifas-Shiman S. L., Redline S., Taveras E. M. 'Television viewing, bedroom television, and sleep duration from infancy to mid-childhood'. *Pediatrics*. 2014 May 1;133(5): e1163–71.

Chang A. M., Aeschbach D., Duffy J. F., Czeisler C. A. 'Evening use of light-emitting eReaders negatively affects sleep, circadian timing, and next-morning alertness'. *Proceedings of the National Academy of Sciences*. 2015 Jan. 27;112(4):1232–7.

Chang A. M., Scheer F. A., Czeisler C. A. 'The human circadian system adapts to prior photic history'. *The Journal of Physiology*. 2011 Mar. 1;589(5):1095–102.

Continente X., Pérez A., Espelt A., López M. J. 'Media devices, family relationships and sleep patterns among adolescents in an urban area'. *Sleep Medicine*. 2017 Apr. 1;32:28–35.

Crowley S. J., Wolfson A. R., Tarokh L., Carskadon M. A. 'An update on adolescent sleep: New evidence informing the perfect storm model'. *Journal of Adolescence*. 2018 Aug. 1;67:55–65.

de Mairan J. J. 'Observation botanique'. *Histoire de l'Académie Royale des Sciences Paris*. 1729.

Descartes R. *Treatise on Man*. 1622.

Duraccio KM, Zaugg KK, Blackburn RC, Jensen CD. 'Does iPhone night shift mitigate negative effects of smartphone use on sleep outcomes in emerging adults?' *Sleep Health*. 2021 Aug 1;7(4):478-84.

Fuligni A. J., Bai S., Krull J. L., Gonzales N. A. 'Individual differences in optimum sleep for daily mood during adolescence'. *Journal of Clinical Child & Adolescent Psychology*. 2019 May 4;48(3):469–79.

Gillette M. U., McArthur A. J. 'Circadian actions of melatonin at the suprachiasmatic nucleus'. *Behavioural Brain Research*. 1995 Dec. 15;73(1–2):135–9.

Kay D. B., Karim H. T., Soehner A. M., Hasler B. P., Wilckens K. A., James J. A., Aizenstein H. J., Price J. C., Rosario B. L., Kupfer D. J., Germain A. 'Sleep–wake differences in relative regional cerebral metabolic rate for glucose among patients with insomnia compared with good sleepers'. *Sleep*. 2016 Oct. 1;39(10):1779–94.

Lewy A. J., Wehr T. A., Goodwin F. K., Newsome D. A., Markey S. P. 'Light suppresses melatonin secretion in humans'. *Science*. 1980 Dec. 12;210(4475):1267–9.

Lund L., Sølvhøj I. N., Danielsen D., Andersen S. 'Electronic media use and sleep in children and adolescents in western countries: A systematic review'. *BMC Public Health*. 2021 Dec.;21(1):1–4.

McClelland G. H., Lynch Jr J. G., Irwin J. R., Spiller S. A., Fitzsimons G. J. 'Median splits, Type II errors, and false–positive consumer psychology: Don't fight the power'. *Journal of Consumer Psychology*. 2015 Oct.;25(4):679–89.

McIntyre I. M., Norman T. R., Burrows G. D., Armstrong S. M. 'Quantal melatonin suppression by exposure to low intensity light in man'. *Life Sciences*. 1989 Jan. 1;45(4):327–32.

Moore R. Y., Eichler V. B. 'Loss of a circadian adrenal corticosterone rhythm following suprachiasmatic lesions in the rat'. *Brain Research*. 1972 Jul. 1;42(1):201–6.

Nagare R., Plitnick B., Figueiro M. G. 'Does the iPad Night Shift mode reduce melatonin suppression?'. *Lighting Research & Technology*. 2019 51(3), pp. 373–83.

Nowozin C., Wahnschaffe A., Rodenbeck A., de Zeeuw J., Hadel S., Kozakov R., Schopp H., Munch M., Kunz D. 'Applying melanopic lux to measure biological light effects on melatonin suppression and subjective sleepiness'. *Current Alzheimer Research*. 2017 Oct. 1;14(10):1042–52.

Orben A., Przybylski A. K. 'Teenage sleep and technology engagement across the week'. *PeerJ*. 2020 Jan. 28;8:e8427.

Powers P., Gavrilovic M., Santana J., Yi S., Spoor A., Campisi J. 'A preliminary study on the effect of mobile device backlight spectrum variation on the quality of sleep among undergraduate students'. *Bios*. 2022 Mar.;92(3):86–93.

Przybylski A. K. 'Digital screen time and pediatric sleep: Evidence from a preregistered cohort study'. *The Journal of Pediatrics*. 2019 Feb. 1;205:218–23.

Reed D. L., Sacco W. P. 'Measuring sleep efficiency: What should the denominator be?'. *Journal of Clinical Sleep Medicine*. 2016 Feb. 15;12(2):263–6.

Richter C. P. '"Dark-active" rat transformed into "light-active" rat by destruction of 24-hr clock: Function of 24-hr clock and synchronizers'. *Proceedings of the National Academy of Sciences.* 1978 Dec. 1;75(12):6276–80.

Richter C. P. *Biological Clocks in Medicine and Psychiatry.* C. C. Thomas, 1965.

Richter C. P. 'Biological clocks in medicine and psychiatry: Shock-phase hypothesis'. *Proceedings of the National Academy of Sciences of the United States of America.* 1960 Nov.;46(11):1506.

Rollag M. D., Panke E. S., Trakulrungsi W., Trakulrungsi C., Reiter R. J. 'Quantification of daily melatonin synthesis in the hamster pineal gland'. *Endocrinology.* 1980 Jan. 1;106(1):231–6.

Scott H., Biello S. M., Woods H. C. 'Identifying drivers for bedtime social media use despite sleep costs: The adolescent perspective'. *Sleep Health.* 2019 Dec. 1;5(6):539–45.

Scott H., Biello S. M., Woods H. C. 'Social media use and adolescent sleep patterns: Cross-sectional findings from the UK millennium cohort study'. *BMJ Open.* 2019 Sept. 1;9(9):e031161.

Short M. A., Weber N., Reynolds C., Coussens S., Carskadon M. A. 'Estimating adolescent sleep need using dose-response modeling'. *Sleep.* 2018 Apr.;41(4):zsy011.

Smith A. K., Conger J. R., Hedayati B., Kim J. J., Amoozadeh S., Mehta M. 'The effect of a screen protector on blue light intensity emitted from different hand-held devices'. *Middle East African Journal of Ophthalmology.* 2020 Jul.;27(3):177.

Stephan F. K., Zucker I. 'Circadian rhythms in drinking behavior and locomotor activity of rats are eliminated by hypothalamic lesions'. *Proceedings of the National Academy of Sciences.* 1972 Jun. 1;69(6):1583–6.

Taie S., Goldring R. *Characteristics of Public Elementary and Secondary School Teachers in the United States: Results from the 2015–16 National Teacher and Principal Survey.* First Look. NCES 2017–072. National Center for Education Statistics, 2017.

Tavernier R., Heissel J. A., Sladek M. R., Grant K. E., Adam E. K. 'Adolescents' technology and face-to-face time use predict objective sleep outcomes'. *Sleep Health.* 2017 Aug. 1;3(4):276–83.

Thapan K., Arendt J., Skene D. J. 'An action spectrum for melatonin suppression: Evidence for a novel non-rod, non-cone photoreceptor system in humans'. *The Journal of Physiology.* 2001 Aug.;535(1):261–7.

Van der Lely S., Frey S., Garbazza C., Wirz-Justice A., Jenni O. G., Steiner R., Wolf S., Cajochen C., Bromundt V., Schmidt C. 'Blue blocker glasses as a countermeasure for alerting effects of evening light-emitting diode screen exposure in male teenagers'. *Journal of Adolescent Health.* 2015 Jan. 1;56(1):113–19.

Wheaton A. G., Jones S. E., Cooper A. C., Croft J. B. 'Short sleep duration among middle school and high school students – United States, 2015'. *Morbidity and Mortality Weekly Report.* 2018 Jan. 26;67(3):85.

Yoshimura M., Kitazawa M., Maeda Y., Mimura M., Tsubota K., Kishimoto T. 'Smartphone viewing distance and sleep: An experimental study utilizing motion capture technology'. *Nature and Science of Sleep.* 2017;9:59.

Zeitzer J. M. 'Real life trumps laboratory in matters of public health'. *Proceedings of the National Academy of Sciences.* 2015 Mar. 31;112(13):E1513.

Chapter 5

Abramson J. 'Can Hillary Clinton convince in the age of the goldfish?'. The *Guardian*, 17 May 2016. Retrieved 14 September 2022 from https://www.theguardian.com/commentisfree/2016/may/17/hillary-clinton-policy-donald-trump-attention-span

Alzahabi R., Becker M. W. 'The association between media multitasking, task-switching, and dual-task performance'. *Journal of Experimental Psychology: Human Perception and Performance*. 2013 Oct.;39(5):1485.

Anderson B. 'There is no such thing as attention'. *Frontiers in Psychology*. 2011 Sept. 23;2:246.

Anderson B. 'Stop paying attention to "attention"'. *Wiley Interdisciplinary Reviews: Cognitive Science*. 2021 Aug. 25:e1574.

Baumgartner S. E., Wiradhany W. 'Not all media multitasking is the same: The frequency of media multitasking depends on cognitive and affective characteristics of media combinations'. *Psychology of Popular Media*. 2022 Jan.;11(1):1.

Behrens T. E., Muller T. H., Whittington J. C., Mark S., Baram A. B., Stachenfeld K. L., Kurth-Nelson Z. 'What is a cognitive map? Organizing knowledge for flexible behavior'. *Neuron*. 2018 Oct. 24;100(2):490–509.

Bisley J. W., Mirpour K. 'The neural instantiation of a priority map'. *Current Opinion in Psychology*. 2019 Oct. 1;29:108–12.

Blumberg Y. 'You can get more done by working less, studies show – here's how'. CNBC, 7 February 2018. Retrieved 14 September 2022 from https://www.cnbc.com/2018/02/07/science-shows-you-can-get-more-done-by-working-less.html

Brick C., Hood B., Ekroll V., De-Wit L. 'Illusory essences: A bias holding back theorizing in psychological science'. *Perspectives on Psychological Science*. 2022 Mar.;17(2):491–506.

Cave K. R., Bichot N. P. 'Visuospatial attention: Beyond a spotlight model'. *Psychonomic Bulletin & Review*. 1999 Jun.;6(2):204–23.

Cherry E. C. 'Some experiments on the recognition of speech, with one and with two ears'. *The Journal of the Acoustical Society of America*. 1953 Sept.;25(5):975–9.

Consumer Insights, Microsoft Canada. *Attention Spans*. 2015. Retrieved 14 September 2022 from https://dl.motamem. org/microsoft-attention-spans-research-report.pdf

Di Lollo V. 'Attention is a sterile concept; iterative reentry is a fertile substitute'. *Consciousness and Cognition*. 2018 Sept. 1;64:45–9.

Diamond S. *Content Marketing Strategies for Dummies*. John Wiley & Sons Inc., 2016.

Duffy B., Thain M. 'Do We Have Your Attention?' *How People Focus and Live in the Modern Information Environment*. The Policy Institute, February 2022. Retrieved 14 September 2022 from https://www.kcl. ac.uk/policy-institute/assets/how-people-focus-and-live-in-the-modern-information-environment.pdf

Duncan J. 'EPS Mid-Career Award 2004: Brain mechanisms of attention'. *The Quarterly Journal of Experimental Psychology*. 2006 Jan. 1;59(1):2–7.

Fernandez-Duque D., Johnson M. L. 'Attention metaphors: How metaphors guide the cognitive psychology of attention'. *Cognitive Science*. 1999 Jan.;23(1):83–116.

Fisher J. T., Hopp F. R., Weber R. 'Mapping attention across multiple media tasks'. Psyarxiv, 2022. doi:10.33767/ osf.io/txfka

Fuchs A. F. 'Saccadic and smooth pursuit eye movements in the monkey'. *The Journal of Physiology.* 1967 Aug.;191(3):609.

Hari J. *Stolen Focus.* Crown Publishing Group, 2022.

Hommel B., Chapman C. S., Cisek P., Neyedli H. F., Song J. H., Welsh T. N. 'No one knows what attention is'. *Attention, Perception, & Psychophysics.* 2019; 81(7): 2288–303.

Krauzlis R. J., Bollimunta A., Arcizet F., Wang L. 'Attention as an effect not a cause'. *Trends in Cognitive Sciences.* 2014 Sept. 1;18(9):457–64.

Krauzlis R. J., Wang L., Yu G., Katz L. N. 'What is attention?'. *Wiley Interdisciplinary Reviews: Cognitive Science.* 2021 Jun. 24:e1570.

Lui K. F., Wong A. C. 'Does media multitasking always hurt? A positive correlation between multitasking and multisensory integration'. *Psychonomic Bulletin & Review.* 2012 Aug.;19:647–53.

Maybin S. 'Busting the attention span myth'. BBC World Service, *More or Less*, 10 March 2017. Retrieved 14 September 2022 from https://www.bbc.co.uk/news/health-38896790

McSpadden K. 'You now have a shorter attention span than a goldfish'. *Time*, 14 May 2015. Retrieved 14 September 2022 from https://time.com/3858309/attention-spans-goldfish/

Neuharth-Keusch A. J. 'NBA will consider shortening games due to millennial attention spans'. USA Today, 13 January 2017. Retrieved 14 September 2022 from https://eu.usatoday.com/story/sports/nba/2017/01/13/nba-shortening-games-millennial-attention-spans/96535434/

Ophir E., Nass C., Wagner A. D. 'Cognitive control in media

multitaskers'. *Proceedings of the National Academy of Sciences*. 2009 Sept. 15;106(37):15583–7.

Orben A. 'The Sisyphean cycle of technology panics'. *Perspectives on Psychological Science*. 2020 Sept.;15(5):1143–57.

Parry D. A., Le Roux D. B. '"Cognitive control in media multitaskers" ten years on: A meta-analysis'. *Cyberpsychology: Journal of Psychosocial Research on Cyberspace*. 2021 Apr. 26;15(2).

Pea R., Nass C., Meheula L., Rance M., Kumar A., Bamford H., Nass M., Simha A., Stillerman B., Yang S., Zhou M. 'Media use, face-to-face communication, media multitasking, and social well-being among 8- to 12-year-old girls'. *Developmental Psychology*. 2012 Mar.;48(2):327.

Posner M. I., Snyder C. R., Davidson B. J. 'Attention and the detection of signals'. *Journal of Experimental Psychology: General*. 1980 Jun.;109(2):160.

Ritchie S. 'Johann Hari's stolen ideas'. UnHerd, 7 January 2022. Retrieved 14 September 2022 from https://unherd.com/2022/01/johann-haris-stolen-ideas/

Sanbonmatsu D. M., Strayer D. L., Medeiros-Ward N., Watson J. M. 'Who multi-tasks and why? Multi-tasking ability, perceived multi-tasking ability, impulsivity, and sensation seeking'. *PloS One*. 2013 Jan. 23;8(1):e54402.

Simons D. J., Chabris C. F. 'Gorillas in our midst: Sustained inattentional blindness for dynamic events'. *Perception*. 1999 Sept.;28(9):1059–74.

Sweet M. 'Have you been paying attention?'. UnHerd, 16 June 2020. Retrieved 14 September 2022 from https://unherd.com/2020/06/the-myth-that-screens-killed-concentration/

Thain M. 'There are challenges but also potential benefits

of digital distractions'. *The Conversation*, 18 February 2022. Retrieved 14 September 2022 from https://theconversation.com/there-are-challenges-but-also-potential-benefits-of-digital-distractions-177296

Thompson H., Sullivan B. *Getting Unstuck: Break Free of the Plateau Effect.* Plume, 2014.

Uncapher M. R., Wagner A. D. 'Minds and brains of media multitaskers: Current findings and future directions'. *Proceedings of the National Academy of Sciences.* 2018 Oct. 2;115(40):9889–96.

York A. 'Pop songs are getting shorter, but it's about a lot more than lower attention spans'. The *i*, 26 June 2022. Retrieved 14 September 2022 from https://inews.co.uk/opinion/pop-songs-getting-shorter-about-more-than-attention-spans-1704396

Zelinsky G. J., Bisley J. W. 'The what, where, and why of priority maps and their interactions with visual working memory'. *Annals of the New York Academy of Sciences.* 2015 Mar.;1339(1):154–64.

Chapter 6

Angwin J., Grassegger H. 'Facebook's secret censorship rules protect white men from hate speech but not black children'. ProPublica, 28 June 2017. Retrieved 14 September 2022 from https://www.propublica.org/article/facebook-hate-speech-censorship-internal-documents-algorithms

BBC. 'Nick Clegg gets bigger role at Facebook owner Meta'. BBC News, 16 February 2022. Retrieved 14 September 2022 from https://www.bbc.co.uk/news/uk-60410636

BBC. 'EA games: Loot boxes aren't gambling, they're just

like a Kinder Egg'. BBC News, 20 June 2019. Retrieved 14 September 2022 from https://www.bbc.co.uk/news/newsbeat-48701962

BBC. 'Star Wars Battlefront II game faces further backlash'. BBC News, 15 November 2017. Retrieved 14 September 2022 from https://www.bbc.co.uk/news/technology-41997252

Behavioural Insights Team. 'Unconscious bias and diversity training – what the evidence says'. Civil Service HR, 15 December 2020. Retrieved 14 September 2022 from https://www.gov.uk/government/publications/unconscious-bias-and-diversity-training-what-the-evidence-says

Bezrukova K., Spell C. S., Perry J. L., Jehn K. A. 'A meta-analytical integration of over 40 years of research on diversity training evaluation'. *Psychological Bulletin*. 2016 Nov.;142(11):1227.

Brockell G. 'Dear tech companies: I don't want to see pregnancy ads after my child was stillborn'. The *Washington Post*, 12 December 2018. Retrieved 14 September 2022 from https://www.washingtonpost.com/lifestyle/2018/12/12/dear-tech-companies-i-dont-want-see-pregnancy-ads-after-my-child-was-stillborn/

Chalk A. 'Electronic Arts gets $11M loot box fine overturned'. *PC Gamer*, 9 March 2022. Retrieved 14 September 2022 from https://www.pcgamer.com/ea-gets-dollar11m-loot-box-fine-overturned/

Chalk A. 'The Netherlands moves toward an outright loot box ban'. *PC Gamer*, 5 July 2022. Retrieved 14 September 2022 from https://www.pcgamer.com/the-netherlands-moves-toward-an-outright-loot-box-ban/

Coad A., Nightingale P., Stilgoe J., Vezzani A. 'The dark side of innovation'. *Industry and Innovation*. 2021 Jan. 2;28(1):102–12.

Commission for Racial Equality. *Medical School Admissions: Report of a Formal Investigation into St George's Hospital Medical School.* 1988

DCMS. 'Government response to the call for evidence on loot boxes in video games', 18 July 2022. Retrieved 14 September 2022 from https://www.gov.uk/government/consultations/loot-boxes-in-video-games-call-for-evidence/outcome/government-response-to-the-call-for-evidence-on-loot-boxes-in-video-games

Derboo S. 'Double Dragon 3 (Arcade)'. Hardcore Gamer 101, 4 November 2016. Retrieved 14 September 2022 from http://www.hardcoregaming101.net/double-dragon-3-arcade/

Digital, Culture, Media and Sport Committee. *Oral Evidence: Immersive and Addictive Technologies*, HC 1846, 19 June 2019. Retrieved 14 September 2022 from http://data.parliament.uk/writtenevidence/committeeevidence.svc/evidencedocument/digital-culture-media-and-sport-committee/immersive-and-addictive-technologies/oral/103191.html

Dobbin F., Kalev A. 'Why diversity programs fail'. *Harvard Business Review*, July 2016. Retrieved 14 September 2022 from https://hbr.org/2016/07/why-diversity-programs-fail

Drummond A., Sauer J. D., Ferguson C. J., Hall L. C. 'The relationship between problem gambling, excessive gaming, psychological distress and spending on loot boxes in Aotearoa New Zealand, Australia, and the United States – A cross-national survey'. *PLoS One.* 2020 Mar. 23;15(3):e0230378.

Dwoskin E., Tiku N., Kelly H. 'Facebook to start policing anti-Black hate speech more aggressively than anti-White comments, documents show'. The

Washington Post, 3 December 2020. Retrieved 14 September 2022 from https://www.washingtonpost.com/technology/2020/12/03/facebook-hate-speech/

Etchells P. J., Morgan A. L., Quintana D. S. 'Loot box spending is associated with problem gambling but not mental well-being'. *Royal Society Open Science*. 2022 Aug. 17;9(8):220111.

Fermilab. 'Inquiring Minds: Physics questions people ask Fermilab', 28 April 2014. Retrieved 4 August 2023 from https://www.fnal.gov/pub/science/inquiring/questions/atoms.html

Gordon K. 'Microtransactions are great for game companies, less so for players'. NPR, 11 March 2021. Retrieved 14 September 2022 from https://www.npr.org/2021/03/11/975765363/microtransactions-are-great-for-game-companies-less-fun-for-players

Hall L. C., Drummond A., Sauer J. D., Ferguson C. J. 'Effects of self-isolation and quarantine on loot box spending and excessive gaming – results of a natural experiment'. *PeerJ*. 2021 Feb. 3;9:e10705.

Hannah F., Andrews J. 'Loot boxes: I blew my university savings gaming on Fifa'. BBC 5 Live, 9 July 2020. Retrieved 14 September 2022 from https://www.bbc.co.uk/news/business-53337020

Lowry S., Macpherson G. 'A blot on the profession'. *British Medical Journal* (Clinical research edn). 1988 Mar. 3;296(6623):657.

Lynn T., Bancroft J. 'The use of algorithms in the content moderation process'. Centre for Data Ethics and Innovation blog, 5 August 2021. Retrieved 14 September 2022 from https://cdei.blog.gov.uk/2021/08/05/the-use-of-algorithms-in-the-content-moderation-process/

Paluck E. L., Green D. P. 'Prejudice reduction: What works? A review and assessment of research and practice'. *Annual Review of Psychology*. 2009 Jan. 1;60(1):339–67.

Parent Zone. 'The rip-off games', 29 August 2019. Retrieved 14 September 2022 from https://parentzone.org.uk/sites/default/files/2021-12/PZ_The_Rip-off_Games_2019.pdf

Perrotta M. 'Business models of video games: Past, present and future'. Medium, 6 April 2020. Retrieved 14 September 2022 from https://medium.com/@mjperrotta46/business-models-of-video-games-past-present-and-future-2b2aafe8ade1

Petrovskaya E., Zendle D. 'Predatory monetisation? A categorisation of unfair, misleading and aggressive monetisation techniques in digital games from the player perspective'. *Journal of Business Ethics*. 2021 Oct. 20:1–7.

Powell S. 'Sid Meier warns the games industry about monetisation'. BBC News, 28 February 2022. Retrieved 14 September 2022 from https://www.bbc.co.uk/news/entertainment-arts-60304123

SensorTower. 'PUBG Mobile shoots past $8 billion in lifetime revenue'. May 2022. Retrieved 14 September 2022 from https://sensortower.com/blog/pubg-mobile-8-billion-revenue

Smith E. 'Diablo Immortal builds could cost way more than $100,000'. PCGamesN, 30 June 2022. Retrieved 14 September 2022 from https://www.pcgamesn.com/diablo-immortal/builds-costs

Spicer S. G., Fullwood C., Close J., Nicklin L. L., Lloyd J., Lloyd H. 'Loot boxes and problem gambling: Investigating the "gateway hypothesis"'. *Addictive Behaviors*. 2022 Aug. 1;131:107327.

Stilgoe J., Owen R., Macnaghten P. 'Developing a framework for responsible innovation'. In *The Ethics of*

Nanotechnology, Geoengineering and Clean Energy. Routledge, 2020.

Tommy's. 'How to stop pregnancy ads following you after a loss', 14 January 2021. Retrieved 14 September 2022 from https://www.tommys.org/about-us/charity-news/how-stop-pregnancy-ads-following-you-after-loss

Woodhouse J. *Loot Boxes in Video Games.* House of Commons Library, 2021.

Zendle D., Cairns P. 'Video game loot boxes are linked to problem gambling: Results of a large-scale survey'. *PloS One.* 2018 Nov. 21;13(11):e0206767.

Zendle D., Cairns P., Barnett H., McCall C. 'Paying for loot boxes is linked to problem gambling, regardless of specific features like cash-out and pay-to-win'. *Computers in Human Behavior.* 2020 Jan. 1;102:181–91.

Zendle D., Meyer R., Over H. 'Adolescents and loot boxes: Links with problem gambling and motivations for purchase'. *Royal Society Open Science.* 2019 Jun. 19;6(6):190049.

Chapter 7

Aagaard J. 'Beyond the rhetoric of tech addiction: Why we should be discussing tech habits instead (and how)'. *Phenomenology and the Cognitive Sciences.* 2021 Jul.;20(3):559–72.

Armstrong L., Phillips J. G., Saling L. L. 'Potential determinants of heavier internet usage'. *International Journal of Human-Computer Studies.* 2000 Oct. 1;53(4):537–50.

Berridge K. C. 'The debate over dopamine's role in reward: The case for incentive salience'. *Psychopharmacology.* 2007 Apr.;191:391–431.

Berridge K. C., Kringelbach M. L. 'Pleasure systems in the brain'. *Neuron*. 2015 May 6;86(3):646–64.

Berridge K. C., Kringelbach M. L. 'Affective neuroscience of pleasure: Reward in humans and animals'. *Psychopharmacology*. 2008 Aug.;199:457–80.

Brauer L. H., De Wit H. 'High dose pimozide does not block amphetamine-induced euphoria in normal volunteers'. *Pharmacology Biochemistry and Behavior*. 1997 Feb. 1;56(2):265–72.

Bressan R. A., Crippa J. A. 'The role of dopamine in reward and pleasure behaviour – review of data from preclinical research'. *Acta Psychiatrica Scandinavica*. 2005 Jun.;111:14–21.

Brischoux F., Chakraborty S., Brierley D. I., Ungless M. A. 'Phasic excitation of dopamine neurons in ventral VTA by noxious stimuli'. *Proceedings of the National Academy of Sciences*. 2009 Mar. 24;106(12):4894–9.

Cara E. 'That "man flu" study is from *BMJ*'s irresponsible holiday issue (updated)'. Gizmodo, 12 December 2017. Retrieved 6 February 2023 from https://gizmodo.com/ that-man-flu-study-is-yet-another-irresponsible-bmj-hol-1821218722

Chen A. 'Please stop calling dopamine the "pleasure chemical"'. The Verge, 27 March 2018. Retrieved 6 February 2023 from https://www.theverge.com/2018/3/27/17169446/dopamine-pleasure-chemical-neuroscience-reward-motivation

Davidson B. I., Ellis D. A. 'Social media addiction: Technological déjà vu'. *BMJ*. 2019 Jun. 21;365:l4277.

Foulkes G. *Control of Space Invaders and Other Electronic Games*. Hansard, 20 May 1981. Retrieved 6 February 2023 from http://hansard.millbanksystems. com/commons/1981/may/20/control-of-space-invaders-and-other

Fox News. '"Man flu" is real? Researcher says men take longer to recover from viruses, colds', 12 December 2017. Retrieved 6 February 2023 from https://www.foxnews.com/health/man-flu-is-real-researcher-says-men-take-longer-to-recover-from-viruses-colds

Gawin F. H. 'Neuroleptic reduction of cocaine-induced paranoia but not euphoria?'. *Psychopharmacology.* 1986 Aug.;90:142–3.

Ince C., van Kuijen A. M., Milstein D. M., Yürük K., Folkow L. P., Fokkens W. J., Blix A. S. 'Why Rudolph's nose is red: Observational study'. *BMJ.* 2012 Dec. 17;345.

Johnson G., Guha I. N., Davies P. 'Were James Bond's drinks shaken because of alcohol induced tremor?'. *BMJ.* 2013 Dec. 12;347.

Kardaras N. 'It's "digital heroin": How screens turn kids into psychotic junkies'. The *New York Post*, 27 August 2016. Retrieved 6 February 2023 from https://nypost.com/2016/08/27/its-digital-heroin-how-screens-turn-kids-into-psychotic-junkies/

Kardefelt-Winther D. 'Conceptualizing Internet use disorders: Addiction or coping process?'. *Psychiatry and Clinical Neurosciences.* 2017 Jul.;71(7):459–66.

Kardefelt-Winther D., Heeren A., Schimmenti A., van Rooij A., Maurage P., Carras M., Edman J., Blaszczynski A., Khazaal Y., Billieux J. 'How can we conceptualize behavioural addiction without pathologizing common behaviours?'. *Addiction.* 2017 Oct.;112(10):1709–15.

Koepp M. J., Gunn R. N., Lawrence A. D., Cunningham V. J., Dagher A., Jones T., Brooks D. J., Bench C. J., Grasby P. M. 'Evidence for striatal dopamine release during a video game'. *Nature.* 1998 May;393(6682):266–8.

Kringelbach M. L., Berridge K. C. 'The functional

neuroanatomy of pleasure and happiness'. *Discovery Medicine.* 2010 Jun.;9(49):579.

Lanette S., Mazmanian M. 'The smartphone "addiction" narrative is compelling, but largely unfounded'. In *Extended Abstracts of the 2018 CHI Conference on Human Factors in Computing Systems*, 2018 Apr. 20.

Liberzon I., Taylor S. F., Amdur R., Jung T. D., Chamberlain K. R., Minoshima S., Koeppe R. A., Fig L. M. 'Brain activation in PTSD in response to trauma-related stimuli'. *Biological Psychiatry.* 1999 Apr. 1;45(7):817–26.

Nann-Vernotica E., Donny E. C., Bigelow G. E., Walsh S. L. 'Repeated administration of the D 1/5 antagonist ecopipam fails to attenuate the subjective effects of cocaine'. *Psychopharmacology.* 2001 Jun.;155:338–47.

Nutt D. J., Lingford-Hughes A., Erritzoe D., Stokes P. R. 'The dopamine theory of addiction: 40 years of highs and lows'. *Nature Reviews Neuroscience.* 2015 May;16(5):305–12.

Olds J., Milner P. 'Positive reinforcement produced by electrical stimulation of septal area and other regions of rat brain'. *Journal of Comparative and Physiological Psychology.* 1954 Dec.;47(6):419.

Olds J. 'Pleasure centers in the brain'. *Scientific American.* 1956 Oct. 1;195(4):105–17.

Olds J. 'Self-stimulation of the brain: Its use to study local effects of hunger, sex, and drugs'. *Science.* 1958 Feb. 14;127(3294):315–24.

Panova T., Carbonell X. 'Is smartphone addiction really an addiction?'. *Journal of Behavioral Addictions.* 2018 Jun.;7(2):252–9.

Rose S., Dhandayudham A. 'Towards an understanding of Internet-based problem shopping behaviour: The concept of online shopping addiction and its proposed predictors'. *Journal of Behavioral Addictions*. 2014 Jun. 1;3(2):83–9.

RTE. 'Nothing to sneeze at? Study says man flu could be real'. 12 December 2017. Retrieved 6 February 2023 from https://www.rte.ie/news/newslens/2017/1212/926719-man-flu/

Salamone J. D., Correa M., Farrar A., Mingote S. M. 'Effort-related functions of nucleus accumbens dopamine and associated forebrain circuits'. *Psychopharmacology*. 2007 Apr.;191:461–82.

Satchell L. P., Fido D., Harper C. A., Shaw H., Davidson B., Ellis D. A., Hart C. M., Jalil R., Bartoli A. J., Kaye L. K., Lancaster G.L. 'Development of an Offline-Friend Addiction Questionnaire (O-FAQ): Are most people really social addicts?'. *Behavior Research Methods*. 2021 Jun.;53(3):1097–106.

Shoblock J. R., Sullivan E. B., Maisonneuve I. M., Glick S. D. 'Neurochemical and behavioral differences between d-methamphetamine and d-amphetamine in rats'. *Psychopharmacology*. 2003 Feb.;165(4):359–69.

Stevens M. W., Dorstyn D., Delfabbro P. H., King D. L. 'Global prevalence of gaming disorder: A systematic review and meta-analysis'. *Australian & New Zealand Journal of Psychiatry*. 2021 Jun.;55(6):553–68.

Sue K. 'The science behind "man flu"'. *BMJ*. 2017 Dec. 11;359.

Van Rooij A. J., Ferguson C. J., Colder Carras M., Kardefelt-Winther D., Shi J., Aarseth E., Bean A. M., Bergmark K. H., Brus A., Coulson M., Deleuze J. et al. 'A weak scientific basis for gaming disorder: Let us err on the side of caution'. *Journal of Behavioral Addictions*. 2018 Mar.;7(1):1–9.

Wallis D. 'Just click no'. The *New Yorker*, 13 January 1997. Retrieved 6 February 2023 from https://www.newyorker.com/magazine/1997/01/13/just-click-no

Wan C. S., Chiou W. B. 'Psychological motives and online games addiction: A test of flow theory and humanistic needs theory for Taiwanese adolescents'. *CyberPsychology & Behavior.* 2006 Jun. 1;9(3): 317–24.

Wood W., Rünger D. 'Psychology of habit'. *Annual Review of Psychology.* 2016 Jan. 4;67(1):289–314.

Chapter 8

Abeele M. M., Halfmann A., Lee E. W. 'Drug, demon, or donut? Theorizing the relationship between social media use, digital well-being and digital disconnection'. *Current Opinion in Psychology.* 2022 Jun. 1;45:101295.

Albarello F., Novoa Á., Castro Sánchez M., Velasco A., Novaro Hueyo M. V., Narbais F. 'The social dynamics of multiplayer online videogames in Argentinian and Chilean family contexts: The case of Fortnite'. *Global Studies of Childhood.* 2021 Dec.;11(4):302–17.

Bayer J. B., LaRose R. 'Technology habits: Progress, problems, and prospects'. In *The Psychology of Habit: Theory, Mechanisms, Change, and Contexts.* Springer, 2018.

Boyle M. 'Bored? No way. Ditching technology makes life complicated and beautiful'. The *Guardian,* 25 March 2017. Retrieved 10 February 2023 from https://www.theguardian.com/commentisfree/2017/mar/25/boredom-ditched-technology-life-beautiful

Boyle M. 'Environmentalism used to be about defending the wild – not any more'. The *Guardian,* 22 May 2017. Retrieved 10 February 2023 from https://www.theguardian.com/commentisfree/2017/may/22/life-without-technology-environmentalism-defending-wild-sustainability

Chambers C. *The Seven Deadly Sins of Psychology*. Princeton University Press, 2017.

Dunican I. C., Martin D. T., Halson S. L., Reale R. J., Dawson B. T., Caldwell J. A., Jones M. J., Eastwood P. R. 'The effects of the removal of electronic devices for 48 hours on sleep in elite judo athletes'. *The Journal of Strength & Conditioning Research*. 2017 Oct. 1;31(10):2832–9.

Etchells, P. J. 'Blue Monday: There is no such thing as "the most depressing day of the year"'. The *Guardian*, 6 January 2014. Retrieved 10 February 2023 from https://www.theguardian.com/science/head-quarters/2014/jan/06/most-depressing-day-of-year-blue-monday

Fioravanti G., Prostamo A., Casale S. 'Taking a short break from Instagram: The effects on subjective well-being'. *Cyberpsychology, Behavior, and Social Networking*. 2020 Feb. 1;23(2):107–12.

Gunther A. C., Storey J. D. 'The influence of presumed influence'. *Journal of Communication*. 2003 Jun. 1;53(2):199–215.

Hall J. A., Xing C., Ross E. M., Johnson R. M. 'Experimentally manipulating social media abstinence: Results of a four-week diary study'. *Media Psychology*. 2021 Mar. 4;24(2):259–75.

Hanley S. M., Watt S. E., Coventry W. 'Taking a break: The effect of taking a vacation from Facebook and Instagram on subjective well-being'. *Plos One*. 2019 Jun. 6;14(6):e0217743.

Hunt M. G., Marx R., Lipson C., Young J. 'No more FOMO: Limiting social media decreases loneliness and depression'. *Journal of Social and Clinical Psychology*. 2018 Dec.;37(10):751–68.

Liao W. 'Put your smartphone down: Preliminary evidence that reducing smartphone use improves psychological well-being in people with poor mental health' (thesis, Master of Science). University of Otago, 2019 Retrieved 10 February 2023 from http://hdl.handle.net/10523/9427

Meier A. 'Studying problems, not problematic usage: Do mobile checking habits increase procrastination and decrease well-being?' *Mobile Media & Communication.* 2022 May;10(2):272–93.

Nguyen M. H., Büchi M., Geber S. 'Everyday disconnection experiences: Exploring people's understanding of digital well-being and management of digital media use'. *New Media & Society.* 2022 Jul. 5:14614448221105428.

Ofcom. *The Communications Marketing Report*, 4 August 2016. Retrieved 10 February 2023 from https://www.ofcom.org.uk/__data/assets/pdf_file/0020/26273/uk_context.pdf

Przybylski A. K., Nguyen T. V., Law W., Weinstein N. 'Does taking a short break from social media have a positive effect on well-being? Evidence from three preregistered field experiments'. *Journal of Technology in Behavioral Science.* 2021 Sept.;6:507–14.

Radtke T., Apel T., Schenkel K., Keller J., von Lindern E. 'Digital detox: An effective solution in the smartphone era? A systematic literature review'. *Mobile Media & Communication.* 2022 May;10(2):190–215.

Ritchie S. *Science Fictions.* Random House, 2020.

Roberts, D. 'Reboot or die trying'. *Outside*, 2 September 2014. Retrieved 10 February 2023 from https://www.outsideonline.com/culture/books-media/reboot-or-die-trying/

Rosen L. D., Cheever N. A., Carrier L. M. 'The association of parenting style and child age with parental limit setting and adolescent MySpace behavior'. *Journal of Applied Developmental Psychology.* 2008 Nov. 1;29(6):459–71.

Sheldon K. M., Abad N., Hinsch C. 'A two-process view of Facebook use and relatedness need-satisfaction: Disconnection drives use, and connection rewards it'. *Journal of Personality and Social Psychology*. 2011 Apr.;100(4):766–75.

Tal-Or N., Cohen J., Tsfati Y., Gunther A. C. 'Testing causal direction in the influence of presumed media influence'. *Communication Research*. 2010 Dec.;37(6):801–24.

Tromholt M. 'The Facebook experiment: Quitting Facebook leads to higher levels of well-being'. *Cyberpsychology, Behavior, and Social Networking*. 2016 Nov. 1;19(11):661–6.

Turel O., Cavagnaro D. R., Meshi D. 'Short abstinence from online social networking sites reduces perceived stress, especially in excessive users'. *Psychiatry Research*. 2018 Dec. 1;270:947–53.

Vally Z., D'Souza C. G. 'Abstinence from social media use, subjective well-being, stress, and loneliness'. *Perspectives in Psychiatric Care*. 2019 Oct.;55(4):752–9.

Vanman E. J., Baker R., Tobin S. J. 'The burden of online friends: The effects of giving up Facebook on stress and well-being'. *The Journal of Social Psychology*. 2018 Jul. 4;158(4):496–508.

Weinstein N., Przybylski A. K. 'The impacts of motivational framing of technology restrictions on adolescent concealment: Evidence from a preregistered experimental study'. *Computers in Human Behavior*. 2019 Jan. 1;90:170–80.

Wilcockson T. D., Osborne A.M., Ellis D.A. 'Digital detox: The effect of smartphone abstinence on mood, anxiety, and craving'. *Addictive Behaviors*. 2019 Dec. 1;99:106013.

Index